# PLAT(

## in focus

This edition of Plato's *Meno* is designed to serve as a handy 'starter-kit' for the study of this important work. It brings together in one volume a new English translation of the text, a selection of illuminating articles, and an introduction setting the work in its historical context and opening up the key philosophical issues which the various articles discuss.

The book is planned to be accessible to readers with little or no knowledge of Greek. Jane Day's translation of the *Meno* preserves rather more consistency in its renderings of Greek terms than is found in existing English translations, thus providing a more reliable reflection of the details in the original. A glossary briefly introduces some of the key terms and indicates how they are translated. Within the articles, translations of Greek words and phrases have been added where necessary.

The *Meno* is an excellent introduction to Plato and to philosophy, and this edition will be of value to teachers and students of classics or philosophy, and to anyone wishing to study the work in depth.

**Jane M. Day** is a Fellow and Tutor in Philosophy at Lady Margaret Hall, Oxford, and University Lecturer at the University of Oxford.

# ROUTLEDGE PHILOSOPHERS IN FOCUS SERIES

Series editor: Stanley Tweyman
*York University, Toronto*

ARISTOTLE'S *DE ANIMA* IN FOCUS
*Edited by Michael Durrant*

GEORGE BERKELEY: *ALCIPHRON* IN FOCUS
*Edited by David Berman*

CIVIL DISOBEDIENCE IN FOCUS
*Edited by Hugo Adam Bedau*

RENE DESCARTES: *MEDITATIONS ON FIRST PHILOSOPHY* IN FOCUS
*Edited by Stanley Tweyman*

GÖDEL'S *THEOREM* IN FOCUS
*Edited by S. G. Shanker*

DAVID HUME: *DIALOGUES CONCERNING NATURAL RELIGION* IN FOCUS
*Edited by Stanley Tweyman*

WILLIAM JAMES: *PRAGMATISM* IN FOCUS
*Edited by Doris Olin*

JOHN LOCKE: *LETTER CONCERNING TOLERATION* IN FOCUS
*Edited by John Horton and Susan Mendus*

J. S. MILL: *ON LIBERTY* IN FOCUS
*Edited by John Gray and G. W. Smith*

# PLATO'S
# *MENO*

## in focus

*Edited by*
*Jane M. Day*

London and New York

First published 1994
by Routledge
2 Park Square, Milton Park, Abingdon, Oxfordshire OX14 4RN

Simultaneously published in the USA and Canada
by Routledge
711 Third Avenue, New York, NY 10017

First issued in paperback 2014

*Routledge is an imprint of the Taylor and Francis Group, an informa company*

Typeset in 10/12 point Bembo by Florencetype Ltd, Kewstoke, Avon

*British Library Cataloguing in Publication Data*
A catalogue record for this book is available from the British Library

*Library of Congress Cataloging in Publication Data*
Plato's Meno in focus / edited by Jane M. Day
(Routledge philosophers in focus series)
Includes bibliographical references and index.
1. Plato. Meno.   2. Socrates.   3. Virtue.   4. Idea (Philosophy)
I. Day, Jane M. (Jane Mary).   II. Plato. Meno. English.
1994.   III. Series.
B377.P53   1994
170–dc20       93–719

ISBN 13: 978-0-415-00297-4 (hbk)
ISBN 13: 978-1-138-00900-4 (pbk)

**Publisher's Note**
The publisher has gone to great lengths to ensure the quality of this reprint
but points out that some imperfections in the original may be apparent

# CONTENTS

# PREFACE

The *Meno* is an excellent choice for one's first reading in Plato, and to many tastes also for one's first reading in philosophy. This volume is designed primarily for such readers, though I hope that others may also find it useful.

The translation is new. It is based on J. Burnet's edition in the Oxford Classical Texts series (*Platonis Opera* tomus III, 1903, with corrections 1908), with a few divergences noted in footnotes. The marginal numbers and letters are those regularly used by scholars when referring to Plato's works, and derive from H. Stephanus' edition of 1578. In translating, while attempting to capture as much as possible of Plato's lightness of style, I have given the first priority to precision and the second to the maximum possible consistency in translating Greek terms. I have also included a Glossary which briefly introduces some of the key terms and indicates how I have translated them. I particularly hope that my translation may be useful to serious students of philosophy with little or no Greek, for whose needs the existing English translations tend to be rather too free.

I am very pleased with the set of articles that I have been able to include. All of them have proved their worth within my own teaching experience and it adds further to the value of reprinting them here that several of them have not been easily accessible in this country hitherto. In order to maximize the cohesion within the volume, I have given strong preference in selecting articles to those which focus largely or solely on the *Meno* itself, rather than merely being about themes central to the *Meno* without necessarily making the *Meno* central in their treatment. I have also limited the choice to articles as opposed to chapters of books, and to the twenty-year period 1965–85 initiated by Vlastos' influential article '*Anamnesis* in the *Meno*'.

With the agreement of the authors concerned, Greek words and phrases occurring in some of the articles are accompanied or replaced in this reprinting by an English translation. In making these changes, I have not attempted to impose consistency as between translation, transliteration and Greek script, but only to minimize obstacles to reading the articles for those with no Greek, while taking care never to introduce ambiguity as to which Greek word or phrase is being referred to. There remain a few points, especially in Vlastos' footnotes, which will chiefly interest readers who do know Greek: here I have made no attempt to add translations. Greekless readers may be assured that these points do not threaten to undermine their understanding of the article's main arguments.

*Jane M. Day*

# ACKNOWLEDGEMENTS

I should like to express my warm thanks to all the authors, editors and publishers who have enabled this book to exist by giving permission for the articles in it to be included.

I. G. Kidd's 'Socrates' was originally published in Paul Edwards (ed.), *The Encyclopedia of Philosophy* (Macmillan: New York, 1967), vol. 7, pp. 480–5, and is reprinted by permission of the publishers and author.

Gregory Vlastos' '*Anamnesis* in the *Meno*' was originally published in *Dialogue* 4 (1965), pp. 143–67. It is reprinted here, with minor amendments and some additional references supplied by the author, by permission of the editor and author.

Julius Moravcsik's 'Learning as recollection' was originally published in G. Vlastos (ed.), *Plato I: Metaphysics and Epistemology* (1971). The volume was first published by Doubleday, New York, and Macmillan, London, and later reprinted by Notre Dame Press (1978). The article is reprinted here by permission of the editor, author and publishers.

George Nakhnikian's 'The first Socratic paradox' was originally published in *Journal of the History of Philosophy* 11 (1973), pp. 1–17. It is reprinted here by permission of the editor and author.

Nicholas P. White's 'Inquiry' was originally published in *Review of Metaphysics* 28 (1974–5), pp. 289–310. It is reprinted here, with minor amendments, by permission of the editor and author.

I. M. Crombie's 'Socratic definition' was originally published in *Paideia* 5 (1976), *Special Plato Issue*, pp. 80–102. It is reprinted here, with minor amendments, by permission of the editor and author.

Kathleen V. Wilkes' 'Conclusions in the *Meno*' was originally published in *Archiv für Geschichte der Philosophie* 61 (1979), pp. 143–53, and is reprinted here by permission of the editor and author. With the author's permission, transliteration and translation have been introduced for this reprinting at many points where the original contained words or phrases in Greek script.

Alexander Nehamas' 'Meno's paradox and Socrates as a teacher' was originally published in *Oxford Studies in Ancient Philosophy* 3 (1985), pp. 1–30 and is reprinted here by permission of the author and publishers. With the author's permission, a few translations of Greek words and phrases have been added for this reprinting.

Special thanks are due also to Professor Ackrill, Dr D. A. Rees and Dr D. C. Innes, each of whom kindly read the translation and made very helpful suggestions for improvements to it at various points.

# ABBREVIATIONS

The abbreviations for titles of ancient works used by various authors in this volume should be easy to follow, with the help if necessary of the lists in Liddell and Scott's *Greek Lexicon* or the *Oxford Classical Dictionary* or, in the case of Plato, the list of his works on p. 9 of this volume. It may however be helpful to mention the following abbreviations used in the Introduction:

| Plato, | *Apol.* | *Apology* |
|---|---|---|
| " | *Ep., Epp.* | *Letter, Letters* |
| " | *Protag.* | *Protagoras* |
| " | *Rep.* | *Republic* |
| " | *Theaet.* | *Theaetetus* |
| Cicero, | *De Fin.* | *De Finibus* |
| " | *Rep.* | *De Republica* |
| " | *Tusc.* | *Tusculan Disputations* |
| D.L. | | Diogenes Laertius, *Lives of Eminent Philosophers* |

Modern works cited in abbreviated form should in general be easy to identify from the Bibliography to this volume. However, the following abbreviations used in the Introduction and the footnotes to the Translation should be noted:

| Bluck | Bluck, R. S., *Plato's Meno* |
|---|---|
| Sharples | Sharples, R. W., *Plato: Meno* |
| OCT | Oxford Classical Text |

# INTRODUCTION
### Jane M. Day

## I  SYNOPSIS OF THE *MENO*

**Scene**     Athens, 403–402 BC
**Characters**    *Socrates*, in his late sixties.
*Meno*, a young aristocrat from Thessaly visiting Athens.
*Anytus*, Meno's host, an Athenian democratic politician, later to be one of the accusers at Socrates' trial.
*One of Meno's slaves.*

### Summary of the dialogue

#### 70a1–71b8  *Introduction*

Meno asks: does virtue come from teaching? Socrates claims not to know even what virtue *is*, which he says must be settled first. The rest of the dialogue falls into four sections.

#### 1. 71b9–79e4  *What is virtue?*
#### *Meno's unsuccessful attempts at definition*

(a) (71b9–73c5) Meno starts confidently: a man's virtue is the capacity to conduct the city's affairs, helping friends and harming foes, a woman's is running the home well and obeying her husband, and similarly each class of people has its own virtue. Socrates objects that these many varieties of virtue cannot be what *virtue itself* is; their shared name 'virtue' must denote something the same for them all, and it is this which needs defining. He illustrates with other terms: 'health', 'size', 'strength'. Meno initially feels that virtue is different, but eventually capitulates.

1

(b) (73c6–77a5) Meno tries defining virtue as 'the ability to rule over people', but this is soon refuted. First, it excludes children and slaves. Secondly, the qualification 'justly' is needed, yet adding this reintroduces the error of trying to define virtue by giving examples.

Socrates lets Meno have sample definitions of 'shape' and 'colour'. The first is 'Shape is the only thing there is which always accompanies colour'. Meno objects that one might not know what colour was. Socrates next offers 'Shape is the limit of a solid', checking that Meno accepts each term involved. Finally he defines colour, as 'an efflux of shapes, commensurate with and perceptible to sight'. This third definition is Meno's favourite; Socrates prefers the previous one. But all three are left standing as passable models.

(c) (77a5–79e4) Quoting a poet, Meno now defines virtue as 'desiring fine things and having power to achieve them'. This again is refuted. First, Socrates argues that the clause 'desiring fine things' is redundant: 'fine things' simply means 'good things', and everyone wants good things anyway. Second, 'having power to achieve good things' does not amount to virtue unless one adds 'with justice, holiness, temperance, etc.' But since these are *parts* of virtue, adding them merely serves to make the definition circular. They must start afresh, Socrates concludes.

## 2. 79e5–86c3 How can we search for things we do not know? The theory of recollection

(a) (79e5–82b3) Meno cannot answer, and complains that Socrates has paralysed him. Socrates re-emphasizes his own ignorance, but willingly offers to join Meno's search. Meno objects: how can one search without knowing what one is searching for? Socrates underlines how this challenges all search for knowledge. He outlines his reply: the human soul is immortal and has long ago learnt everything. What we call 'learning' is really recollection and, because all nature is interrelated, every memory can lead eventually to every other. To demonstrate, Socrates asks Meno to call one of his slaves.

(b) (82b4–85b7) Socrates sets the slave a geometrical problem: given that a square with sides two feet long has an area of four square feet, how long are the sides of a square with double this area? The slave confidently answers 'four feet', and is refuted, then tries 'three feet', and is refuted again. By now he is paralysed – just like Meno. But they start afresh, and although Socrates still supplies only questions and not answers, the slave soon grasps how he could solve the problem.

(c) (85b8–86c3) Socrates draws two conclusions from the slave's success. First, *all* apparent learning is really recollection of truth within oneself, so the human soul must possess knowledge *at all times*, and therefore must be immortal. Secondly – and indeed the one point in the argument that Socrates claims to be totally sure about – we should persevere in searching for what we do not know.

### 3. 86c4–96d1 Does virtue come from teaching?
### Discussion using the hypothetical method

(a) (86c4–89c4) Meno assents, but asks to return to his original question whether virtue comes from teaching. Socrates protests, but consents, on condition that they start 'from a hypothesis', i.e. by stipulating what sort of thing virtue would have to be if it *did* come from teaching (that is, he adds, from recollecting). It would have to be knowledge, he claims. He then argues as follows: virtue is good and therefore beneficial, nothing is beneficial unless rightly used, right use requires wisdom, therefore virtue must be wisdom of some sort. Socrates and Meno conclude from this that virtue is knowledge and therefore does come from teaching.

(b) (89c5–95a1) Abruptly, Socrates expresses doubts. If virtue comes from teaching, there should surely be teachers of it, but are there any? At this point Anytus arrives and Socrates asks him who could teach Meno 'the wisdom and virtue by which people run homes and cities finely'. In general the appropriate teachers of a subject are the professionals, so would the appropriate teachers of virtue also be the professionals, i.e. the Sophists?

Anytus is outraged: the Sophists simply corrupt their followers! Indeed, cities should expel them. Socrates expresses disbelief that Protagoras and other well-respected Sophists should be so totally bad, and wonders how Anytus knows, since he says himself he has never met one. He asks again, who *could* teach Meno virtue? 'Any

3

among the "fine and good" of the Athenians, if he will take their advice' is Anytus' reply. Socrates challenges the claim that men with virtue can teach it to others. As men of notable virtue he mentions Themistocles, Aristides, Pericles and Thucydides. These men's sons all achieved distinction in many skills through teaching, but none did so in virtue. Yet the fathers surely *wished* their sons to achieve virtue, Socrates argues, so virtue cannot come from teaching. Anytus takes this as an insult. Warning Socrates to be careful, he leaves.

(c) (95a2–96d1) Socrates and Meno decide that no one's claim to teach virtue survives examination. Many of the 'fine and good' do not even claim this for themselves, while the Sophists' claims to teach virtue are widely disputed. But if there are no teachers there are no learners, and therefore virtue does not come from teaching.

### 4. 96d1–100c2 Provisional conclusions

Meno wonders how, then, virtue does come. Socrates replies that they went wrong in assuming earlier that only knowledge provided right guidance. In fact, *true opinion* also does so. True opinions lack the stability of knowledge, until transformed into knowledge by 'reasoning out the explanation'. But they provide no less practical benefit than knowledge while they last. Thus *either* knowledge *or* right opinion could make men good and beneficial to their cities. Either way, virtue does not come by nature. But neither does it come from teaching, so it cannot be knowledge. Therefore, virtue must be right opinion, coming not through rational means but by divine dispensation, like the utterances of soothsayers and seers – that is, unless a genuine teacher of virtue can be found.

Meno expresses assent, Socrates reiterates that to achieve clear knowledge it is essential to investigate first what virtue is in itself, and so they part.

## II PLATO'S LIFE[1]

Plato was born in about 427 BC,[2] the son of Ariston and Perictione, both of whom seem to have come from eminent Athenian families. He had two elder brothers Glaucon and Adeimantus, who feature prominently in the *Republic*, and a sister Potone, whose son

Speusippus was later to succeed him as head of the Academy. He never married.

During the half-century before Plato's birth, Athens had enjoyed a period of unrivalled political, commercial and cultural splendour dating from 480–479 BC when the Greeks had finally repulsed Persia's attempts to conquer their country. Athens' ascendancy culminated in the 'Periclean Age' of the 440s and 430s, when both Persia and Sparta formally recognized the Athenian Empire. The building of the Parthenon symbolized the confidence of the era, and the Athenians regarded themselves as both the educators of Greece and its leaders in democracy.

Socrates, born about 470 BC, had lived through much of this period. For Plato, however, Athens' greatness was in the past. In 431 BC Sparta and other cities, feeling increasingly threatened by Athens, had started the Peloponnesian War which was finally to lead to Athens' defeat in 404 BC, while in 429 BC Pericles himself and many others had died in the plague which swept Athens that year. Plato grew up against a background of decline in Athens' power, and indeed must have served in the Athenian army during its period of military defeat.

Plato's father died during his childhood, and his mother subsequently married Pyrilampes, by whom she had another son, Antiphon (as we learn from an engaging family vignette at 126a–127a of Plato's *Parmenides*). Pyrilampes had been a supporter of the Periclean democracy. Two other members of Plato's family, his mother's brother Charmides and her cousin Critias, became notorious as leading oligarchs. Critias was a member of the puppet oligarchic government set up by Sparta in Athens in 404 BC and known as the 'Thirty Tyrants', and Charmides supported him.

Plato himself grew up assuming he would enter politics, as we learn from the Seventh Letter (324b8–325c5). However, in the end he never found a party he felt he could join. He had been repelled by democracy's irresponsible workings during the last years of the Peloponnesian War, but even more so by the lawless acts of the Thirty Tyrants. Finally, when a more moderate democracy was established in 404 BC and his hopes rose again, it was not long before Socrates was impeached by leading democrats, and condemned to death by a democratically constituted jury, on the charges of 'refusing to recognize the gods recognized by the City and introducing other new divinities' and of 'corrupting the youth'.[3] To Plato, who describes Socrates at *Phaedo* 118a16–17 as

5

'of all the men of his generation whom we have known, the best, wisest, and most just', this was a profoundly unholy act. Plato's own standing must also have been affected, since he was publicly known as one of the three friends of Socrates who offered surety for him at his trial (*Apology* 37b6). His thoughts of entering politics were postponed, this time, as it turned out, for ever, though according to the Seventh Letter (325c5–326a2) it was only gradually that he began to conceive his true vocation.

Socrates died in 399 BC. Afterwards, tradition relates that Plato, with others of Socrates' friends, withdrew from Athens for a while to Megara, joining the Megarian philosopher Euclides.[4] It is generally agreed among scholars that Plato's writing life began at about this time or soon after. When the Corinthian War broke out in 395 BC he would presumably have been called up to serve in Athens' army again, since he was still of military age, though we have no record of this. There was also a tradition, which may or may not be true, that he visited Cyrene and Egypt during this period.[5]

Then, aged 'about forty' according to the Seventh Letter (324a6), Plato paid a visit to Italy and Sicily. There is every reason to accept Cicero's statements that his primary purpose was to visit Archytas of Tarentum and other Pythagoreans in Italy.[6] Archytas himself was a great mathematician (as well as, apparently, a successful politician and general), and many aspects of Pythagoreanism had enormous attraction for Plato, including particularly their conception of number as the underlying principle ordering the world, their almost mystical sense of the kinship of all nature, and their belief in immortality.[7] On a more practical level, their actual organization would have been of interest to him. It seems clear that by the time Plato came to Italy he must have been close to formulating his project of founding the Academy, if indeed he had not already done so,[8] and the Pythagorean societies were among the models on which he could draw.

From Italy, the Seventh Letter (326d 7–327b 6) reports that Plato went on to Syracuse in Sicily, at that time ruled by the tyrant Dionysius I. Here he encountered a form of government he had not experienced in Athens – the most brilliant and successful despotism of the Greek world at this time. His description of tyranny at *Republic* 565d–587e shows he was far from dazzled (though obviously the tyrant in the *Republic* is an idealized monster, not to be equated with any real individual). In Syracuse Plato formed a close friendship with Dionysius' brother-in-law,

Dion, a young man of 20, whom he found to be the most eager student of philosophical ideals that he had ever met, and who quickly became converted to a life 'holding virtue dearer than pleasure or luxury' (*Ep.* 7, 327b3–4). This rather irritated other members of Dionysius' court, who were less impressed. Later traditions add that Dionysius then expelled Plato or even had him sold into slavery.[9] These stories have no good authority, though it is quite plausible to suppose that Plato was genuinely kidnapped and held to ransom not by any agents of Dionysius but simply by Aeginetans, who were raiding Athenian shipping during 389–387 BC.[10] This could be the basis for later embroidery. Plato's times were not peaceful.

The next known fact about Plato is his founding of the Academy. There is every reason to suppose, with most scholars, that this took place soon after his return from Sicily to Athens. For the rest of his life Plato was the head of this institution, which was then to continue its own existence until dissolved, together with other pagan institutions, by Justinian in AD 529. Its total lifespan was thus over nine hundred years. The Academy can lay claim to be the first university[11] of which anything is clearly known, although it had antecedents in Isocrates' school of rhetoric founded shortly earlier and, more importantly, in the Pythagorean institutions in Italy. It was an institute of both teaching and research. A major part of its aim and motivation was to train young people for the service of the state. But (in contrast with Isocrates) Plato was committed to starting from intensive studies in mathematics and philosophy, and the Academy's main fame was in these fields, although it seems it also produced various advisory consultants who assisted cities in drawing up codes of laws.[12] As to methods of teaching, there is evidence that Plato gave some formal lectures,[13] but also that such lectures formed a comparatively minor part of the Academy's activities, far more important being the give and take of oral discussion, which Plato defends[14] as well as uses in his dialogues. The Academy attracted members and students from all over Greece. It seems clear that, as in modern universities and colleges, there was a distinction between young students passing through and long-term members engaged in research and teaching, though it is not known what the formal distinctions were. Its long-term members included the eminent mathematicians Theaetetus (who is commemorated in Plato's dialogue of that title, and who was there from the formation of the Academy until his death in

369 BC) and Eudoxus, along with Speusippus and Xenocrates, later to be elected as heads of the institution in turn, and, most famous of all in the long run, Aristotle, who came to the Academy aged about 17 in 367 BC and remained until Plato's death twenty years later.[15]

One may safely assume that much of Plato's energy went into the Academy for the rest of his life. However, twenty years after his first visit to Sicily, the Seventh Letter records that he again became involved in Syracusan politics.[16] He was offered through Dion, and felt he must accept, a chance to set a new ruler in the path of true statemanship; Dionysius I had died, Dion's young nephew Dionysius had succeeded him, and Dion begged Plato to take this opportunity of exerting influence. Plato apparently made two visits, first in 367 and again in 362 BC, 'moved', as Guthrie aptly puts it (History of Greek Philosophy IV, p. 25), 'by that pathetic and mistaken shame which the naturally theoretical and contemplative spirit feels at failing to meet a challenge to action for which it is, in fact, entirely unsuited'. The outcome was humiliating failure. Dionysius showed many signs of eagerness for Plato's approval but none of real conversion. Political intrigue was rife, and in the end, hearing that some of Dionysius' soldiers were out for his blood, Plato was thankful that, with Archytas' help, he succeeded in leaving Sicily alive.

From then until his death thirteen years later, Plato stayed in Athens. The Seventh and Eighth Letters[17] serve as evidence of continuing interest in Syracuse, but it may be assumed that his main energies were focused on the Academy and on writing. Several of his major works, including the Laws, must date from this period.

Plato died in 347 BC. The following list gives the main dates.

| | |
|---|---|
| ?427 BC | Birth of Plato |
| 404 BC | End of Peloponnesian War; the Thirty Tyrants |
| 403 BC | Restoration of democracy in Athens |
| 399 BC | Death of Socrates |
| ?Between 389 and 387 BC | First Sicilian visit |
| ?Not long after 387 BC | Foundation of the Academy |
| 367–366 BC | Second Sicilian visit |
| 362–360 BC | Third Sicilian visit |
| 347 BC | Death of Plato |

# III THE DATE OF THE *MENO* AND ITS PLACE IN THE DEVELOPMENT OF PLATO'S THOUGHT

Plato's dialogues have not come down to us with dates attached, and we have only a single statement from any contemporary source about their chronology, this being Aristotle's in the *Politics* (1264b26) that the *Laws* was written later than the *Republic*. However, using this datum, and by a painstaking comparison of stylistic details in the *Republic*, the *Laws*, and Plato's other works, scholars have succeeded in establishing the following division of the dialogues into three groups, early, middle, and late.

| Early | | Middle | Late |
|---|---|---|---|
| *Apology* | | *Phaedo* | *Sophist* |
| *Crito* | *Protagoras* | *Symposium* | *Statesman* |
| *Io* | *Euthydemus* | *Republic* | *?Timaeus* |
| *Hippias Minor* | *Gorgias* | *Phaedrus* | *Critias* |
| *Laches* | *Menexenus* | *Parmenides* | *Philebus* |
| *Euthyphro* | *Meno* | *Theaetetus* | *Laws* |
| *Lysis* | *?Cratylus* | | |
| *Charmides* | | | |
| *Hippias Major* | | | |
| (if genuine) | | | |

This grouping is confirmed by a number of cross references between different dialogues: for instance the *Phaedo* refers to the *Meno's* argument for the theory of recollection, while among later dialogues the *Sophist* and *Statesman* refer to the *Theaetetus*, and the *Timaeus* to the *Republic*. It also succeeds impressively in providing a broadly coherent logical framework, and is very generally agreed among scholars, except that the dating of the *Cratylus* and the *Timaeus* remains disputed. Fortunately for us these questions do not impinge on the *Meno*.

Stylistic analysis gives no clear result about the order of dialogues within each group. For the two later groups, cross-references and other fairly obvious clues indicate an order approximating to that which I have listed (except for the doubt about the *Timaeus*). The point of greatest interest for the *Meno* is that the earliest middle-period works seem clearly to be the *Phaedo*, *Symposium* and *Republic*.

Within the early group of dialogues there are no such explicit guides to their order. However, there are many indications of a subtler nature that the *Meno* comes late in the group. It is generally accepted that Plato's earliest works were the *Apology*, the *Crito*, and most or all of the others in the leftmost column above. These form the group often labelled 'short Socratic dialogues'. They are shorter even than the *Meno*, and vividly portray Socrates as it seems he was in real life, the self-styled 'gadfly' who went around Athens finding difficulties in everyone's views, demanding definitions and then refuting them all, exposing everyone's ignorance but apparently leaving the difficulties worse than when he started. Meno wittily sums up this picture in his analogy between Socrates and the torpedo fish which 'torpifies whoever comes near' (*Meno* 80a4–8). However, in the *Meno* Plato goes on, in the slave-boy episode, to show how being refuted can lead to positive results – which is certainly not the outcome in these other dialogues. In the *Meno* we see Plato consciously reflecting on Socrates' procedure and providing a defence of it which goes beyond anything in Socrates' own thought.

The *Protagoras* also is generally agreed to be earlier than the *Meno*. Its picture of Socrates is on a much grander scale than that in the short Socratic dialogues, but essentially similar. The *Protagoras* and *Meno* have many points of contact. In particular, while several other early dialogues discuss specific virtues, only these two discuss virtue as a whole. Also, they are both alike concerned with the teaching of virtue, and both reach the dilemma that virtue seems to be knowledge yet not to come from teaching. These very points of contact emphasize the development from the *Protagoras* to the *Meno*. For instance, the *Protagoras* ends with the proposition that what virtue itself is needs to be settled before discussing whether it comes from teaching. This, however, is precisely where the *Meno* begins, while where the *Meno* ends is far beyond this point, for despite Socrates' ritual protestations against discussing anything else about virtue before defining it, he in fact manages perfectly well to make at least a start, by using the 'hypothetical method' which here makes its début in Plato. Another contrast is that the *Protagoras*, like the short Socratic dialogues, shows none of the mathematical, metaphysical and religious interests prominent in the *Meno*. In the *Protagoras* 'knowledge' is uncompromisingly this-worldly; in the *Meno* the theory of recollection points towards a link between knowledge and eternal truths which would set the

Socratic saying 'Virtue is knowledge' in an entirely new light – though the *Meno* itself does not develop this suggestion.

The remaining early dialogues, the *Euthydemus*, *Gorgias* and *Menexenus* (omitting the *Cratylus* from present consideration), are generally agreed to be close in date to the *Meno*. Their order is disputed, but I would myself agree with E. R. Dodds (*Plato, Gorgias*, pp. 18–30) and Bluck (pp. 108–20) that it was most probably as in the table above; *Euthydemus* first, *Gorgias* and *Menexenus* next, and *Meno* last. All three of the *Euthydemus*, *Gorgias* and *Meno* discuss statesmanship and the part played in it by knowledge, and there are many resonances among them. However, in some important ways the *Gorgias* and *Meno* resemble the middle-period dialogue the *Phaedo*, rather than the *Euthydemus*, while in others the *Meno* is like the *Phaedo* rather than either the *Euthydemus* or the *Gorgias*. The *Gorgias* and *Meno* are both like the *Phaedo* in showing far more Pythagorean influence than the *Euthydemus* or any earlier dialogue, and they also come much closer to the *Phaedo*'s picture of Socrates as a philosopher with positive views. But only the *Meno* shares with the *Phaedo* the two key themes which most clearly mark the transition from early- to middle-period Plato, the theory of recollection and the hypothetical method.

To turn now briefly to the *Meno*'s actual date of composition, we have no direct evidence, but in all probability it was written soon after Plato's first visit to Italy and Sicily – thus during or soon after 385 BC. The new Pythagorean influence shown in the *Gorgias* and *Meno* would thus stem partly from Plato's personal meetings with Archytas and other Pythagoreans. This date also links the *Meno* with another major event in Plato's life, the founding of the Academy, and we can clearly see within the dialogue how much the theme of education dominated Plato's thoughts at this time. But alongside these new interests which the *Meno* reflects, the Socrates of the Socratic dialogues still remains an important force.

So much for the *Meno*'s background and immediate context. It is equally interesting to see what it points forward to, and especially its relationship with Plato's most famous doctrine, the Theory of Forms, first to be explicitly presented in the classic 'Platonist' dialogues *Phaedo, Symposium* and *Republic*. A brief description of this will help to set the *Meno* in perspective with it.

In *Republic* Book X Plato makes Socrates say 'Our custom is to posit a single form in each case, from each set of many things to

11

which we apply the same name', adding that it is the form, not any of the many instances, which is what the quality in question actually *is*. This in itself does not go far beyond the *Meno* (and other early dialogues), except for Socrates' increased self-consciousness about his method. However, in the *Phaedo, Symposium* and *Republic* further contrasts, far stronger than any before, are drawn between forms and their instances. To take Plato's favourite example, the form 'beauty', it is argued that since this is by definition what beauty actually is, it must be beautiful absolutely and without qualification, independently of place and time, for to suppose otherwise would be self-contradictory. By contrast, the *instances* – that is, all the things ordinarily called beautiful – are beautiful only in particular respects and contexts, and at particular times; thus one and the same thing will be beautiful at one time, in one context or in one respect, while ugly in others. The same applies to other forms – justice, largeness, equality, etc. Hence arises Plato's famous 'two world' theory of reality. Our familiar world of the senses contains only instances, not forms, since the senses cannot show us what beauty, largeness, justice, etc. are in themselves. Therefore, Plato concludes, the forms must constitute a wholly separate world, not perceptible but knowable by the intellect. Only the forms really *are* what they are, since only they are what they are *in themselves*, while instances of forms are what they are only derivatively, through 'partaking in' or 'resembling' the relevant forms. In the *Republic*, there is yet a further development. One form, that of the Good, is singled out as supreme, the ultimate explanation of why the other forms are as they are and, correspondingly, the ultimate goal and ground of all knowledge.

On this theory, knowledge cannot come from the senses. This point is central in the *Phaedo*'s new argument for the theory of recollection. Starting from the obvious fact that our knowledge of, for example, equality is indeed *triggered* by perception – by seeing equal stones and sticks – Socrates points out that we are well aware that such things are 'equal' only in a qualified sense and thus cannot actually be equality itself. But this awareness is only possible, he argues, if we have a latent knowledge of equality independent of all sense experience, i.e. from before birth, which is then forgotten at birth but which sense experience reactivates.

The aim of philosophy on this theory is to know the forms – especially, in the *Republic*, the form of the Good. Such knowledge is the highest happiness of which human beings are capable. It also has practical value, since only in its light can human affairs be guided aright, and hence the *Republic*'s ideal of philosopher-statesmen. However, the *Republic* does not allow that even a philosopher can strictly have *knowledge* of practical instances of beauty, justice, etc.; it argues that these are intrinsically unknowable, on the grounds that only what fully *is* can be known and only forms fully *are*, and relegates them to 'opinion'.

Everyone must agree that the full Theory of Forms just outlined is not to be found explicitly in the *Meno*. The mere fact that Socrates there describes virtue, strength, etc. as *eidē* or 'forms' (72c7; 72d8; 72e5) does not in itself imply that they are seen as *Platonic* forms existing separately from their instances, since obviously the word *eidē* could not acquire this technical use until the theory was spelt out. What matters is what the *Meno* says or does not say about these 'forms'; and the position is that although the *Meno* emphasizes that one form has many instances and that the form is what, for example, virtue or shape 'actually is', it does not remotely suggest that the forms are what they are more perfectly than the instances, or that they are *separate from* rather than *present within* them. It is the *Phaedo*'s new argument for the theory of recollection which first adds these points. Nor does the *Meno* exclude knowledge of the perceptible world; indeed the example of the road to Larisa assumes that there can be such knowledge. A reader of the *Meno* who had not also read or heard about the *Republic* would I think be hardly likely to attribute a two-world theory of reality to Plato.

However, for those who have read the *Republic* and other middle-period dialogues it is easy to see that such a theory is at least near the horizon. In particular, the theory of recollection linking knowledge with truths known from all eternity becomes reworked into the *Phaedo*'s argument that knowledge must ultimately derive from acquaintance with the eternal forms, while the *Meno*'s emphatic contrast between knowledge and opinion is taken up and further developed in the *Republic*, and both the *Phaedo* and the *Republic* expand on the hypothetical method which the *Meno* first introduces.

These links are so clear that various commentators have felt that the full Theory of Forms must be not only near the horizon but implicitly already present in the *Meno*. I think myself that this is a distortion. But the question is a controversial one which cannot be sensibly discussed except through detailed consideration of particular topics in the *Meno*; in fact it is a recurrent motif throughout this volume.

## IV  THE DRAMATIC SETTING OF THE *MENO*

The *Meno* is among those of Plato's dialogues which stand out most strongly as works of literature as well as philosophy, each character being a distinct individual who joins in the discussion after his own manner. Moreover, the people are not merely vivid stage characters, but except for Meno's slave they are known historical people. We cannot compare the portraits with the originals as Plato's contemporaries could, but all the evidence suggests that they were strikingly telling as likenesses, as well as in their own right.

### Time and place

The dialogue represents a conversation between Socrates and Meno, a young aristocrat from Thessaly. The place is somewhere unspecified in Athens. The dramatic date is clear within a year or two. Meno is the same person whom Xenophon describes in the *Anabasis* as one of the Greek mercenaries employed by Cyrus in his unsuccessful attempt on the Persian throne; he was in Asia Minor by 401 BC[18] and died, executed by the king of Persia, in 400 BC.[19] The dramatic date of Plato's *Meno* is therefore before 401 BC. On the other hand it cannot be many years earlier, since Meno was 'still a youth'[20] (i.e. not yet 21) during the expedition. Also, Anytus is introduced in the *Meno* as currently holding office as a democratic politician. The dramatic date must therefore be during 403–402 BC, when democracy was newly restored in Athens after the fall of the Thirty Tyrants.

### Characters

Plato's portrait of Socrates has already been briefly discussed above in describing the *Meno*'s place among Plato's writings (pp. 10–11), and for full discussion of Socrates the reader should turn on to the article in this volume by Kidd (pp. 73–87), so no more need be said here.

Meno is portrayed in vivid detail. He is marked out from the start as confident and assertive: 'Can you tell me, Socrates . . .?', he begins – the *Meno*'s abrupt opening is unique among Plato's dialogues. It quickly emerges that Meno is rich, well born, and young and beautiful enough to attract lovers. Bearing in mind that in Plato's Greece it was a common fashion for older men to be homosexually attracted towards boys in their mid to late teens, we should picture Meno as being 18 or 19 years old. His taste for discussions about virtue is already well developed; he has heard Gorgias on the subject enthusiastically and, doubtless helped by Gorgias' guidelines, has also enjoyed giving talks about it himself. Now he is keen to hear Socrates' views – especially if they are expressed in the style to which Gorgias has accustomed him. He is self-willed in discussion, and several times gets his way, most notably when Socrates agrees to forsake his own principles and discuss whether virtue comes from teaching before settling what it is. He is also prepared to object boldly to Socrates' procedures, the most striking example being his challenge at 80d5–6, 'But how can you find out what you don't know at all?', which changes the whole course of the dialogue. What he is repeatedly *not* prepared to do is to struggle on when the going gets tough. He is keen for answers, but impatient of the effort needed to achieve real understanding. Indeed, one aspect of the challenge to Socrates just mentioned is, as Socrates points out, that 'weak-willed people love to hear it' because it rationalizes laziness (81d7). Doubtless related is Meno's haziness about the points he has actually accepted in discussion. For instance, he happily assents to the proposition that virtue must involve justice and temperance (73b), but then twice needs reminding of it (73d; 78d). Again, after seeming highly impressed by Socrates' conversation with the slave-boy and by the conclusions which Socrates draws from this, he goes straight on afterwards as though it had never taken place.

For all these weaknesses, Plato's Meno is not an unsympathetic figure – self-willed but at least free from sullenness – even when he goes on strike he does it prettily – and ready to be appreciative even if he does not retain points very well. There is a big contrast between Plato's picture and that which Xenophon gives of unmitigated greed and general odiousness.[21] It is clear that Xenophon's portrait is exaggerated (he himself admits that points in it are disputable), but it is also clear that Meno's short career after the imagined conversation with Socrates was tarnished and ended miserably. Plato must of course have written on the assumption that his readers knew this, and the knowledge gives an extra poignancy to his picture of a young man of promise but little staying power, wanting to discuss how people acquire virtue but without time or patience really to work out any answer.

No such leniency is shown towards Anytus. He is introduced at *Meno* 90a as a popular Athenian democratic politician, and from other sources we know that he had been exiled from Athens by the Thirty Tyrants[22] and was one of those involved in the successful *coup* which restored democracy.[23] He was later one of the prosecutors at Socrates' trial. Xenophon's *Apology* claims that he was partly motivated by a personal grudge[24] but this finds no support in Plato. What the *Meno* suggests is that Anytus felt himself deeply threatened by Socrates, not so much personally as in his capacity as one of the 'fine and good', or in other words of the leading members of the Athenian establishment (see, particularly, 95a). Initially he is prepared to humour Socrates' questions with good grace, but he soon lapses into the kneejerk reactions of sheer prejudice, and finally storms out with a barely disguised threat. Socrates meanwhile seems happy to provoke him, and comes close to positive rudeness, both in the patronizing tone with which he first introduces him (90a–b), and in the bluntness with which he later exposes Anytus' prejudices. The effect conveyed is that these two men *could not* but become totally antipathetic to one another.

Finally, even Meno's slave has character. To some degree, his function is to be colourless; as Bluck says, he 'merely represents someone who is completely uneducated' (p. 28). However, he develops colour as he goes on. By the time he admits defeat, at 84a1–2, he is beginning to be a real person, and he is even more so by the time he reaches his solution to the problem at 85b – though it is still Socrates who underlines his identity for him: 'you, *Meno's slave*, say . . .'. Even this sketch is finely drawn.

## Dialogue form and interpretation

The special delight of reading Plato is his use of the dialogue form; it is also the special bugbear of those who want to read him as a philosopher. By writing dialogues rather than treatises Plato brings about two distinct effects. First and more obvious, the sharpness of interplay between viewpoints which he achieves by this method enables him to bring philosophy wonderfully to life as a dramatic spectacle. Second, by writing dialogues Plato distances himself from all his characters, including even Socrates; that is, one cannot just assume that any of them straightforwardly represent Plato's own views. Without a doubt, he used this way of writing quite deliberately for educative, not only artistic, purposes. The effect it achieves when used genuinely – that is, nót in such a way that one speaker can be immediately recognized as the author's mouthpiece – is that it forces the reader's attention on to the argument, never letting him surrender comfortably to the authority of any speaker. Plato is in fact trying to do for us, his readers, what he shows Socrates trying to do for Meno: trying to make us think for ourselves rather than simply collect views from an authority. At the same time Plato is also giving *himself* opportunity to explore and develop ideas in his writing, without being necessarily committed to them. That this is happening in the *Meno* is made abundantly clear at the end: '*On the basis of this reasoning*', Socrates concludes, 'we find that virtue apparently comes to men by divine dispensation. But we shan't have clear knowledge about it, until . . . we first try to search what [virtue] is in itself' (100b4–6).

So can we tell at all what Plato's own views were from his dialogues? In theory, the answer should be no, but in practice this is implausibly extreme, and a much more plausible view is that one can draw *some* conclusions by careful reading, and by noticing the nuances of the discussion. By this approach one can in fact trace the broad line of development in Plato's thought from the early destructive dialogues to the full Theory of Forms of the *Phaedo, Symposium* and *Republic*, and on into conscious criticism of this in later dialogues, that has been outlined in the previous section of this Introduction. But the tentative and questing nature of Plato's philosophy makes its interpretation always a matter of great subtlety.

## V  PHILOSOPHICAL THEMES AND ISSUES IN THE *MENO*

### Meno's question 'Does virtue come from teaching?'

Throughout my translation in this volume, I have used 'virtue' for the Greek term *aretē* and 'comes from teaching' for *didakton*.

*Aretē* is a wider term than 'virtue', covering all kinds of good quality of animate or inanimate subjects. On these grounds the translation 'excellence' is sometimes preferred. However, within the *Meno*, *aretē* is being used in its common narrower meaning, to

17

refer specifically to the qualities most to be valued in human beings. 'Excellence' is too vague to translate this well; for instance, the question 'Does excellence come from teaching?' hardly even makes sense unless one explains what sort of excellence is meant. The traditional translation 'virtue' seems to me still the best available, though in using it one should certainly not assume that Greek and modern views coincide as to what *constitutes* virtue.

*Didakton* is poised in meaning between what is taught and what can be taught, and 'comes from teaching' seems to me the translation which captures this best, while also reflecting the presupposition within Meno's question that virtue arises in only one way.

The question whether virtue comes from teaching was, as Nehamas points out in his article in this volume (pp. 221–48), a commonplace of Socrates' time. Broadly speaking, in early Greek society virtue had been thought of as the natural endowment of the well born, but by the fifth century BC a 'rise of the (male!) meritocracy' was under way, leading to a demand for education from those wishing to compete, which the Sophists saw themselves as meeting. Of the various Sophists, Protagoras firmly identified what he taught as *virtue*, including within this term both political effectiveness and also moral qualities such as justice (Plato, *Protag.* 319–23). By contrast, Gorgias laughed at the idea of anyone's teaching virtue and professed only to make people clever orators (*Meno* 95c). A source other than Plato reflecting current debate as to whether virtue comes from teaching is the *Dissoi Logoi*, a series of theses and counter-theses on various topics dating from the period 403–395 BC.

Both the *Dissoi Logoi* and Plato's own *Protagoras* contain evidence of an awareness that virtue might result from a combination of factors rather than just one. So why do not only Meno, but also Socrates in his final argument that virtue does not come from teaching, ignore any such possibility? The answer to this must wait until we come to the interpretation of the last part of the *Meno*. Meanwhile, let me refer the reader to section I of Nehamas' article (pp. 222ff) for illuminating further discussion of Meno's question's historical background.

## Socrates' question 'What is virtue?' – Socratic definition

Socrates' immediate response to Meno's question whether virtue comes from teaching, is that he cannot say how virtue comes until he knows what virtue *is*. He generalizes the point: knowledge of *what* a thing is must come before knowledge of *what sort* of thing it is. To illustrate, he points out that one must know who Meno is before one can know what sort of a person he is. So, he asks Meno, what is virtue?

It soon becomes clear, despite this illustration, that Socrates is not suggesting that a reply could or should be given by simply pointing. He is demanding some single description which covers all cases of virtue, that is, some kind of definition. But exactly what kind of definition he is seeking is far from clear. The topic of Socratic definition is succinctly outlined by Kidd in his article on Socrates in this volume (pp. 84–5) and explored in depth by Crombie in his subtle and illuminating article 'Socratic definition' (pp. 172–207 of this volume). Here I would just like to introduce the subject by tracing how it arises in the *Meno*.

No successful definition of virtue emerges in the *Meno*, but there is evidence relevant to deciding what form Socrates demands that a successful definition should take. Some points come from Socrates' objections to the various proposed definitions of virtue offered by Meno. First, a definition must be unitary: Socrates will not accept a list of different varieties of virtue as saying what virtue is. Second, it must include all and only those items which are genuine instances of virtue. Third, it must not be circular.

Further evidence is provided by the three sample definitions which Socrates offers Meno at 75–6 – two of shape and one of colour:

(a) shape is the only thing there is which always accompanies colour;
(b) shape is the limit of a solid;
(c) colour is an efflux of shapes, commensurate with, and perceptible to, sight.

Socrates says that he demands no more than a definition similar to (a) for virtue, but Meno objects to (a), on the grounds that it would be useless to define shape in this way for anyone who did not know what colour is, and Socrates, while still maintaining that (a) is objectively true, concedes to Meno that constructive discussion needs to avoid terms which are not understood by both parties. As between (b) and (c), Socrates prefers (b). Meno's favourite is (c), but Socrates suggests that he might change his mind if he underwent a full training in philosophy (a gag for the Academy?). In fact, all three definitions can be faulted for not picking out the right phenomena; I leave this exercise to the reader. More importantly for present purposes, the three definitions differ in *form*. To use Crombie's terminology (pp. 172–4 and pp. 188–9), (a) serves to identify shape, (b) defines shape by analysing the concept, and (c) defines colour in terms of a theory of colour vision. The difference between (b) and (c) is that between a conceptual and a real definition. It seems from this section of the *Meno* that Socrates regards all three forms of statement as acceptable models, but is inclined to prefer the conceptual definition, (b), to the real definition, (c).

However, this is difficult to reconcile with other evidence within the *Meno* and elsewhere. First, it seems particularly strange that Socrates is ready to accept a statement such as (a), which does not say what shape is in itself, but only provides a fact about it. This is not what Socrates first said he wanted for virtue, and in the *Euthyphro* a proposed definition of holiness is rejected on these very grounds of only providing a fact about its subject rather than saying what the thing itself is. Possibly Socrates' point at *Meno* 75 is that to provide *any* single factor common to all cases of virtue would represent an advance over Meno's attempts so far. But this must remain a speculative suggestion, as Socrates does after all drop (a) very quickly. Second, a question which opens up much deeper doubts about the meaning of Socrates' question 'What is virtue?' is that the preference Socrates states for the answer (b) over (c) is inconsistent with the kind of answer which he elsewhere seems to demand. For instance, in the last part of the *Meno* Socrates seems to suggest that the proposition 'Virtue is a form of knowledge' is at least a possible and partial statement of what virtue is (only possible, rather than definite, because it is presented only as a hypothesis; and only partial, not complete, because it does not specify which particular kind of knowledge virtue might be). But, as Crombie points out, this proposition 'Virtue is a form of knowledge' clearly is not one which is implicit in the *concept* of virtue; if it is true at all, it must be so on a more factual level, as a matter of what virtue in practice consists in. So if 'Virtue is knowledge' is part of any kind of definition of virtue, it must be part of a real, rather than of a conceptual definition, that is, like (c) rather than like (b).

How is this discrepancy to be resolved? Also, is it fully correct to say that Socrates is seeking *any* kind of definition when he asks 'What is virtue?' As Crombie notes, his readiness to consider an answer such as 'Virtue is knowledge' suggests that his real target might be to identify the psychological roots of virtue rather than to define it (p. 189). I think that this point does not counterweigh the evidence that Plato's Socrates is at least *aiming* to define virtue. However, many 'ifs' and 'buts' need to be added, and it is time for me to pass the reader on to Crombie's article.

### Everyone desires good things and no one desires bad things – the Socratic paradox

On the argument of *Meno* 77c–78b Guthrie (*History of Greek Philosophy* IV, p. 246) aptly comments, 'One must admit that Plato lets Socrates make a wickedly sophistical use of ambiguity when he likes. Witness the way in which he uses Meno's last attempt at a definition [i.e. 'virtue is desiring fine things and having the power to achieve them'. Ed.] as an opportunity to prove his favourite thesis that no one does wrong willingly.' Nakhnikian's article, 'The first Socratic paradox' (pp. 129–51 of this volume) is exemplary in its patient, fair and tough-minded unravelling of Socrates' arguments, and well exposes the falsehood of Socrates' claim that no one can desire bad things. The claim is false, Nakhnikian shows, even of situations where the agent knows that it is he himself who will suffer, let alone of cases where the interests of different people conflict.

Socrates' argument does suggest a very interesting point which was later to be emphasized by Aristotle and which Nakhnikian does not deny, namely that every desire incorporates a perception of its object as in *some* way good. But this by no means saves Socrates' thesis, since being in some way good need not imply being wholly, or even preponderantly, good. Thus Meno's proposal that virtue is 'desiring fine things and having the power to achieve them' is not refuted by anything that Socrates says. Indeed, it seems rather a promising definition.

21

## How can we search for what we do not know? –
## Meno's paradox and the theory of recollection

The first third of the *Meno* is largely negative in outcome, much like the earlier Socratic dialogues, but the section which follows strikes a new and more positive note. At 80d Socrates suggests that he and Meno, since they both seem equally ignorant about virtue, should start again and try together to find out what it is. Meno responds with 'Meno's paradox': How can you search for something when you don't know at all what that thing is? For in such a situation how do you even know what to look for? It is Socrates' response in turn to this that has given the *Meno* its unique place in the history of philosophy. Knowledge, he replies, is essentially innate in the soul from all eternity, and what we call learning is really the recollection of truths once known but since forgotten. The search for knowledge is never hopeless, because any item can be recovered if the memory is suitably prompted. To illustrate this, Socrates shows how an uneducated slave can solve a geometrical problem without guidance other than a series of questions. Furthermore, though more tentatively, Socrates claims that this phenomenon entails that the human soul must be immortal.

This part of the *Meno* is of critical importance both within Plato's thought and within the whole history of ideas. Within Plato's thought, it marks the watershed between Socratic philosophy and Plato's own developing metaphysics. Within the whole history of ideas, however, its major importance is that here, for the first time on record, the possibility of achieving knowledge *a priori* – that is, from the mind's own resources rather than from experience – is articulated, demonstrated, and seen as raising important philosophical questions.

Four articles in this volume are directly focused on the issues which arise in this section: those by Vlastos, Moravcsik, White and Nehamas. Vlastos' valuable article, '*Anamnesis* in the *Meno*' (see pp. 88–111), takes its start from the demonstration with the slave which Socrates gives as proof that 'learning' is recollecting, and which offers, as Vlastos remarks, 'a chance, rare in Greek philosophy, to compare a philosophical theory with the data which make up its ostensible evidence'. So what are these data? Socrates takes a slave, who speaks Greek and knows how to count but is uneducated in geometry, poses a geometrical question which the slave answers incorrectly, and then goes on to pose a series of further questions, in answering which, the slave first realizes that his original answer was wrong, and finally, after various further false attempts, manages to answer correctly. According to Socrates, these data show that one can have knowledge without having been taught. In one sense, Socrates' claim is clearly false, because in an obvious sense he himself is teaching the slave: he is stimulating the slave's thoughts and supplying the diagrams. But the important truth remains that he is not *handing over* an answer but enabling the slave to find one for himself. As Vlastos rightly emphasizes, the slave does not simply read the answer off the diagrams but has to reason it out logically. Socrates is thus justified in claiming that knowledge can be gained from within oneself, in the sense of being grasped through one's own powers of reason. However, a second point which must be added is that this is true of only some, not all, types of knowledge. It is true of mathematics but not of history or botany, for instance. To generalize, it applies to knowledge based on logical necessity but not to knowledge based on experience.

Vlastos highlights both these points, and they both contribute to his interpretation of Plato's conclusions. He distinguishes between what he calls the 'minimal sense' of the theory of recollection and the doctrine in its 'full strength'. Its minimal sense is that demonstrative knowledge is independent of sense-experience, and Vlastos powerfully argues for Plato's pioneering role in formulating this principle and thus establishing that there can be non-empirical knowledge. The full-strength doctrine, however, adds the exaggerated claim that *all* knowledge is non-empirical. This leads straight into the Theory of Forms, which in Plato's view was needed to provide suitably non-empirical *objects* for knowledge. It also, Vlastos argues, demands a doctrine of reincarnation; indeed he suggests that Plato's belief in reincarnation came first, and was the historically necessary catalyst which made his recognition of non-empirical knowledge possible.

Vlastos' article raises various points of controversy. The reader will enjoy picking out some of these as he passes on from Vlastos to Moravcsik, White and Nehamas. Two others which I should like to add are the following. First, Vlastos seems to be reversing the direction of Plato's argument when he suggests that belief in reincarnation was a precondition for Plato's recognition of non-empirical knowledge. Socrates' argument runs *from* the slave's success *to* immortality (to immortality, incidentally, not to reincarnation). Indeed, Socrates claims to be more certain that success in inquiry is possible than he is about the later steps of the argument. Second, when Vlastos speaks of 'the full-strength doctrine of the *Meno*' he is blurring chronology: It was not until after the *Meno* was written that Plato published the Theory of Forms, or denied that there could be knowledge based on experience; in fact at *Meno* 97b Socrates asserts that knowledge of the road to Larisa not merely can, but must, be so based! However, these points by no means negate the usefulness of Vlastos' distinction between 'minimal' and 'full strength' senses of the theory of recollection for the purposes of analysis.

Moravcsik's article, 'Learning as recollection' (see pp. 112–27), forms an interesting complement to that by Vlastos. Moravcsik acknowledges indebtedness to Vlastos, but his article has a very different slant. Whereas Vlastos emphasizes the theory of recollection's historical significance, Moravcsik focuses on its meaning in logical terms. Starting from Meno's paradox which the theory of recollection professes to solve, he points out that this paradox applies only to learning by deliberate *inquiry* (as opposed to learning by chance or as the result of external agency). He agrees with Vlastos that Plato's discussion covers only non-empirical or, in Moravcsik's preferred terminology, *a priori* knowledge, and adds further arguments for this, although he also rightly points out that Plato never makes the limitation explicit. However, he goes on to argue for an important clarification: the truths which Socrates claims are reached by recollection are not, on this theory, viewed as knowable purely by *deduction*. If they were, there would be no need to postulate *memory* to explain how they are reached. Moravcsik is surely right here. It can be misleading to speak of the theory of recollection as concerned purely with deductive knowledge, since from the theory's own point of view the knowledge concerned is not purely deductive.

Finally, Moravcsik discusses the logical status of the theory of recollection itself: is it empirical hypothesis, *a priori* proposition, or mere metaphor? He argues that, like the knowledge it covers, so it too is in Plato's view something recollectable, thus *a priori* but not purely deductive or analytic. While Moravcsik's logical categories are to some extent anachronistic as applied to Plato (as he himself also recognizes), it is nevertheless illuminating to try to apply them, in order to find the intersection between Plato's and modern thought. But it is time to pass the reader on to Moravcsik himself.

The next article, White's 'Inquiry' (see pp. 152–71), is a lively and searching discussion concentrating on Meno's paradox. As White points out, Plato's elaborate reply to this paradox seems at first highly puzzling. Surely one can perfectly well search for something one does not know, provided that one has some specification of what one is searching for. Why does Plato not simply make Socrates point this out?

This is the question which White explores in his article, and he does so on two levels. First, he shows how the paradox could have arisen for Plato specifically out of his own work. He quotes evidence from the *Meno* and earlier dialogues showing how Plato felt *both* (a) that every claim to know a given object must be authenticated by a specification of that object, *and* (b) that every specification of a given object must be authenticated by checking with the object itself, a combination of demands which clearly forms a vicious circle and which could well have given Meno's paradox a special sting for Plato. But second, White explores various wider implications of the paradox, beyond its particular interest for Plato. One such implication is that a fully purposive project of inquiry must be literally *defined* by the specification from which it starts. There can be no room for refining one's initial specification as one goes along, without also making room for the paradox to rearise. (Incidentally, to draw out a point which White does not emphasize, this shows how pertinent Meno's paradox is to his and Socrates' situation regarding virtue; they have agreed on no clear specification of it at all.) White also suggests further interesting ramifications of the paradox, for which let me refer the reader to his article. He amply demonstrates that the paradox has more than a purely historical interest.

White's article closes with a salutary demonstration that Plato's own theory of learning as recollection is no solution whatever to Meno's paradox, since it immediately gives rise to a paradox of recollection which is exactly analogous to the original paradox of inquiry.

We come lastly to Nehamas' article, 'Meno's paradox and Socrates as a teacher' (see pp. 221–48), which provides a yet further viewpoint contrasting with and complementing all three preceding articles. Nehamas offers an illuminating analysis of Meno's paradox as it arose for Plato in reflecting on Socrates and on the Socratic method of doing philosophy, and of the theory of recollection as answering the paradox on this specific front. After pointing out that Meno's paradox poses a threat for Socrates and Meno only because they are both alike totally ignorant about virtue, Nehamas asks why they should not solve their problem simply by finding someone with the requisite knowledge to teach them both. He answers by demonstrating from the *Protagoras* and elsewhere that Plato had already ruled out this solution, on the ground that, unless one already knows for oneself what virtue is, one cannot even know which teacher's views are sound. The only kind of person from whom it would be safe to seek help would thus be someone like Socrates, whose method involved no presumption that he himself had knowledge. But how can a student actually *learn* anything, if he is not to draw on his teacher's knowledge? As Nehamas rightly says, this can only be shown possible by solving Meno's paradox. (Indeed, though Nehamas does not say this, the problem of finding a sound teacher can be seen with hindsight as simply one application of the more general problem raised by Meno.)

The demonstration with the slave disarms the paradox by showing how Socratic questioning *can*, in fact, lead towards knowledge by stimulating the learner to form and test his own opinions. The test involved is simply that of whether these opinions can stand up as the questioning continues, and it is in this test that Nehamas finds the nub of Plato's primary answer to Meno: one can know what one does not know, because one's lack of knowledge is revealed in one's inability to answer continued questions, while the continued ability to answer suggests that knowledge has now been reached. Nehamas emphasizes how crucially this test depends on the actual questioning process, with the result, as he puts it, that 'Plato's resolution of Meno's paradox is dialectical rather than logical' (p. 240).

In identifying the episode with the slave, rather than the theory of recollection, as Plato's primary answer to Meno, Nehamas disagrees with White, who claims that Plato's primary answer to Meno is the theory of recollection, while the episode with the slave is there to support the theory. Nehamas' analysis seems clearly closer than White's to the order of Plato's reasoning, as I have mentioned above (pp. 23–4). However, as Nehamas himself allows, it is only when Plato introduces the theory of recollection that he moves on from demonstrating how Socratic questioning does in practice lead to learning to explaining how this is possible. Thus Nehamas' article leaves untouched White's main arguments about the logic of Meno's paradox and the objective inadequacy of

Plato's solution. However, Nehamas' concern is different; it is to trace how *Plato* saw his response to Meno's paradox. On this front I think that, by and large, White's arguments do not touch Nehamas. But this question, and many further interesting points raised by Nehamas and by the other authors in this section, I must now leave for the reader to pursue for himself.

## The *Meno*'s hypothetical conclusions

After the high hopes of progress raised by the slave-boy episode and the theory of recollection, the rest of the *Meno* comes as a puzzling surprise. Meno accepts Socrates' arguments superficially, but he has not really grasped them, as his next words show. First, he still wants to ask whether virtue comes from teaching before settling what virtue itself is, thus disregarding all that Socrates has said about the importance of asking questions in the right order. Second, he blithely asks both to 'consider' and to 'hear about' the subject, when 'hearing about' a subject is precisely the route to knowledge which has just been ruled out. Meno's relapse is not surprising in itself: the surprise is that Socrates apparently goes along with it, and not only agrees to discuss whether virtue comes from teaching before defining what it is, but also tacitly lets Meno slip out of the hot seat in discussion, supplying all the positive ideas himself from this point on.

The puzzlement arising from these points extends to the whole of the rest of the *Meno*. Socrates begins by stating that his answer will have to rest on hypotheses since it cannot be based on knowledge. This restores some respectability to proceedings from Socrates' point of view, but gives little help to the reader in trying to interpret what follows. Next Socrates argues that virtue must come from teaching, on the grounds that all knowledge does so, and that virtue is knowledge. Then, however, he turns about, and argues that virtue does *not* come from teaching, and therefore is not knowledge, on the grounds that no actual teachers of virtue can be identified. Finally he suggests that, instead of being knowledge, virtue is 'right opinion' achievable only by divine favour, though he emphasizes that this conclusion is only provisional and would be overthrown immediately if a genuine teacher of virtue should appear.

What conclusions does Plato intend to convey by this whole discussion? This question forms the subject of Wilkes' interesting and suggestive article, 'Conclusions in the *Meno*' (see pp. 208–20), which I should like to introduce by giving a sample of interpretations previously advanced by others.

Broadly speaking the last part of the *Meno* can be interpreted in two contrasting ways:

(a) Plato is here abandoning the uncompromising Socratic view that virtue must always be knowledge, and while holding to the *ideal* that virtue should be knowledge he now recognizes a second legitimate form of virtue consisting in 'right opinion' (*orthē doxa*).

(b) The true conclusion of the *Meno* is that virtue is knowledge and comes from teaching, as argued at 87–9, while the whole subsequent argument is ironical and consciously fallacious.

Among the many commentators taking the first of these views are A. E. Taylor, Gould, Bluck and Sharples. In Taylor's view (*Plato, the Man and his Work*, pp. 138–45), the main purpose of the *Meno*'s final argument is 'to distinguish between a higher and a lower kind of goodness' (p. 144), thus adumbrating the doctrine of the *Republic*, where even in Plato's ideal state only the philosopher-rulers have virtue based on knowledge, while the other citizens have only a secondary kind of virtue resting not on knowledge but on simple loyalty to the state's sound traditions. Plato in the *Meno*, Taylor thinks, recognizes that even a non-ideal state such as Athens is bound to include enough good elements within its tradition to form the basis for some kind of virtue, though at the same time emphasizing how shadowy such virtue must be in comparison with true virtue based on knowledge, if only this could be achieved. Gould's view (*Plato's Ethics*, pp. 133–41) is broadly similar to Taylor's but sees Plato as placing perhaps even a slightly higher value on 'right opinion'. He points out that the *Meno* never suggests that opinions need be acquired at second hand, and claims that the essential difference between knowledge and opinion in the *Meno* is simply that opinion fails to rise above particular instances and reach basic principles (which Gould equates with Forms). Among Plato's writings Gould sees the *Meno* as 'the first place where the second-best appears in conjunction with *epistēmē* as something of value' (p. 141).

Bluck (pp. 19–43) in one way differs strongly from Taylor, in that he rejects the proposition that Plato recognized virtue based on 'right opinion' in any Greek city. However, he agrees with Taylor and Gould on the broader proposition that there *could* be a kind of virtue based on right opinion, and that this would be a prototype of the ordinary citizens' virtue in the *Republic*. The big difference between any actual state and the *Republic*'s ideal one, Bluck points out, is that the *Republic*'s ideal state is guided by people with genuine knowledge, and it is from this that the opinions of the rest derive their truth. Sharples (pp. 10–15) generally supports Bluck on all these points.

Bluck's major objection to Taylor is that the dominant feature in the *Meno*'s treatment of Anytus and other actual public figures is irony, making it absurd to suppose that Plato saw them as in any way like the citizens in the *Republic*, and on this point Bluck seems unquestionably correct. However, Bluck's own attempt to find in the *Meno* some type of virtue based on opinion, *other* than that which might be claimed for the so-called 'fine and good' in actual Greek cities, seems equally far fetched. When Socrates at the very end of the *Meno* expresses the hope that some day virtue can be passed from one person to another, the clear implication is that the virtue thus passed on will be knowledge, since the *Meno* envisages no way of passing on virtue other than by teaching, and maintains that nothing can be taught other than knowledge. This framework simply does not allow for the idea developed in the *Republic* that a form of virtue based on right opinion could be transmitted from person to person.

Thus the attempt to locate a legitimate form of virtue based on right opinion within the *Meno* runs into problems whether we identify this with the virtue of the 'fine and good' in Greece or whether we try to contrast the two.

Wilkes' article develops the other main method of interpreting the *Meno*, which takes the dialogue's true conclusion to be that virtue is knowledge, and the argument against this to be ironical. She points out that the hypothesis 'Virtue is knowledge' is known to represent Socrates' own view, while the question 'Can virtue be taught?' is equated at 86c7 with 'Can it be recollected?', and therefore the later argument for virtue's unteachability, resting as it does on the claim that no one teaches virtue in the 'orthodox' sense of handing it over like a parcel, is simply irrelevant. Also, the proposition that true opinion with all its instability could add up to virtue cannot be seriously attributed to either Socrates or Plato.

Wilkes therefore interprets *Meno* 87–9 as presenting what Plato sees as the true conclusion about virtue, namely that it is knowledge and hence 'teachable' in the sense of 'recollectable'. She claims that Meno reaches true opinion at 89a–c just as the slave did at 85a–b. She interprets Socrates' later arguments as deliberately disrupting Meno's true opinion, to which Meno lays himself open by not noticing that the sense of 'teaching' has been changed. The implication of Socrates' procedure is, she suggests, that in order to provoke Meno to further thought it is better to leave him with a false opinion which he finds unsatisfactory, than with a true one which he may find so satisfactory that he mistakes it for knowledge. However, she suggests that the last argument does incidentally provide a seriously intended demonstration that virtue cannot be taught by orthodox means. Finally, at the end of the dialogue, she interprets the allusion to a genuine teacher of virtue as hinting towards Socrates himself as fulfilling this role.

Any reader of Wilkes' article would, I think, find it difficult to revert to the interpretation which takes Plato to be seriously identifying virtue with right opinion; her case against it is overwhelming. There are just three comments I should like to make by way of addition or qualification to her treatment.

First, and a very minor point, it is questionable whether Plato thought he had validly shown even that virtue cannot come from orthodox teaching, as Wilkes claims (p. 215). As I have mentioned above (p. 18), Plato's own earlier work, the *Protagoras*, shows awareness that virtue might result from a combination of factors rather than just one. In that dialogue Protagoras claims that success demands *both* suitable teaching *and* aptitude in the pupil, and Socrates has no answer (*Protag.* 323–8). Plato could hardly have forgotten this argument between writing the *Protagoras* and the *Meno*. This point in fact reinforces Wilkes' broader claim that the argument in the *Meno* against the teachability of virtue is ironical, since it suggests that Plato saw his own argument as fallacious even when applied to 'orthodox' teaching.

My second point again reinforces Wilkes' broader conclusions. She suggests that in the *Meno* 'aretē is not only the product, it is also the process of inquiry' and as such is already displayed in searching for knowledge even before knowledge is reached (pp. 216–17). If true this would be devastating for the principle that virtue is knowledge, since virtue clearly cannot be knowledge if it can be displayed when knowledge is not yet present. But I do not think it is true. Wilkes infers it from Socrates' statement at 86b–c that men become 'better people' by trying to achieve knowledge than if they do not even try. But this remark need not imply that these people's state already amounts to 'virtue', and I do not think it can be meant to do so, especially in view of Socrates' argument soon afterwards (88a–d) that good qualities only amount to virtue when knowledge is present to direct them rightly. Thus there is no case here for diluting the thesis that virtue is knowledge.

However, the third point I would like to make is that I think we would be going too far if we interpret this thesis as being what Plato intends us to understand as the *Meno*'s true conclusion about virtue. The *Meno* does indeed give the impression that Socrates *would like* to show that virtue is knowledge. However, it must not be forgotten that the entire last part of the dialogue is represented as hypothetical – as resting in mid-air until the nature of virtue is established – and it is hardly legitimate to represent it as reaching any conclusion firmly. Plato presents *neither* 'Virtue is true opinion' *nor* 'Virtue is knowledge' as a firm conclusion. Socrates' last words include the reminder that they know nothing yet for sure about virtue (100b4), and at 89c8–9 he has specifically said that it is unsound to assert a conclusion unless it seems right 'always' (i.e. stands up to critical examination), which he then immediately proceeds to claim is not the case with the conclusion that virtue is knowledge. He and Meno, that is to say, have no business to maintain that virtue is knowledge unless they can defend their claim against objections – and the objections to the claim that virtue is knowledge are not in fact answered in the *Meno*.

I do not think this point can really be answered by Wilkes' suggestion that Socrates is deliberately disrupting Meno's true opinion for pedagogic purposes. Her analogy between Meno at 89 and the slave-boy at 85 will not work, for the reason that Socrates, Meno and the reader all know that the slave's answer at 85 is correct, even if the slave does not, whereas Socrates emphasizes that neither he nor anyone else knows the answer to questions about virtue, thus no one is in a position to recognize whether Meno's opinion at 89 actually is true or not.

Let us also not forget what a weak argument 87–9 has actually offered for this thesis that virtue is knowledge – one that is hardly more satisfactory than the later argument against it. First, Socrates has failed to show that knowledge is necessary for virtue. He claimed this on the grounds that virtue must produce beneficial results and only knowledge can achieve this, but as he later points out, true opinions produce exactly the same results as knowledge while they last. Now, the greater stability of knowledge over opinion might well form the basis of some *new* argument that knowledge is necessary for virtue, but the fact remains that the original argument fails and has not been replaced. Second, Socrates needed to show not just that knowledge is necessary for virtue but that it is *sufficient* to ensure virtue. Otherwise his argument could not support the conclusion that virtue is knowledge and comes from teaching, but only the conclusion that virtue *involves* knowledge and that teaching has some contribution to make *towards* virtue. But 87–9 omits altogether to argue that knowledge is sufficient to ensure virtue, and in fact of course it is not, for reasons similar to those brought by Nakhnikian in this volume against the Socratic paradox (pp. 137ff.): it is possible to act against what one knows to be for the best through weakness of will, or even to do so wilfully (e.g., if one's own interests conflict with other people's, to take the most obvious case). Thus even if knowledge is necessary for virtue it does not follow that virtue actually *is* a form of knowledge.

In fact Socrates' own conclusion is, to be precise, not 'Virtue is knowledge' but 'Virtue is wisdom' – in Greek, *phronēsis*, not *epistēmē* – and his claim gains a certain plausibility from this choice of words. *Phronēsis*, like its translation 'wisdom', is a term normally used so as to *imply* right action as well as true reasoning. However, in this respect 'knowledge' and 'wisdom' diverge; 'wisdom' implies right use but 'knowledge' does not. On the other hand, it is knowledge, rather than wisdom, which can plausibly be claimed to come from teaching. Wilkes correctly remarks that Socrates equates the two terms. But this does not make his argument any the better. All in all, it can hardly be claimed that the reader of the *Meno* has objective grounds for preferring the argument that virtue is knowledge to its counterpart.

Therefore if we are to take it as the one of the two which Plato intends more seriously, it must be because *he* indicates this is so. What does the text suggest is his view? He clearly expresses an unresolved doubt as to whether knowledge is *necessary* for virtue. His position on the question whether knowledge is *sufficient* for virtue is less clear. Perhaps he moves tentatively towards recognition that it is not, when he lists memory and quickness of learning as themselves things which require to be rightly used in order to be beneficial, but this must remain uncertain. It would be unjustified to suggest that Plato had the errors of 87–9 clearly formulated in his mind. However, it is only fair to recognize that he did in fact get in before his critics in rejecting its argument as *somehow* unsound.

To sum up. As Wilkes so amply demonstrates, the *Meno* does not propose the view that any form of virtue is right opinion. However, I would suggest that it does not propose the view that virtue is knowledge, either. It begins to explore these possibilities, but gets no further than negative results. The dialogue ends genuinely inconclusive about both Meno's and Socrates' questions about virtue, even though with positive signs of planning as to how to reach answers to questions in future.

At which point I close this Introduction, and leave the reader to the pleasure of picking his own way through all the many arguments within and around the *Meno*.

## NOTES

1 Plato mentions himself only twice in the dialogues (*Apol.* 38b6, *Phaedo* 59b10), but other members of his family feature more often. There are two main sources for his life: 1) the Platonic Letters, especially the Seventh. Doubts have been raised about the authenticity of all the Letters, but the Seventh, or at least its autobiographical part, is generally accepted as genuine, as is also the Eighth; 2) Diogenes Laertius' life of Plato in his *Lives of Eminent Philosophers* (hereafter D.L.). This is a rather uncritical work of the third century AD which, however, quotes some sources close to Plato's lifetime. For further details about sources see W. K. C. Guthrie, *History of Greek Philosophy* IV, pp. 8–10.
2 D.L. 3.2 quotes this date from Apollodorus, mentioning also a variant date two years earlier.
3 Xenophon, *Memorabilia*, 1.1.1. and D.L. 2.40 quote this as the actual wording.
4 D.L. 3.6, quoting Plato's pupil Hermodorus.
5 D.L. 3.6, and for Egypt also Strabo 17.29, but both accounts as they stand contain impossibilities. Cicero (*De Fin.* 5.29.87 and *Rep.* 1.10.16) also mentions Egypt, and perhaps carries a little more weight.
6 Cicero *De Fin.* 5.29.87, *Rep.* 1.10.16, *Tusc.* 1.17.39.
7 For extended discussion of Pythagoreanism see Guthrie, *History of Greek Philosophy* I, pp. 146–319 and his references, and for Archytas in particular see ibid., pp. 333–6. Sharples suggests (p. 2) that Archytas to some extent inspired Plato's conception of the philosopher-statesman, but this goes against *Ep.* 7, 326a2–5, *Rep.* 497a9–b2, and indeed *Meno* 100a, all of which imply that no philosopher-statesman has actually existed.

8 *Ep.* 7, 326a5–b4 indicates that Plato by now at any rate believed that the cure for society's ills lay in education, even if he had not yet planned to found an establishment.

9 Diodorus 15.7, Plutarch, *Dion* 5, and D.L. 3.20 give differing variants of this story.

10 See G. C. Field, *Plato and his Contemporaries*, p. 18, who attributes this suggestion to Eduard Meyer.

11 Despite the many differences between the Academy and most modern universities, the term 'university' still seems essentially correct. See further, Field, op. cit., pp. 30–48 and Guthrie IV, pp. 19–24.

12 See Guthrie IV, pp. 23–4.

13 Including the famous 'Lecture on the Good', on which see Guthrie IV, pp. 21–2.

14 E.g., at *Protag.* 334c7–336b3, *Theaet.* 148e6–150d8, and of course also *Meno* 82a4–85d, 1.

15 D.L. 3.46 lists various members of the Academy. See further, Guthrie, *History of Greek Philosophy* V, pp. 446–92.

16 *Ep.* 7, 327d7–330c1; 337e3–341b3; 345c2–350b5.

17 Dion's death, which did not occur until 353 BC, is presupposed in *Epp.* 7 and 8 *passim.*

18 *Anabasis* I.2.6.

19 *Anabasis* II.6.29.

20 *Anabasis* II.6.28.

21 *Anabasis* II.6.21–29.

22 *Hellenica* II.3.42.

23 Lysias XIII.78.

24 Xenophon, *Apology* 29–31.

# TRANSLATION OF THE *MENO*

*Jane M. Day*

**Meno: Socrates: One of Meno's slaves: Anytus**

*Meno*  Can you tell me, Socrates – does virtue come from 70a
teaching? Or does it come not from teaching but from practice? Or
does it come to people neither from practice nor from being learnt,
but by nature or in some other way?

*Socrates*  Well, Meno, in the past it was for horsemanship and
wealth that the Thessalians were famous among the Greeks and
admired, but now, I think, it is for wisdom too, especially your  b
friend Aristippus' fellow-citizens in Larisa. You owe all this to
Gorgias. When he went to that city, he won over the most eminent
people as lovers for his wisdom – both those within the Aleuad
family (including your own lover Aristippus) and those among the
other Thessalians. In particular he trained you in the habit of
answering any questions anyone asks with the grand confidence
that suits people with knowledge, just as he himself too volunteers  c
to be asked anything that anyone in the Greek world may wish, and
never leaves anyone unanswered. But here in Athens, my dear
Meno, the opposite has happened. A sort of drought of wisdom has
developed, and it seems that wisdom has left these parts for yours.
At any rate, if you want to ask one of the people here such a  71a
question there's no one who won't laugh and say: 'Well, stranger,
perhaps you think I'm some specially favoured person – I'd certainly need to be, to know whether virtue comes from teaching or
in what way it does come – but in fact I'm so far from knowing
whether it comes from teaching or not, that actually I don't even
know at all what virtue itself is!'

And that's the situation I'm in too, Meno. I'm as impoverished as  b
my fellow-citizens in this respect, and confess to my shame that I

don't know about virtue at all. And if I don't know what something is, how could I know what that thing is like? Or do you think it possible, if someone doesn't know who Meno is at all, that this person should know whether he's beautiful or rich, or whether he's well-born, or whether he's the opposite of all these? Do you think that possible?

*Meno*   No I don't. But is it really true about *you*, Socrates, that you don't even know what virtue is? Is this the report about you   c that we're to take home with us?

*Soc.*   Not just that, my friend, but also that I don't think I've yet met anyone else who does, either.

*Meno*   What? Didn't you meet Gorgias when he was here?

*Soc.*   Yes I did.

*Meno*   You mean you didn't think he knew?

*Soc.*   I don't remember things very well, Meno, so I can't now say what I thought about him then. But perhaps he does know, and perhaps you know what he used to say, so remind me what that was. Or if you like, *you* tell me yourself, for I expect you think the   d same as he does.

*Meno*   Yes I do.

*Soc.*   Well then, let's leave him out of it, since after all he isn't here – and Meno, by all the gods, what do you yourself say that virtue is? Tell me and don't keep it back. Make it a really lucky false statement I've uttered, if what comes to light is that you and Gorgias do know, all the time I've been saying I'd never yet met anyone who did.

*Meno*   But it's not hard to tell you, Socrates. First, if it's virtue   e for a man you wish to know, that's easy: virtue for a man is the ability to conduct the city's affairs and, in so doing, to help his friends, hurt his foes, and take good care not to get hurt himself. Or if it's virtue for a woman you wish for, that's not hard to describe: she must run the home well, looking after everything in it and obeying her husband. And there is another virtue for a child, whether female or male, and another for an older man, free or slave, whichever you wish. And there are a great many other   72a virtues, so that there's no perplexity about saying what virtue is. For there is virtue for every field of practice and time of life, in connection with every activity, and for every one of us; and vice too in the same way, I think, Socrates.

*Soc.*   I seem to be having a lot of luck, Meno, if in searching for just one virtue I've found a positive swarm of virtues in your possession. But Meno, to follow up this metaphor of swarms: if I had asked about the nature of a bee and what that is, and b you had said that bees were many and varied, how would you answer me if I then asked, 'Do you say they are many and varied and different from one another *in respect of being bees?* Or is it not at all in *this* respect that they differ, but in some *other* respect, such as beauty or size or something else like that?' Tell me, how would you answer if you were asked that?

*Meno* I would say that in respect of being bees they are no different from one another.

*Soc.* Then if I said next, 'Well, tell me then, Meno, what do you c say this thing itself is, in respect of which they are not different but all the same?', I expect you would have an answer for me?

*Meno* Yes I would.

*Soc.* Then it's the same with the virtues too: even if they are many and various, they must still all have one and the same form which makes them *virtues.* Presumably it would be right to focus on this in one's answer and show the questioner what virtue actually *is.* Or don't you understand what I mean?                                    d

*Meno* I think I understand. But I don't yet grasp the question quite as clearly as I'd like to.

*Soc.* Well, is it only about virtue, Meno, that you think as you do – that there is one for a man, another for a woman, and so on – or do you think the same about health and size and strength too? Do you think there is one health for a man and another for a woman? Or is it the same form in every case, if it really *is* health, whether in a man or in anything else?                                    e

*Meno* With health, I think it is the same in both man and woman.

*Soc.* And isn't it so with size and strength too? If a woman is strong, won't it be the same form, the same strength, that makes her strong? What I mean by 'the same' is that whether strength is in a man or in a woman makes no difference with respect to its being *strength.* Or do you think it does make a difference?

*Meno* No I don't.

*Soc.* Well, will whether *virtue* is in a child, in an old man, in a 73a woman or in a man make any difference with respect to its being *virtue?*

*Meno* I think this is somehow no longer like those other cases, Socrates.

*Soc.* Well now, didn't you say that for a man, virtue was running a city well and for a woman, running a home well?

*Meno* Yes I did.

*Soc.* And is it possible to run a city or home or anything else well without running it temperately and justly?

*Meno* No indeed.

*Soc.* And to run it temperately and justly will mean running it b with temperance and justice, won't it?

*Meno* It must.

*Soc.* So they both need the same things if they're going to be good – both the man and the woman: – justice and temperance?

*Meno* Apparently they do.

*Soc.* And what about a child or old man? Surely they could never come to be good by being undisciplined and unjust?

*Meno* No indeed.

*Soc.* But rather, by being temperate and just?

*Meno* Yes.

*Soc.* So people are all good in the same way, since they all come c to be good by attaining the same things?

*Meno* It seems so.

*Soc.* Now presumably they would not have been good in the same way if the virtue they'd had were not the same?

*Meno* No indeed.

*Soc.* Well then, since virtue is the same for everyone, try to remember and tell me what Gorgias, and you with him, say it is.

*Meno* What else but the ability to rule over people, if what you are searching for is some one thing covering them all. d

*Soc.* That is indeed what I'm searching for. But does a child have the same virtue too, Meno, or a slave – the ability to rule over his master? Do you think he would still *be* a slave, if he were the ruler?

*Meno* I don't think so at all, Socrates.

*Soc.* It's certainly unlikely, my good chap. For consider this too. You say 'ability to rule'. Won't we add to this the words 'justly, and not unjustly'?

*Meno* Yes, I think so. For justice is virtue, Socrates.

*Soc.* Virtue, Meno, or *a* virtue? e

*Meno* What do you mean by that?

*Soc.* The same as I would with anything else. For instance, if you like, with roundness, I'd say that it's *a* shape, not simply that it's shape. The reason I'd say this is that there are also other shapes.

38

*Meno*  You're quite right, since I too say that besides justice there are also other virtues.

*Soc.*  What are these? Tell me. Just as I'd name some other 74a shapes if you told me to, so you tell me some other virtues.

*Meno*  Well then, courage is virtue in my opinion, and so are temperance and wisdom and grandeur, and all the many others.

*Soc.*  The same thing has happened to us as before, Meno. Once again, though in a different way from last time, we've found many virtues while searching for one. But as for the one virtue which extends through all these, that we can't discover.

*Meno*  No, I still can't pin down what you're searching for – one b virtue covering them all, as with the other examples.

*Soc.*  Fair enough. But I'll do my best to get us closer[1] if I can. You understand, I expect, that it's the same with everything – if someone asked you about the example I mentioned just now, 'What is shape, Meno?', and you told him that it was roundness, and he said to you as I did, 'Is roundness shape, or *a* shape?', I expect you'd tell him that it's *a* shape.

*Meno*  Yes indeed.

*Soc.*  Your reason being that there are also other shapes?      c

*Meno*  Yes.

*Soc.*  And if he went on to ask you what these were, you'd tell him?

*Meno*  Yes I would.

*Soc.*  And again with colour, if he asked you in the same way what that was, and when you said 'White', the questioner then took you up with 'Is white colour, or *a* colour?', you'd say it was *a* colour, because there are in fact others too?

*Meno*  Yes I would.

*Soc.*  And if he told you to mention some other colours, you'd mention some other things which are in fact colours no less than d white is?

*Meno*  Yes.

*Soc.*  Well, if he pursued the argument as I did and said, 'We keep ending up with many – not that way please, but since you refer to these many things by the one name and say that none of them fails to be a shape even though they are positively inconsistent with each other, tell me what this is, which includes round no less than

---

[1] 'get . . . closer' translates Bluck's reading προσβιβάσαι. OCT has προβιβάσαι, 'help . . . on'.

straight, and which you call shape when you say that roundness is a
shape no less than straightness is? – Or don't you say this?'           e

*Meno*  Yes I do.

*Soc.*  'Well, when you say it are you saying that roundness is no
more round than straight, or straightness no more straight than
round?'

*Meno*  Certainly not, Socrates.

*Soc.*  'Yet you do say that straightness is no more a *shape* than
roundness is, and the same the other way about?'

*Meno*  What you say is true.

*Soc.*  'Then what is this thing which has this name "shape"? Try
to tell me'. Well, if when asked this question, whether about shape  75a
or about colour, you said, 'But I don't even understand what you
want, man, and I don't know what you mean, either', he would
perhaps be surprised and say, 'Don't you understand that I'm
searching for the thing which is *the same* in all of these?' Or would
you have no answer in this case either, Meno, if someone asked
you, 'What is it in roundness and straightness and the other things
you call shapes, that is the same in all of them?' Try and tell me, to
get some practice for your answer about virtue.

*Meno*  No! You tell me, Socrates.                                      b

*Soc.*  You'd like me to do you a favour?

*Meno*  Yes indeed.

*Soc.*  Then you'll be ready to tell me about virtue in your turn?

*Meno*  Yes I will.

*Soc.*  Well then, I must do my best; it's a fair deal.

*Meno*  Yes indeed.

*Soc.*  Well now, let's try to tell you what shape is. See whether
you accept that it's this: let us say that shape is the only thing there
is which always accompanies colour. Will that do for you, or is it
something different you are searching for? I'd be pleased enough if
you could tell me about virtue even in this sort of way.                c

*Meno*  But that's silly, Socrates.

*Soc.*  How do you mean?

*Meno*  Shape, according to your account, is what always accompanies colour. Right. But now if someone were to say he didn't
know colour, and raised the same problem about that as about
shape, what kind of answer do you think the one you've given
would be?

*Soc.*  A true one! And if the questioner were one of the wise, one
of those disputatious debaters, I'd say to him 'I have said my      d

say. If it's not right, then it's your job to take up the argument and prove me wrong.' However, if friends, like you and me today, wished to engage in discussion with one another, then they should reply in some milder way more appropriate to discussion. And perhaps what's more appropriate to discussion is to give answers which are not only true but also in terms which the questioner has first agreed he knows.[2] So I'll try to answer you like that. – Tell me, do you call something an 'end'? I mean something such as a  e limit or boundary – I mean the same by all of these; perhaps Prodicus would disagree with us, but I dare say you do speak of things as having a limit or coming to an end. That's the kind of thing I wish to express – nothing complicated.

*Meno*  I do speak like that, and I think I understand what you mean.

*Soc.*  Next, do you call something a 'plane' and something else a  76a 'solid' – the planes and solids in geometry, for instance?

*Meno*  Yes I do.

*Soc.*  Well then, that's enough for you to understand what I say shape is. I say that, for every case of shape, shape is that in which a solid comes to its limit, or summing this up, I'd say that shape is the limit of a solid.

*Meno*  And what do you say colour is, Socrates?

*Soc.*  You are quite outrageous, Meno! You bother an old man with your demands for answers, but you yourself won't use your memory and tell me what Gorgias says virtue is.  b

*Meno*  But I will, Socrates, once you've told me this.

*Soc.*  One could tell blindfold, Meno, just from the way you talk, that you're beautiful and still have lovers.

*Meno*  How so?

*Soc.*  Because you do nothing but make demands when you speak, as favourites always do – after all they're the kings while their season lasts. Perhaps you've also discovered my own suscepti-  c bility to beauty. So I'll do you the favour and answer you.

*Meno*  Yes indeed, *do* do me the favour.

*Soc.*  Would you like me to answer like Gorgias then, to make it easy for you to follow?

*Meno*  Yes, of course, I would.

---

[2] 'which the questioner has first agreed he knows' translates Bluck's reading ὧν ἂν προσομολογῇ εἰδέναι ὁ ἐρωτῶν. OCT has προσομολογῇ ὁ ἐρωτώμενος, 'which the person being questioned agrees further that he knows'.

*Soc.* Well then, do you and he follow Empedocles and say that things give off effluxes?

*Meno* Very much so.

*Soc.* And that there are channels into and through which the effluxes pass?

*Meno* Yes indeed.

*Soc.* And some of the effluxes fit into some of the channels, while others are too small or too big?     d

*Meno* That is so.

*Soc.* And you also call something 'sight'?

*Meno* Yes I do.

*Soc.* From this then 'grasp what I say to thee' as Pindar said: – colour is an efflux of shapes, commensurate with and perceptible to sight.

*Meno* I think that is an excellent answer you've given, Socrates.

*Soc.* Yes – I've given it the way you're used to, perhaps. And besides, I expect you realize you could use it to say what sound is too, or smell, or many other such things.     e

*Meno* Yes indeed.

*Soc.* Yes, it's a showy kind of answer, Meno, so you prefer it to the one about shape.

*Meno* Yes I do.

*Soc.* All the same, O son of Alexidemus, I am sure myself that it's not a *better* one – the other was. And I expect you wouldn't think so either, if only you didn't have to leave before the mysteries, as you were saying yesterday, but could stay and be initiated instead.

*Meno* Well, I would stay if you'd tell me many more things like     77a
this, Socrates.

*Soc.* Well, I certainly shan't lack the will to tell you such things, for both your sake and my own; it's rather that I might not be *able* to tell you many. But come on, now you try and do what you promised for me, and say what virtue is as a whole. Stop making many out of one, as the jokers say whenever someone breaks something, and instead say what virtue is, leaving it whole and sound. After all, I've provided you with the models.     b

*Meno* Well then, Socrates, I think virtue is, as the poet says, 'To glory in fine things and hold the power'. That's what *I* say virtue is, too: desiring fine things and having the power to achieve them.

*Soc.* Do you say that desiring *fine* things means having a desire for *good* things?

*Meno*   Yes, certainly.

*Soc.*   Is that assuming that some people desire bad things and others good ones? Don't you think everyone desires good things, c my good chap?

*Meno*   No I don't.

*Soc.*   But some people desire bad things?

*Meno*   Yes.

*Soc.*   Supposing the bad things to be good, do you mean? Or do they still desire them even when they know they are bad?

*Meno*   Both, I think.

*Soc.*   Really? You think someone can still desire bad things even when he knows they are bad?

*Meno*   Certainly.

*Soc.*   How do you mean 'desires'? Is it 'desires that they should happen to him'?

*Meno*   Yes, that – what else?                                    d

*Soc.*   Is this in the belief that the bad things benefit everyone to whom they happen, or while knowing that they always harm their possessor?

*Meno*   There are some people who believe the bad things are beneficial; there are also others who know they are harmful.

*Soc.*   But do the people who believe the bad things are beneficial really know they are *bad*, do you think?

*Meno*   No, I don't think that at all.

*Soc.*   Then clearly this first group don't desire bad things, do they, seeing these ones don't know the things *are* bad. Isn't it things e they supposed to be *good* that they desire, even while in fact these things are bad? So the people who don't know the things are bad and suppose them to be good clearly desire *good* things. Or don't they?

*Meno*   Yes, these ones perhaps do.

*Soc.*   Next, the ones whom you say desire bad things while believing that bad things harm everyone to whom they happen – they know they are going to be harmed by them, presumably?

*Meno*   They must do.

*Soc.*   But don't they suppose that people who are suffering 78a harm are miserable to the degree that they are being harmed?

*Meno*   They must do that, too.

*Soc.*   And that people who are miserable are wretched?

*Meno*   Yes, so I'd suppose.

*Soc.*   And does anyone wish to be miserable and wretched?

*Meno*   I don't think so, Socrates.

*Soc.*   So no one wishes for bad things then, Meno, if no one wishes to be that. For what else *is* it to be miserable, but to desire bad things and get them?

*Meno*   Perhaps what you say is true, Socrates, and no one wishes b for bad things.

*Soc.*   Well, you were saying just now that virtue was wishing for good things and having the power, weren't you?

*Meno*   Yes, that is what I said.

*Soc.*   Then in what you said the 'wishing' applies to everyone, and as far as this goes no one is better than anyone else – isn't that so?

*Meno*   Apparently.

*Soc.*   But if one person *is* better than another, it's clear he must be better in having the power.

*Meno*   Yes indeed.

*Soc.*   So what virtue seems to be on your account is this: power to achieve good things.   c

*Meno*   My opinion is exactly as you now understand it, Socrates.

*Soc.*   Let's look at this too then to see whether what you say is true, for it may be that it's well said. Virtue is the ability to achieve good things, you say?

*Meno*   Yes I do.

*Soc.*   And the things you call good would be things like health and wealth, wouldn't they?

*Meno*   I mean both getting gold and silver, and also honours and high office in one's city.

*Soc.*   And there's nothing else you mean by good things, apart from things like these?

*Meno*   No, I mean all the things like these.   d

*Soc.*   Right. And so achieving gold and silver is virtue, says Meno the hereditary guest-friend of the Great King. Do you add the words 'justly and holily' to the 'achieving'? Or does that make no difference for you, and even if someone achieves them *un*justly you call it virtue just the same?

*Meno*   Certainly not, Socrates.

*Soc.*   But rather, vice?

*Meno*   Yes, definitely.

*Soc.*   So it seems that the achievement must be accompanied by justice or temperance or holiness or some other part of virtue, or e else it will not be virtue despite achieving good things.

*Meno* Yes, how could it be virtue without these?

*Soc.* And *not* to achieve gold and silver either for oneself or for anyone else, when to do so wouldn't be just – isn't this non-achievement also virtue?

*Meno* Apparently.

*Soc.* So the achievement of this sort of good thing can't be virtue any more than the non-achievement can. Rather, it seems that whatever comes about with *justice* will be virtue, and what comes about without anything of that kind will be vice. 79a

*Meno* I think it must be as you say.

*Soc.* Then didn't we say a little while ago that each of these things – justice, temperance, and everything of that kind – was a *part* of virtue?

*Meno* Yes.

*Soc.* So you're playing games with me, are you, Meno?

*Meno* How so, Socrates?

*Soc.* A moment ago I asked you not to break virtue up or cut it in pieces and gave you models of how to answer, and you've disregarded all that and tell me that virtue is the ability to achieve good things with justice – and you say justice is a part of virtue? b

*Meno* Yes I do.

*Soc.* Then it follows from what you yourself agree, doesn't it, that what virtue is, is to do everything one does with some part of virtue? For justice and each of these things is a part of virtue, you say. So why am I saying this? Because I asked you to tell me about virtue as a whole, but far from telling me what *virtue* is you just say that any action is virtue provided it's done with a part of virtue – as though you'd already said what the whole of virtue was, so I'd c recognize it even if you cut it up into parts.

So the same question has to be put to you all over again I think, my dear Meno. What *is* virtue, if any action can be virtue when done with a part of virtue? – for that's what is being said if one claims that every action done with justice is virtue. Or don't you think the same question has to be put again? – do you suppose one can know what a part of virtue is without knowing virtue itself?

*Meno* No, I don't think so.

*Soc.* No, and if you remember when I answered you about d shape a moment ago, I believe we rejected this kind of answer, which tries to answer in terms of things which are still being searched for and not yet agreed on.

*Meno* Yes, and we were right to do so, Socrates.

*Soc.* Well then, my good chap, neither must you suppose that, while we're still searching for what *virtue* is as a whole, you can explain it to anyone by answering in terms of its parts or saying anything else in that same old way, without the same question having to be put again: What *is* this 'virtue' about which you say   e what you do? Or do you think I'm talking nonsense?

*Meno* No, I think what you say is right.

*Soc.* Well, answer all over again then: what do you – and your friend too – say virtue is?

*Meno* Socrates, I used to hear even before I met you how all you ever do is to be perplexed and to make other people perplexed too,   80a and what I feel now is that you're applying your spells and potions to me and positively mesmerizing me, till I'm brimful of perplexity. If a little joke's in order, I think that what you're just exactly like, both in looks and everything else, is that flat-fish the sea torpedo. The torpedo fish always torpifies whoever comes near and gets into contact with it, and I think you've done something of the same sort to me now too, for I'm truly torpid in both mind and   b mouth and I've got no answer for you. And yet I've spoken a great many words about virtue in front of many people on thousands of occasions, and did it very well too – at least, so I thought. But now I can't even say what virtue is at all. And I think you're well advised in not taking ship and going abroad from Athens, for if you were a visitor in another city doing things like this, you would probably be arrested as a sorcerer!

*Soc.* You're a rascal, Meno – you almost had me tricked.

*Meno* Just how, Socrates?

*Soc.* I know why you played 'what you're like' with me.   c

*Meno* Why then, do you suppose?

*Soc.* So that I'd say what *you*'re like back. I know how all beautiful boys enjoy hearing what they're like – they come out of it well, for if one is beautiful the things one is like are beautiful too, I suppose – but I'm not going to say what you're like back. As for me, if the torpedo fish is torpid itself and that's how it makes other people torpid too, I *am* like it, but not otherwise. For it's not that I myself have the solutions when I make other people perplexed, but that I'm utterly perplexed myself and that's how I come to make other people perplexed as well. That's how it is with virtue now; I   d on my side *don't* know what it is, while you on yours *did* know, perhaps, till you came into contact with me, while now you're just like someone who *doesn't* know. All the same I'm ready to consider it with you and join you in searching for what it might be.

*Meno*   And how are you going to search for this when you don't know at all what it is, Socrates? Which of all the things you don't know will you set up as target for your search? And even if you actually come across it, how will you know that it *is* that thing which you didn't know?

*Soc.*   I know what you mean, Meno. Do you see what a disputa-   e tious argument you're bringing down on us – how it's impossible for a person to search either for what he knows or for what he doesn't? He couldn't search for what he knows, for he knows it and no one in that condition needs to search; on the other hand he couldn't search for what he doesn't know, for he won't even know what to search for.

*Meno*   And don't you think that's a fine argument, Socrates?   81a

*Soc.*   No I don't.

*Meno*   Can you tell me why?

*Soc.*   Yes I can. I've heard men and women wise in matters divine –

*Meno*   Saying what?

*Soc.*   Something both true and beautiful in my opinion.

*Meno*   What is it, and who are the people saying it?

*Soc.*   The people saying it are those priests and priestesses who have made it their concern to be able to give an account of their practices; Pindar says it too and many other divinely inspired poets.   b And as for what they say, it's this – but consider if you think what they say is true. They say the soul of man is immortal; sometimes it comes to an end – which people call dying – while at other times it is reborn, but it never perishes. So because of this one should live out one's life in the holiest possible way, since for those from whom

'Persephone receives
Requital for long grief, their souls she yields
In the ninth year once more to the sun above;
From whom grow noble kings, and men                                   c
Swift in strength and great in wisdom;
And to the end of time men call them heroes holy.'

Well, since the soul is immortal, and has been born many times and seen both what is here, and what is in Hades, and everything, there is nothing it has not learnt. So no wonder it's possible that it should recollect both virtue and other things, as after all it did

47

know them previously. For seeing that the whole of nature is akin
and the soul has learnt everything, there's nothing to prevent
someone who recollects – which people call learning – just one
thing, from discovering everything else, if he's courageous and
doesn't give up searching; – for searching and learning are just
recollection. So we shouldn't be persuaded by that disputatious
argument. That argument would make us lazy, and weak-willed
people love to hear it, but this one makes us industrious and eager e
to search. It's because I'm confident that this one is true that I'm
ready to search with you for what virtue is.

*Meno*  Yes Socrates – but what do you mean by saying we don't
learn, but what we call learning is recollection? Can you teach me
how that is so?

*Soc.*  Only a minute ago I said you were a rascal, Meno, and now
you ask me if I can teach you – I who say there's no teaching, 82a
only recollecting – obviously all to show me up as immediately
contradicting myself.

*Meno*  No by Zeus, Socrates, I didn't speak with any such
thought, but out of habit. But if there's any way you can show me
that it is as you say, do show me.

*Soc.*  Well, it's not easy, but all the same I'm ready to do my
best for your sake. Call me one of these many attendants you have,
whichever one you wish, so that I can demonstrate on him for b
you.

*Meno*  Yes, certainly. Come here!

*Soc.*  First, is he Greek and does he speak Greek?

*Meno*  Very much so; he was born in our home.

*Soc.*  Observe carefully then which of the two things he shows
himself to be doing, recollecting or learning from me.

*Meno*  I shall do.

*Soc.*  Tell me now, boy, you know that a square figure is like
this?

*Boy*  Yes I do.

*Soc.*  So a square figure is one which has all these four lines c
equal?

*Boy*  Yes indeed.

*Soc.*  And it is one which also has these lines through the middle
equal, isn't it? [*See Figure 1, opposite. Throughout his conversation
with the slave we must imagine Socrates drawing figures as he describes
them.*]

*Boy*  Yes.

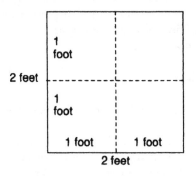

*Figure 1*

*Soc.* And there could be both bigger and smaller figures like this, couldn't there?

*Boy* Yes indeed.

*Soc.* Well, if this side were two feet long and this other side two feet, how many feet big would the whole be? Think of it like this: if it had been two feet this way and only one foot that way, wouldn't the figure have been two feet times one?

*Boy* Yes.

*Soc.* But since it's two feet that way also, doesn't it come to two times *two*?                                                                    d

*Boy* It does.

*Soc.* So it comes to two times two feet?

*Boy* Yes.

*Soc.* Well, how many are two times two? Work it out and tell me.

*Boy* Four, Socrates.

*Soc.* Well, there could be another figure twice the size of this one but like it, couldn't there, having all its lines equal just like this one?

*Boy* Yes.

*Soc.* How many feet big will it be, then?

*Boy* Eight.

*Soc.* Well now, try to tell me how long each line of that one will be. The line for this one is two feet long; what about the line for that one which is twice the size?                                              e

*Boy* Clearly it'll be twice the length, Socrates.

49

*Soc.* Do you see, Meno, how I'm not teaching him anything but instead asking him everything? And at present he supposes he knows what kind of line the eight-foot figure will come from – or don't you think he does?

*Meno* Yes I do.

*Soc.* And does he know?

*Meno* No indeed.

*Soc.* But he supposes it will come from a line twice the length?

*Meno* Yes.

*Soc.* Then watch him recollecting in order, as one has to do.

Now, you tell me. You say that a figure twice the size comes from a line twice the length? I mean a figure like this one, not long 83a one way and short the other, but it's to be equal in each direction just like this one, only twice the size, eight feet big – but see whether you still think it will comé from the line twice the length.

*Boy* I do.

*Soc.* Well, *this* line comes to twice the length of this one, doesn't it, if we add on another of the same length starting here?

*Boy* Yes indeed.

*Soc.* Then this is the line you say the eight-foot figure will come from, if there came to be four lines of the same length.

*Boy* Yes.                                                                b

*Soc.* Let's draw four equal lines starting from it, then. Isn't this what you say would be the eight-foot figure?

*Boy* Yes indeed.

*Soc.* And inside it, aren't there these four figures, of which each one is equal to this four-foot figure? [*See Figure 2, opposite*]

*Boy* Yes.

*Soc.* How big is it then? Isn't it four times the size?

*Boy* Yes, of course.

*Soc.* So what's four times the size is twice the size?

*Boy* No, by Zeus.

*Soc.* But how many times the size *is* it?

*Boy* Four times.

*Soc.* So it's not a figure *twice* the size that comes from a line twice the length, my boy, but one *four times* the size.                  c

*Boy* What you say is true.

*Soc.* For four times four is sixteen, isn't it?

*Boy* Yes.

*Soc.* But what line does an *eight*-foot figure come from? From this line comes a figure four times the size, doesn't it?

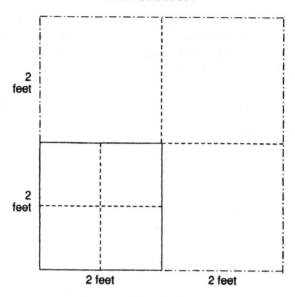

*Figure 2*

*Boy*   I agree.

*Soc.*   And this quarter-size[3] figure comes from this half-length line, doesn't it?

*Boy*   Yes.

*Soc.*   Right. The eight-foot figure is twice the size of this one and half the size of that one, isn't it?

*Boy*   Yes.

*Soc.*   Won't it be from a line bigger than this one but smaller than that? Or not?

*Boy*   I think that is so.                                                         d

*Soc.*   Fine; always answer what you think. And tell me, wasn't this line two feet long and the other one four feet?

*Boy*   Yes.

*Soc.*   So the line for the eight-foot figure needs to be bigger than this two-foot line, but smaller than the four-foot one.

*Boy*   It does.

*Soc.*   Then try to tell me how long a line you say it is.          e

*Boy*   Three feet.

*Soc.*   Well, if it's to be three feet long, we'll add on half as much

---

3  'quarter-size' translates Bluck's reading τέταρτον. OCT has τετράπουν, 'four-foot'.

again of this line and that will be three feet, won't it? – these two feet here, plus this one more. And over here in the same way there will be these two feet here plus this one more, and here comes the figure you say. [*See Figure 3, below*]

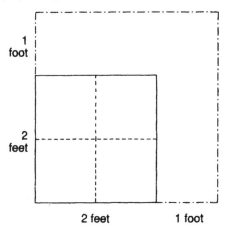

*Figure 3*

*Boy*  Yes.

*Soc.*  Then if it's three feet this way and three feet this way, doesn't the whole figure come to three times three feet?

*Boy*  Apparently.

*Soc.*  And how many feet are three times three?

*Boy*  Nine.

*Soc.*  And how many feet big did the figure which is twice the size have to be?

*Boy*  Eight.

*Soc.*  So a three-foot line is still not what an eight-foot figure comes from, either?

*Boy*  No indeed.

*Soc.*  But what line *is*? Try to tell us exactly, and if you don't wish to put a number to it, *show* us what it is instead.

*Boy*  But by Zeus, Socrates, *I* certainly don't know.  84a

*Soc.*  Are you observing again, Meno, what stage he's reached now in recollecting? At first he didn't know what the baseline of the eight-foot figure was, just as he still doesn't know it now either, but at that time he supposed he *did* know, and answered boldly like someone with knowledge, and didn't think he was perplexed. But now he *has* begun to think he's perplexed, and besides not knowing, he doesn't suppose he knows either.                                                b

*Meno*  What you say is true.

*Soc.*  And isn't he in a better state now in relation to the thing he doesn't know?

*Meno*  I think that is so too.

*Soc.*  Well, in making him perplexed and torpifying him like a torpedo fish does, we've done him no harm, have we?

*Meno*  No, I don't think so.

*Soc.*  In fact it seems we've done him a service towards finding the real answer, for now he'd gladly search for what he doesn't know, whereas then he'd have supposed he could speak well with ease in front of many people and on many occasions, about how a figure twice the size has to have its baseline twice the length.          c

*Meno*  It seems so.

*Soc.*  Well, do you think he would have attempted to search out or learn what he supposed he knew but in fact didn't, till he fell into perplexity on coming to think he didn't know, and began longing for knowledge?

*Meno*  I don't think so, Socrates.

*Soc.*  So he has benefited from being torpified?

*Meno*  I think so.

*Soc.*  Now look what he'll go on from this state of perplexity to discover as he searches with me, while I do nothing but ask questions, not teach him. Watch out in case you ever find me d teaching and instructing him instead of drawing out his own opinions.

You tell me, this is our four-foot figure, isn't it? You understand?

*Boy*  Yes I do.

*Soc.*  And we could add on to it this other equal one here.

*Boy*  Yes.

*Soc.*  And this third one equal to each of the others?

*Boy*  Yes.

*Soc.*  Then we could fill in this one in the corner as well, couldn't we?

*Boy*  Yes indeed.

*Soc.*  And these would come out four equal figures, wouldn't they?

*Boy*  Yes.

*Soc.*  Now then, how many times the size of this one here does e this whole thing here come to?

53

*Boy*   Four times the size.

*Soc.*   While what we had to get was one twice the size. Or don't you remember?

*Boy*   I do indeed.

*Soc.*   Then there's a line here from corner to corner, isn't there, cutting each of the figures in two?                                           85a

*Boy*   Yes.

*Soc.*   And these four lines come out equal, don't they, and surround this figure here? [*See Figure 4, below*]

*Boy*   Yes they do.

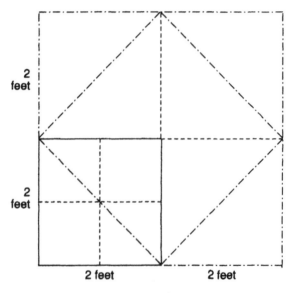

*Figure 4*

*Soc.*   Now consider. How big is this figure?

*Boy*   I don't understand.

*Soc.*   Of these four figures here, hasn't half of each been cut off and enclosed by each line? Or is that not so?

*Boy*   Yes.

*Soc.*   Then how many bits of that size are there inside here?

*Boy*   Four.

*Soc.*   And how many inside here?

*Boy*   Two.

*Soc.* And how much is four as compared to two?

*Boy* Twice as much.

*Soc.* Then how big does this figure come out?

*Boy* Eight feet big.                                                                         b

*Soc.* And what line does it come from?

*Boy* This one.

*Soc.* The one stretching from corner to corner of the four-foot figure?

*Boy* Yes.

*Soc.* What the experts call that is the diagonal. So if the diagonal is the name of this line then you, Meno's boy, say that a figure of twice the size would come from the diagonal.

*Boy* Yes indeed, Socrates.

*Soc.* What do you think, Meno. Has he answered with any opinions but his own?

*Meno* No, only with his own.                                                  c

*Soc.* And yet he certainly didn't *know*, as we said a little while ago.

*Meno* What you say is true.

*Soc.* But he certainly had these opinions in him – or didn't he?

*Meno* Yes.

*Soc.* So someone who doesn't know something, whatever it may be he doesn't know, has true opinions in him about the very thing he doesn't know?

*Meno* It appears so.

*Soc.* And at present it's as though in a dream that these opinions have just been aroused in him. But if someone questions him many times and in many ways about the same things as now, you may be sure he will end up knowing them as precisely as anyone does.      d

*Meno* It seems so.

*Soc.* And it won't be through being taught by anyone that he knows, will it, but through being questioned, recovering the knowledge from within him for himself?

*Meno* Yes.

*Soc.* And recovering knowledge which is within one for oneself is recollecting, isn't it?

*Meno* Yes indeed.

*Soc.* Well, the knowledge which this boy has now – he either acquired it sometime or else always had it, didn't he?

*Meno* Yes.

*Soc.* Then if he always had it, it follows that he was always in a state of knowledge. On the other hand, if he acquired it sometime, it could certainly not be in his present life that he has done so. Or has someone taught him geometry? For he will do just the same e with anything in geometry or any other subject of knowledge. *Has* someone taught him everything, then? Presumably you should know, especially as he's been born and brought up in your home.

*Meno* No, I know that no one ever taught him.

*Soc.* And does he have these opinions or not?

*Meno* Apparently he must do, Socrates.

*Soc.* And if that is without acquiring them in his present life, doesn't it clearly follow that he had them and had learnt them at 86a some other time?

*Meno* Apparently.

*Soc.* And that means the time when he was not a human being, doesn't it?

*Meno* Yes.

*Soc.* Well, if both during the time that he is a human being, and during the time that he is not, there are going to be true opinions within him which become knowledge when aroused by questioning, isn't[4] his soul going to be for *all* time in a state of having learnt? For it's clear that at every time he either is, or is not, a human being.

*Meno* Apparently.

*Soc.* Then if the truth about the things which are is in our souls b always, the soul must be immortal, must it not? So shouldn't you boldly try to search for and recollect what you happen not to know – that is, not to remember – at present?

*Meno* I think that is well said, somehow or other, Socrates.

*Soc.* Yes, I think so too, Meno. I wouldn't be absolutely adamant about the rest of the argument, but that we shall be better people, more manly and less slothful, by supposing that one should enquire about things one doesn't know, than if we suppose that when we don't know things we can't find them out either and needn't search for them – *this* is something for which I absolutely c *would* fight, both in word and deed, to the limit of my powers.

*Meno* That too is well said I think, Socrates.

*Soc.* Then since we agree that one should search for what one doesn't know, would you like us to try to search together for what virtue may be?

---

[4] 'isn't . . .?' translates Bluck's reading ἆρ'οὐ. OCT has ἆρ'οὖν, 'then is . . .?'

*Meno* Yes indeed. But no – what I'd like best to consider and hear about is what I first asked: should we make the attempt on virtue as something that comes from teaching, or as coming to d people by nature, or in what way?

*Soc.* Well, Meno, if I were the one who ruled not just over myself but over you as well, we wouldn't consider whether or not virtue comes from teaching before first searching for what virtue itself is. But since on the contrary it's you who, while not even attempting to rule over yourself – to keep yourself free, no doubt – attempt to rule over me instead, and succeed too, I'll give way to you – what else can I do? So it seems we have to consider what e something is like when we still don't know what it is. Then please slacken your rule just one little bit at least, and consent to start from a hypothesis in considering whether virtue comes from teaching or whatever. By 'starting from a hypothesis' I mean doing what geometricians often do when considering questions they get asked – about a figure for instance, whether the given figure can be inscribed in a given circle as a triangle. 'I don't yet know whether 87a this figure *is* such as this', one of them might say, 'but I think I have a sort of hypothesis which helps with the question, as follows: *if* this figure is such that, when laid out on its given baseline, it leaves remaining a figure similar to that one which has been laid out itself, *then*, I think, one consequence follows, and a different one on the other hand if this *cannot* be done to it. So once I've set up a hypothesis, I'll willingly tell you what follows about inscribing the b figure in the circle and whether or not it can be done.' Let us deal with virtue in this same way, too. As we don't know either what it is or what it's like, let us examine whether or not it comes from teaching by setting up a hypothesis, and saying 'What *kind* of thing among those belonging to the soul would virtue have to be, for it to come from teaching or not come from teaching?' Now first, if it's a different kind of thing from knowledge, would it, or would it not, come from teaching? – or as we were saying just now, recollecting; let's treat it as making no difference which name we use – but *would* c it come from teaching? Or is at least this much clear to everyone, that a person isn't taught anything but knowledge?

*Meno* Yes, I think so.

*Soc* But if virtue *is* some sort of knowledge, clearly it *must* come from teaching?

*Meno* Of course.

*Soc.* So we've quickly disposed of the first point, how if it's one kind of thing virtue would come from teaching, but if it's another, it wouldn't.

*Meno* Yes indeed.

*Soc.* Next, then, it seems we have to examine whether virtue *is* knowledge or some different kind of thing.

*Meno* Yes, I think that should be examined next.          d

*Soc.* Well then, we say virtue is good, don't we, and this hypothesis 'Virtue is good' is a firm one for us?

*Meno* Yes indeed.

*Soc.* Then if there's anything else, apart from knowledge, that is good, in that case virtue may perhaps not be any sort of knowledge. If on the other hand there's nothing good that is not included within knowledge, then we'd be right to suspect that virtue is some sort of knowledge.

*Meno* That is so.

*Soc.* Now, virtue is what makes us good?

*Meno* Yes.

*Soc.* And if good then beneficial, for everything good is bene-   e
ficial, isn't it?

*Meno* Yes.

*Soc.* So virtue too is beneficial?

*Meno* It must be, from what has been agreed.

*Soc.* Then let's examine what kinds of thing benefit us, taking them one by one. We say health does so, and strength, and beauty, and of course wealth – these and things like them are what we call beneficial, aren't they?

*Meno* Yes.

*Soc.* But we say these same things also sometimes do harm – 88a
or would you say that's not so?

*Meno* No, I'd say it is so.

*Soc.* Consider then: what is the guiding principle which makes each of them beneficial or harmful to us as the case may be? Isn't it when guided by *right use* that they are beneficial, and when not, harmful?

*Meno* Yes indeed.

*Soc.* Well then, let's go on and examine the things in the soul too. Are there things you call temperance, justice, courage, quickness in learning, memory, grandeur, and everything like these?

*Meno* Yes there are.

*Soc.* Consider then: among these things, aren't those which   b
you think are not knowledge but something other than knowledge,

sometimes harmful while at other times beneficial? Courage, for instance, if it's not wisdom but just a sort of boldness – when people are bold without reason they get harmed, don't they, but when they're bold with reason they benefit?

*Meno*  Yes.

*Soc.*  And isn't it the same with temperance and with quickness in learning: *with* reason both learning and discipline are beneficial, but *without* reason they are both harmful?

*Meno*  Yes, very much so.

*Soc.*  To sum up, then, everything the soul endeavours or c endures under the guidance of wisdom ends in happiness, doesn't it, and the opposite under the guidance of folly?

*Meno*  It seems so.

*Soc.*  So if virtue is a thing in the soul and must necessarily be beneficial, it has to be wisdom, since none of the things in the soul are either beneficial or harmful in themselves, but it's the addition of wisdom or folly which makes them either harmful or beneficial. d According to this argument, once granted that virtue is beneficial, it has to be some sort of wisdom.

*Meno*  Yes, I think so.

*Soc.*  Now what is more, isn't it the same with the other things which we were saying just now are sometimes good and sometimes harmful – wealth and things like that? Just as we found that wisdom made the things in the soul beneficial when it guided the rest of the soul, so again with these other things too, it's by using e and guiding them rightly that the soul makes them beneficial, and by doing so wrongly that it makes them harmful – isn't that so?

*Meno*  Yes indeed.

*Soc.*  And is it the wise soul which guides rightly, and the foolish one which guides wrongly?

*Meno*  It is.

*Soc.*  Then it can be said about everything, can't it, that everything else a person has depends on his soul, and the things within the soul itself depend on wisdom, if they're going to be good; and 89a by this argument what is beneficial will be wisdom. And we say virtue is beneficial?

*Meno*  Yes indeed.

*Soc.*  So we say virtue is wisdom – either the whole or a part?

*Meno*  I think what you're saying is finely said, Socrates.

*Soc.*  Then if that is so, good people do not come into being by nature.

*Meno* I think not.

*Soc.* Yes, and presumably there's this point as well. If good b people came into being by nature, presumably we'd have had people who could recognize children with good natures, and we'd take the ones they pointed out and guard them in the Acropolis, sealing them up much more carefully than gold bullion, so that no one should corrupt them and when they grew up they could come to be useful to their cities.

*Meno* Very likely so, Socrates.

*Soc.* Well, since good people don't come to be so by nature, is it c by learning?

*Meno* I think that must necessarily follow. And it's clear on the basis of the hypothesis, Socrates, that virtue comes from teaching if it's knowledge.

*Soc.* Perhaps, by Zeus. But I'm afraid we may not have done so finely in agreeing on that.

*Meno* Yet it seemed finely said a moment ago.

*Soc.* But I'm afraid it needs to seem finely said not only a moment ago but also in the present and the future, if there's to be anything sound about it.

*Meno* What's all this? What do you see to make you dissatisfied d with it, and doubtful about virtue being knowledge?

*Soc.* I'll tell you, Meno. It's not the statement that it comes from teaching *if* it's knowledge that I retract as other than finely said. But as to whether it *is* knowledge, consider whether you think I'm reasonable in my doubts about *that*. Tell me this: if *anything at all* – not just virtue – comes from teaching, must there not be teachers and learners of it?

*Meno* Yes, I think so.

*Soc.* And conversely, given something of which there were no e teachers or learners, shouldn't we be making a fair guess if we guessed that this didn't come from teaching?

*Meno* That is so – but don't you think there are teachers of virtue?

*Soc.* Well, I've often searched to see if there were any teachers of it, but for all my efforts I can't find any. And yet I make the search in company with many people, and for choice with the ones I suppose to be most experienced in the matter. And look, Meno, we're in luck now, too – here's Anytus just sat down beside us; let's invite him to share our search. It would make good sense; first, 90a Anytus here had a father Anthemion who was wise as well as rich –

he didn't come to be rich by sheer chance or by a gift from someone (like Ismenias the Theban who has just taken over the fortune of Polycrates) but by achieving it through his own wisdom and diligence; and besides that, he was a citizen who didn't seem to be arrogant, or pompous and disagreeable, but a peaceful, modest man. Besides, he brought up and educated Anytus well, in the view b of the Athenian public – at any rate, they elect him to the highest offices. Obviously this is the right kind of person to have with one in the search for whether or not there are teachers of virtue and who they are. So do join your guest-friend Meno and myself, Anytus, in our search for who the teachers of this subject might be. Consider it like this: if we wished Meno here to become a good doctor, what teachers would we send him to? Wouldn't it be to c doctors?

*Anytus* Yes indeed.

*Soc.* What if we wished him to become a good cobbler? Wouldn't it be to cobblers?

*Any.* Yes.

*Soc.* And the same for everything else?

*Any.* Yes indeed.

*Soc.* Now tell me this about the same examples as before. We'd do well to send him to doctors if we wished him to become a doctor, we say. In saying this, do we mean we'd be acting sensibly d in sending him to the people who profess the skill rather than to those who don't, people who charge a fee precisely on these grounds and advertise themselves as teachers for anyone who wants to go and learn? Isn't it with this in mind that we'd do well to send him?

*Any.* Yes.

*Soc.* And it's the same with flute-playing and everything else, isn't it? If we wish to make a flute-player of someone, it would be e very foolish to refuse to send him to the people who undertake to teach the skill and charge fees, and instead bother other people[5] who neither claim to be teachers, nor have a single pupil, in the subject we expect them to teach the person we're sending. Don't you think it would be very irrational?

*Any.* Yes I do, by Zeus, and very ignorant too.

*Soc.* Finely spoken. Well then, possibly you'll join me now in

---

[5] OCT includes here an additional phrase, ζητοῦντα μανθάνειν παρὰ τούτων, 'seeking to learn from them', which I have followed Bluck in omitting.

planning for your guest-friend Meno here. He's been telling me for  91a
a long time, Anytus, how he desires the wisdom and virtue through
which people run homes and cities finely, look after their parents,
and know how to receive and send off both fellow-citizens and
guest-friends from abroad in the manner worthy of a good man. So
consider: who would be the right people to send him to for this  b
virtue? Or is it quite clear, on the basis of what we've just said, that
it would be those who profess to be teachers of virtue and advertise
themselves as available to anyone in Greece who wishes to learn,
fixing and charging fees for it?

*Any.* And who are these you are speaking of, Socrates?

*Soc.* Surely you too must know – they're the men people call
Sophists.

*Any.* By Heracles, Socrates, say no such thing! Let none of my  c
friends or associates, whether Athenian or guest-friend from
abroad, be seized by such madness as to go to them and be made
havoc of – since *they're* just plain havoc and corruption to everyone
in their company.

*Soc.* What do you mean, Anytus? Are these people so uniquely
different from all the others who claim to know how to provide a
service, that they not merely fail to do any benefit to what's put in
their hands as the others do, but actually corrupt it? And this is  d
what they openly think fit to charge money for? Well, I for one
can't believe you. For I know that Protagoras, one man alone, got
more money from this branch of wisdom, than Pheidias who
produced such outstandingly fine works, and ten other sculptors all
combined. Besides, a man who works on old shoes or repairs
clothes couldn't take people in for one month if he returned the  e
clothes or shoes in a worse state than he'd received them in, but
would soon go starving if he did such things. Surely it's incredible
to suggest that Protagoras took in the whole of Greece for more
than forty *years*, corrupting those in his company and sending them
away in a worse state than he received them in – for I believe that
when he died he had lived for nearly seventy years and practised his
art for forty – and in all that time, and up to this very day, he has
lost none of his good reputation – and not only Protagoras, but a
great many others too, some who came before him and others even  92a
now still alive. Are we to say on your argument, then, that they
defraud and make havoc of young men *knowingly*, or do they take
themselves in too? Are we to judge them to be as crazy as that,
these men whom some say are the wisest of people?

*Any.* *They're* far from being crazy, Socrates – no, it's much more the young men who give them the money, and even more than these it's their relatives who let them, but most of all by far it's b the cities who allow these men entry and don't expel them, whether they be visitors or natives who start such activities.

*Soc.* Has one of the Sophists wronged you, Anytus, or why are you so angry with them?

*Any.* By Zeus, no; *I've* never yet been in any of their company, and I wouldn't allow anyone else in my family to be, either.

*Soc.* So you've had no experience at all of the men?

*Any.* And I hope I never shall have.

*Soc.* Then, my good sir, how could you know whether there's c any good or bad in this business, if you've had no experience at all of it?

*Any.* Easily – after all, I know who these people are, whether I've had experience of them or not.

*Soc.* Perhaps you've got second sight, Anytus, for from what you yourself say I'd be puzzled how you know about them otherwise. However, we weren't enquiring whom Meno should join in order to acquire *vice* – let that be the Sophists if you wish – but tell d us instead, and do this hereditary friend of yours a service by telling him – whom in our great city should he join to become distinguished in the *virtue* I just described?

*Any.* Why haven't *you* told him?

*Soc.* Well, I did mention the people I supposed were teachers of these things, but you say I was just talking nonsense and perhaps there's something in what you say. No, you take your turn and tell e him which Athenians he should go to. Name whom you wish.

*Any.* But why need he hear one person's name? Anyone he meets from among the fine and good of the Athenians will make him better than the Sophists would, without exception, if he's ready to take advice.

*Soc.* And did these fine and good people come to be as they are by sheer chance – never having learnt from anyone but all the same able to teach others what they never learnt themselves? 93a

*Any.* I expect they learnt in their turn from people who were fine and good in the past. Or do you not think there have been many good men in this city?

*Soc.* Yes, Anytus, I do think there are men here who are good at public affairs, and that there have been in the past, no less than there are. But have they really also been good *teachers* of their own virtue? For that's what our discussion is actually about. What we've been considering all this time is not whether there are any good men here or not, nor whether there have been any in the past, but b whether virtue comes from teaching. And in considering that, the question we're considering is whether the good men, either of nowadays or of the past, knew how to pass on the virtue they themselves possessed to other people as well, or whether this is something which people can't pass on or receive from one another. That is what Meno and I have been searching for all this time. So consider it like this, starting from what you yourself say. Wouldn't you say that Themistocles was a good man?　　　　　　　　　　c

*Any.*　Yes I would, more than anybody in fact.

*Soc.*　Then if anyone were a teacher of his own virtue, wouldn't Themistocles have been a good teacher of his?

*Any.*　Yes, I suppose so, if he'd wished to be.

*Soc.*　But don't you suppose he *would* have wished other people to become fine and good, and especially his own son, presumably? Or do you suppose he begrudged him this and it was on purpose that he didn't pass on the virtue he himself possessed? Haven't you d heard how Themistocles had his son taught to be a good horseman? He used to balance on a horse standing upright, and throw the javelin from on horseback in that position, and perform many other marvels which his father trained him to do, so as to make him wise in everything which depended on good teachers. Or haven't you heard this from older people?

*Any.*　I have.

*Soc.*　So no one could blame his son's *nature* for being bad.

*Any.*　No, perhaps not.　　　　　　　　　　　　　　　　　　e

*Soc.*　But as to his being a good or wise man in the ways in which his father was – have you ever yet heard, from anyone either young or old, that Cleophantus son of Themistocles was *that*?

*Any.*　No indeed.

*Soc.*　Well, do we suppose Themistocles *wished* to train his son in these other ways but make him no better than his neighbours in the wisdom he possessed himself – if virtue comes by teaching, that is.

*Any.*　By Zeus, perhaps not.

*Soc.*　So you see what kind of teacher of virtue *he* was – the man you yourself agree to be the very best of all those in the past. But let's consider someone else – Aristides son of Lysimachus. Or don't 94a you agree that he was a good man?

*Any.* Yes I do – definitely.

*Soc.* And didn't he too give his son Lysimachus the finest training in Athens in everything which depended on good teachers? But do you think he made him better than anyone else *as a man*? I expect you've been in this man's company and can see for yourself what he's like. Or if you like, take that grandest of wise men Pericles. You know he brought up two sons, Paralus b and Xanthippus?

*Any.* Yes, I do.

*Soc.* Well, as you yourself know, he taught those sons to be horsemen second to none in Athens, also he trained them till they were second to none in music and athletics and everything else which depends on skill – and did he really not *wish* to make them good men? I should think he wished it; what I suspect is that it doesn't come from teaching. Again, in case you were to suppose it's just a few and the least worthy of the Athenians who've turned out powerless in this matter, think how Thucydides also brought c up two sons, Melesias and Stephanos. He trained those sons well in every way, while as wrestlers they were the finest in Athens – he gave one to Xanthias to teach and the other to Eudoros, these being thought the finest wrestlers of their time, I believe – or don't you remember?

*Any.* Yes, so I've heard.

*Soc.* Isn't it clear then, if Thucydides taught his sons everything in the cases where he had to spend money to teach them, that he d would never have omitted to teach them in the case where he could have made them good men without having to pay a thing – *if* that subject came from teaching? Or was Thucydides not a worthy person perhaps, not someone with vast numbers of friends among Athenians and the allies? He belonged to a great family and held great power in Athens and in all Greece; so if virtue did come from teaching he could have found either someone in Athens or a guest-friend from somewhere else who would make his sons good men, if he hadn't got time himself because of his public duties. But in fact, Anytus my friend, I suspect virtue doesn't come from e teaching.

*Any.* Socrates, I think you speak ill of people very easily. I'd advise you to be careful, if you're ready to take my advice. Maybe in other cities too it's easier to harm people than to do them good, but it certainly is here, as I suppose you know yourself. 95a

*Soc.* Meno, I think Anytus is angry, and I'm not surprised – for in the first place he supposes I'm speaking ill of those people, secondly he believes he's one of them himself. Well, if he ever comes to know what kind of thing speaking ill is, he'll stop being angry, but he doesn't know at present. But you tell me, aren't there fine and good men in your city too?

*Meno* Yes indeed.

*Soc.* Well then, are they ready to offer themselves as teachers b for young people, and do they agree that they're teachers and that virtue comes from teaching?

*Meno* No by Zeus, Socrates; on the contrary, you'd sometimes hear from them that it comes from teaching, but sometimes that it doesn't.

*Soc.* So are we to say that people for whom not even this is agreed can be teachers in the subject?

*Meno* I don't think so, Socrates.

*Soc.* What next then? These Sophists, the only people who announce themselves as such – do you think *they're* teachers of virtue?

*Meno* Well with Gorgias, Socrates, the thing I find most re- c markable is that you'd never hear him professing that, and in fact he laughs at the others whenever he hears them professing it. No, he thinks that what he has to do is make people clever speakers.

*Soc.* So *you* don't think the Sophists are teachers of virtue either?

*Meno* I can't say, Socrates. I'm in the same state as most people – sometimes I think they are, sometimes not.

*Soc.* Do you know, it's not only you and these other people in public life who sometimes think virtue comes from teaching and sometimes not. Do you know, the poet Theognis says the very d same thing.

*Meno* In which verses?

*Soc.* In the elegiacs, where he says:

'Take food and drink with men whose power is great,
And sit by them, and on their pleasure wait:
From noble men is learnt nobility
And minds grow rotten through bad company.'                    e

You see how in *these* lines he speaks of virtue as something which comes from teaching?

*Meno* Apparently so, at least.

*Soc.* But elsewhere he shifts his ground a bit and says:

> 'Could mind be formed and set in man by art,
> Many and great the fees men would impart.'

– to those who could do this, and –

> 'No good man's son would ever bad become,
> Hearkening to wise words. But never could      96a
> The best of teaching make a bad man good.'

Do you observe how he says opposite things himself about the same subject?

*Meno* Apparently.

*Soc.* Well, can you tell me any other subject where those claiming to be teachers, far from being agreed to be capable of teaching others, aren't even agreed to know the subject themselves, but instead are agreed to be poor at the very subject of which they say b they're teachers, while the people who *are* agreed to be fine and good themselves say one minute that this comes from teaching and the next that it doesn't? Would you say then that people who are so confused about a subject could properly count as teachers of it?

*Meno* No I wouldn't, by Zeus.

*Soc.* Then if neither the Sophists, nor the people who are fine and good themselves, are teachers of the subject, clearly no one else could be?

*Meno* I don't think so.

*Soc.* And if there are no teachers, there are no learners either? c

*Meno* I think it is as you say.

*Soc.* And we did agree that where there are no teachers or learners of a subject, this subject doesn't come from teaching?[6]

*Meno* We did.

*Soc.* And there appear to be no teachers anywhere of virtue?

*Meno* That is so.

*Soc.* And if no teachers, no learners either.

*Meno* Apparently so.

*Soc.* So virtue can't be something which comes from teaching.

*Meno* It seems not, if we've considered the question rightly. d And so I really do wonder, Socrates, whether there are any good men at all, or if some *do* become good, what their method of becoming it might be.

---

[6] 'doesn't come from teaching' translates Bluck's reading μὴ διδακτὸν εἶναι. OCT has μηδὲ . . ., 'doesn't come from teaching, either'.

*Soc.* I'm afraid, Meno, that you and I are rather poor specimens – Gorgias has not trained you adequately nor Prodicus me. We must turn our attention more than ever to ourselves then, and search for someone who will somehow or other manage to make us better. I say this looking back at our search a moment ago and how e ridiculous it was that we didn't notice it's *not* only with knowledge as guide that men do things well and rightly. Perhaps that is the gap through which the understanding of how good men come into being is escaping us.

*Meno* What do you mean, Socrates?

*Soc.* This. We were right to agree that good men must be beneficial and that this could not be otherwise, weren't we?    97a

*Meno* Yes.

*Soc.* And presumably we were also doing fine when we agreed that they will be beneficial if they guide our affairs aright?

*Meno* Yes.

*Soc.* But as to not being able to guide aright without having wisdom, we don't look as though we've been right to agree to that point.

*Meno* So what do you mean?

*Soc.* I'll tell you. If someone who knew the road to Larisa, or wherever else you like, went there and guided others, he'd guide them rightly and well, wouldn't he?

*Meno* Yes indeed.

*Soc.* And what if it were someone who had a *right opinion* as to b what the road was, but had never been there and didn't know it? Wouldn't he too guide aright?

*Meno* Yes indeed.

*Soc.* And so long as he has right opinion about what the other person has knowledge of, presumably he will be no worse as a guide through having true opinion without being wise on the matter, than someone who *is* wise on it.

*Meno* No, not at all.

*Soc.* So true opinion is no worse a guide in acting rightly than wisdom, and this is the point we missed out just now in considering what sort of thing virtue is, when we said that only wisdom can c guide right action. In fact there is also true opinion.

*Meno* It does seem so.

*Soc.* So right opinion is no less beneficial than knowledge.

*Meno* Except, Socrates, that someone with knowledge would be successful all the time, while someone with right opinion would sometimes be successful and sometimes not.

*Soc.* What do you mean? Wouldn't someone who had right opinion all the time be successful all the time, so long as his opinion is right?

*Meno* It must be so, it appears to me. So in that case, Socrates, I wonder why on earth knowledge is so much more valuable than d right opinion, and what makes either of them different from the other.

*Soc.* Do you know what makes you wonder, or shall I tell you?

*Meno* Do tell me.

*Soc.* It's because you haven't paid attention to the statues of Daedalus – but perhaps you haven't got any in your parts.

*Meno* Why do you say that?

*Soc.* Because they too escape and run away if they are not tied down, but stay in place if they are.

*Meno* What about it? e

*Soc.* It's of no great value to own one of Daedalus' productions that's loose, any more than a runaway slave – for it won't stay – but to own one that's tied down is worth a lot; they are very fine works. So what am I thinking about in saying this? True opinions. True opinions too are a fine thing and altogether good in their effects so long as they stay with one, but they won't willingly stay long and 98a instead run away from a person's soul, so they're not worth much until one ties them down by reasoning out the explanation. And that is recollection, Meno my friend, as we agreed earlier. And when they've been tied down, then for one thing they become items of knowledge, and for another, permanent. And that's what makes knowledge more valuable than right opinion, and the way knowledge differs from right opinion is by being tied down.

*Meno* By Zeus, Socrates, it does seem likely to be something of that kind.

*Soc.* Well of course I'm only speaking myself from what looks b likely, not from knowledge. However, I don't at all think it merely looks likely that right opinion and knowledge are different kinds of things. No, if there's anything I would say I know – and few enough such things there are – this is one thing I *would* include among those I know.

*Meno* And you're quite right in saying that, Socrates.

*Soc.* Well, am I not also right in saying that when true opinion is the guide it is no worse than knowledge at carrying out the activity of every field of practice?

*Meno*  I think what you're saying is true there too.

*Soc.*  So right opinion will be no worse and no less beneficial c than knowledge, for practical purposes, nor will a man who *has* right opinion be any worse or less beneficial than one with knowledge.

*Meno*  That is so.

*Soc.*  Now we've agreed that a good man is a beneficial one?

*Meno*  Yes.

*Soc.*  Well then, since it's not only through knowledge that there can be men who are good and beneficial to their cities, given that there are such, but also through right opinion, and since people don't have either of these by nature – neither knowledge nor true opinion[7] – or do you think people do have either of them by d nature?

*Meno*  No I don't.

*Soc.*  Then since it's not by nature, people can't be good by nature, either.

*Meno*  No indeed.

*Soc.*  And since it's not by nature, the next thing we were considering was whether it came from teaching.

*Meno*  Yes.

*Soc.*  And it seemed, didn't it, that virtue *would* come from teaching if it were wisdom?

*Meno*  Yes.

*Soc.*  And indeed that it must be wisdom if it *did* come from teaching?

*Meno*  Yes indeed.

*Soc.*  And that if there were teachers it would come from teach- e ing, but otherwise not?

*Meno*  Just so.

*Soc.*  But in fact we agreed there aren't any teachers of it?

*Meno*  That is so.

*Soc.*  Thus we have agreed that it does *not* come from teaching and is *not* wisdom?

*Meno*  Yes indeed.

*Soc.*  But we do agree that it's something *good*?

*Meno*  Yes.

*Soc.*  And that a thing is beneficial and good if it guides aright?

[7] I have followed Bluck in omitting the obelized οὔτ ἐπίστητα recorded in OCT at this point.

*Meno*   Yes indeed.

*Soc.*   And that there are only the two things – true opinion and   99a
knowledge – which guide aright so that by having them a human
being could guide aright – for things which come out right by mere
chance don't come about through human guidance – but where a
*human being* guides anything in the right course, the two things
involved are true opinion and knowledge.

*Meno*   I think so.

*Soc.*   And since virtue doesn't come from teaching it can no
longer be knowledge either, can it?

*Meno*   Apparently not.

*Soc.*   So of the two things which are good and beneficial we   b
have dismissed one, and it can't be knowledge that is the guide in
public life.

*Meno*   I don't think so.

*Soc.*   So it isn't by any sort of wisdom, or by being wise, that
men like Themistocles or the others that Anytus here mentioned a
moment ago guide their cities. And that's why they can't make
other people like they are themselves – because it's not through
knowledge that they are as they are.

*Meno*   It seems to be as you say, Socrates.

*Soc.*   If it's not by knowledge, then, it only remains for it to
come about by good opinion. That's what statesmen employ in   c
setting their cities to rights, and as far as wisdom is concerned they
are no different from soothsayers or seers – for these too say many
true things in their trances without knowing what they are talking
about.

*Meno*   Perhaps it *is* like that.

*Soc.*   And don't men deserve to be called divine, Meno, when
they have many great successes in what they do and say, all without
thought?

*Meno*   Yes indeed.

*Soc.*   So we'd be right both to apply the word 'divine' to the
soothsayers and seers we were just speaking of, along with all the   d
poets, and also to say that statesmen are not the least among these
in being divinely entranced, inspired and possessed by the god as
they must be when they speak successfully on many great issues
without knowing what they are talking about.

*Meno*   Yes indeed.

*Soc.*   And you know, Meno, women do call good men 'divine',
and the Spartans, whenever they pay tribute to a good man, say,

71

'He's a divine man'.

*Meno*  And apparently they speak rightly, Socrates – though  e
Anytus here may not like you saying it.

*Soc.*  That's not my concern. I'll be discussing with him again
later, Meno, but as to us now, if we've done finely in our search
and in what we've been saying in this whole discussion, then virtue
can't come either by nature or from teaching, but comes to people,
when it does, by divine dispensation without thought – unless there  100a
were to be a statesman such that he could make someone else
a statesman too. If there were, he could be described as being,
among the living, rather like Homer describes Teiresias as being
among the dead, when he says of him:

> He alone [of those in Hades] had life and mind;
> >                                    the rest were shadows.

That is just what such a man would be like in this world –
something real among shadows in terms of virtue.

*Meno*  I think that is most finely said, Socrates.  b

*Soc.*  Well then, Meno, on the basis of this reasoning we find
that virtue apparently comes to people, when it does, by divine
dispensation. But we shan't have clear knowledge about it, until
before searching for how virtue comes to people we first try to
search out what it is in itself. But just now, it's time for me to go
somewhere, and you please try and convince your guest-friend
Anytus here of everything you've been convinced of yourself, so as
to soften him down – for if you convince *him*, you will be doing the  c
Athenians a service too.

# SOCRATES

## I. G. Kidd

Socrates (*c.* 470–399 BC), of Athens, was perhaps the most original, influential and controversial figure in the history of Greek thought. Very little is known about his life. He died by drinking hemlock after having been condemned to death for 'not believing in the gods the state believes in, and introducing different new divine powers; and also for corrupting the young', according to the indictments recorded in Plato's *Apology* and Xenophon's *Apology*. Philosophy before him was 'pre-Socratic'; he was the 'hinge', or the orientation point, for most subsequent thinkers and the direct inspiration of Plato. There is no agreement, however, on the exact nature of Socrates' philosophical contribution or on whether anything certain can be said of the historical Socrates. This controversy is known as the Socratic problem, which arises because Socrates wrote nothing on philosophy, unless, perhaps, jottings of self-examination not for publication (cf. Epictetus, *Discourses* II. I, 32). Not only a historical problem is involved in the nature of the evidence, but also a philosophical puzzle in the character of Socrates embedded in Plato's dialogues.

Two extreme answers which would put an end to further controversy have been put forth in this century. Professors John Burnet and A. E. Taylor have argued that the Socrates of Plato's dialogues, and only he, is the historical Socrates, and agnostics suggest that we know nothing of Socrates, the earliest reports being versions of a literary myth of no greater historical validity than stage Agamemnons.

There are two arguments for the latter view. (1) None of the primary evidence is historical in purpose or character. Aristophanes' comedy *The Clouds* (423 BC) is a satire on intellectuals, and Socrates, the chief character, is a mere type. The Socratic dialogues of Socrates' friends and admirers (Plato and the fragmentary minor Socratics – for example, Antisthenes and Aeschines) were not intended as biography but as live philosophy, mostly written well after Socrates' death, where 'Socrates' illustrates the writers' arguments, which differ from one another. Xenophon also knew Socrates, but much in his memoirs is probably secondhand and tainted with the suspect fancies of Greek apologetics. It is demonstrable that the first two chapters of Xenophon's *Memorabilia* are a reply to a literary pamphlet written some time after 394 by the Sophist Polycrates. This pamphlet put a fictitious prosecuting speech into the mouth of Anytus, one of Socrates' accusers. Aristotle, who was not born until fifteen years after Socrates' death, probably derived his historical assessment from the earlier suspect literature; anyway, his 'historical' comments are often protreptic interpretations for his own philosophy. The frequent references in later antiquity must derive from these suspect sources or from an oral tradition hardening into collected 'Sayings of Socrates' (see Hibeh Papyrus 182), an equally untrustworthy source. (2) All the evidence is riddled with contradiction, and not only of details. The whole presentation of one reporter is scarcely consistent with that of another; indeed, the Socratics were bitterly critical of one another. There are no objective facts against which to resolve these inconsistencies.

It should, however, be protested against extreme agnosticism that contradiction among the reports cannot by itself prove them all wholly mythical. Doubt thrown on part of a historical anecdote does not necessarily invalidate the whole. It does not follow from two contradictory pieces of evidence that neither of them can be true or be explained. We are looking for a common stimulus to divergent interpretations where cancellation by naive abstraction proves nothing. Contradiction should lead to a critical examination of the value of a piece of evidence against the background and context of the individual reporter. Second, literary genres are never mutually exclusive. None of the evidence can be thus dismissed. Who can say that Plato's Socrates is a figment of his literary imagination or that Aristophanes did not reflect current opinions of Socrates? *The Clouds* itself helped to create a historical prejudice about Socrates which was later used against him at his trial; Plato's *Apology* is geared to this historical atmosphere. Polycrates' fictional speech probably embodied another part of the historical prejudice, and Xenophon's account is not invalidated because it is a reply to a fictional speech although its value for us is limited by our knowledge of Xenophon. Aristotle can be shown to have distinguished (*Metaphysics* 987a29 ff and 1078b9 ff) between the Platonic and the historical Socrates in the history of a subject, the Theory of Forms, on which twenty years in the Platonic Academy must have made him expert. There is no reason to suspect misrepresentation.

It seems to follow that while the sceptics are right in not accepting any evidence *per se* as having firsthand historical certainty, all the evidence has a right to be regarded as historical interpretations of varying value, from which it may be difficult but not impossible to separate historical plausibility. It is clear this could not be done by simple corroboration but by an estimate of the peculiarities of each reporter's view of Socrates. Only by an intensive study of Plato and the others may we hope to gauge the 'lenses' through which they saw Socrates and thus interpret their evidence. Then and only then may corroboration play a significant part.

The question arises whether one reporter should take precedence over the rest. The likeliest candidate is Plato, but he should not be taken as absolutely as Burnet and Taylor take him. For although they argued that it was unlikely that Plato would misrepresent his revered master, it is still more improbable that a man of Plato's ability could postpone his own philosophical progression and, contrary to his Socrates' methods, preach another's philosophy until after he was 60, when the character of Socrates retired into the background of Plato's dialogues. Nor is it easy to see why a historical criterion should work for Plato's Socrates and not for other writers of the same genre. But it is impossible to believe that the development of 'Socrates'' doctrine in the course of the dialogues, which were written after his death, can be other than Plato's; Aristotle was right to make his distinction. Plato's Socrates, too, is an interpretation. Weight should be given, however, to Plato's sincere attachment to Socrates and to his insight into Socrates' thought. Also, although Socratic doctrine must still be disentangled from a study of the development of Plato's thought (and probably never will be to everybody's satisfaction), Plato does give by far the most coherent and convincing picture of Socrates' personality. That Plato thought this personality of prime philosophical importance is the most fruitful thing we know of the historical Socrates. From such principles a plausible account of Socrates may be attempted.

## EARLY LIFE AND PERSONAL CIRCUMSTANCES

Our sources insist that Socrates was remarkable for living the life he preached. But information is sparse. He was the son of Sophroniscus (only in later sources described as a stone-mason), of the deme Alopeke, and Phaenarete, a midwife, an occupation translated by Socrates into philosophical activity. The father was a close friend of the son of Aristides the Just, and the young Socrates was familiar with members of the Periclean circle. Later, he was obviously at home in the best society, but he had no respect for social status. His financial resources were adequate to entitle him to serve as a hoplite in the Peloponnesian War, where his courage in the campaigns of Potidaea, Delium, and Amphipolis is offered as evidence that there was a complete concord between his words and character. His later absorption in philosophy and his mission made him neglect his private affairs, and he fell to a level of comparative poverty, which was in tune with his arguments on the unimportance of material goods and his own simple needs. He was probably more in love with philosophy than with his family, but that his wife Xanthippe was a shrew is a late tale and that he was not without interest in parental and filial duties is obvious in his thought for his sons' future in Plato's *Crito*. But all personal considerations, including his own life, were subordinated to 'the supreme art of philosophy'; tradition holds that by refusing to compromise his principles, he deliberately antagonized the court which was trying him for impiety and forced an avoidable death penalty. Plato's *Crito* and *Phaedo*, set during Socrates' last days, give a moving and convincing picture of a man at one with himself.

## CONTEMPORARY PHILOSOPHY

In Plato's *Phaedo* (96a) Socrates describes his youthful enthusiasm for philosophies that concentrated on physical descriptions of the universe, which were then in vogue, and his subsequent disillusionment with all material explanations of causation. Although the tone and context of Plato's Theory of Forms forbid literal acceptance of the whole passage, the general outline is probably correct. The contemporary Ion of Chios recorded that as a young man Socrates was a pupil of Archelaus. Archelaus' teacher, Anaxagoras, was linked with Socrates' name to stir a prejudice which persisted from Aristophanes' *Clouds* to the trial. But by the time we have any descriptive picture of Socrates, he had abandoned any interest in physics and was immersed in ethical and logical inquiries. It is more helpful to see Socrates against the background of the Sophists. Almost the only information to be derived with any certainty from *The Clouds* is that Socrates (then about 47) was regarded as a Sophist. Polycrates was still attacking him as such after his death, and Plato and Xenophon go to great pains to distinguish him from other Sophists. The Sophists were itinerant professors teaching for a fee the skill (*sophia*) of *aretē* (excellence, in the sense of how to make the best of yourself and get on). Socrates was the Athenian Sophist inasmuch as his life was dedicated to the same new intellectual inquiry into education – the science of effecting *aretē*. He might claim that he took no fees and gave no formal instruction, but he would start and dominate an argument wherever the young and intelligent would listen, and people asked his advice on matters of practical conduct and educational problems. Sophists frequently studied language and rhetoric as an obvious key to private and political success; Socrates' interest in words and arguments was notorious. Plato lightheartedly compared him with Prodicus, the specialist in subtle discriminations of the meanings of apparently synonymous words. The terrorist government of Thirty banned any public utterance by him. His very method of argument, dialectic, characterized by destructive cross-examination, could be confused with, and sometimes in Plato falls to the level of, the combative eristic technically practised by Sophists, who concentrated almost exclusively on technique. The similarities are real. The distortion arises from seeing Socrates simply as the Athenian counterpart of the Sophistic phenomenon. Plato suggests that he differed fundamentally in moral purpose and intellectual standards and so should be contrasted to them.

## POLITICAL AND SOCIAL INFLUENCE

Like all generalizations, the classification of Socrates as a Sophist carries such half-truths as the charge, reflected in Polycrates' pamphlet, that Socrates was politically dangerous, the enemy of democracy, and the inspiration of the notorious politicians Alcibiades and Critias. The politician Anytus could not formally bring this charge at the trial since the effective deployment of political attack in the courts was barred by the amnesty decree of 403 BC. But the anti-Sophistic prejudice was real enough in the sensitive restored democracy, which remembered its earlier animosity against supposed political interference by freethinking, unscrupulous Sophists in Pericles' circle.

Nevertheless, in the strict sense the political influence of Socrates is a mirage. The only two public acts recorded by his apologists (see Plato's *Apology* 32b–d) were refusals to involve himself in state actions he thought wrong; both were courageous personal protests of no political significance. In the *Apology* (31d; cf. *Gorgias* 521c–e, 473e) Socrates explicitly denies political participation. Nor was he a power behind the scenes, for his friends Critias and Charmides when in power tried ineffectively to muzzle his caustic comments (Xenophon, *Memorabilia* I. 2, 32 ff). The association with Alcibiades is testified to by the rash of 'Alcibiades dialogues' by the Socratics, and Socrates could not fairly disown his influence by simply denying that he was responsible because he had no financial contract or profession as a teacher. But his influence was always personal, not political. No characteristic political philosophy emerged from the Socratics; even Plato may have conceived his doctrine of philosopher-kings through pondering the injustice of Socrates' conviction and death rather than from what Socrates had said (*Epistle* VII 324c–326b).

However, in the wider Greek sense of 'political' there was reason for fearing Socrates as a social force. Where *aretē*, education, and state were fused in one image (see Plato, *Protagoras* 325c–326e), an educator critical of received assumptions was a revolutionary. Socrates not only publicly raised such fundamental questions as 'What is *aretē*?' and 'Who are its teachers?', but also by discrediting through their own representatives the accepted educational channels and by creating a climate of questioning and doubt, he was suspected by conservative minds of the dangerous game of discomfiting all authority before a circle of impressionable youths and subtracting from the state the stability of tradition (see the encounter with Anytus in *Meno* 90a–95a). It was also apparent that the values by which Socrates lived, his indifference to material wealth and prosperity, and his freedom from desire and ambition were themselves a living criticism of the actual social and economic structures of Athens. In fact, Socrates claimed the right of independent criticism of all institutions and of politicians who did not seem to know what they were doing or compromised their principles; the Athenian democracy was distinguished merely by relying on a majority of ignoramuses. But he did not oppose the authority of law, and in Plato's *Crito* he rejected his friends' plan to smuggle him out of the country by putting forward a theory of social contract imbued with the true Athenian's emotional regard for his country as for a parent. He claimed that he had ruined himself financially in service to the state; yet his unsettling effect on the young and his persistent criticism were intolerable to any establishment. A gadfly, however patriotic (*Apology* 30e), will, if it does not go away by itself, eventually be removed as a poisonous nuisance. That Socrates was not attacked until he was 70 argues that his influence was not so wide as has been suspected (that is, that many did not take him seriously), unless he was saved by the power of his friends or by the charm and sincerity of his own personality.

## RELIGION

The charge made against Socrates of disbelief in the state's gods implied un-Athenian activities which would corrupt the young and the state if publicly preached. Meletus, who brought the indictment, counted on an anti-intellectualist smear that had precedents in the impiety trials of Pericles' friends. The prejudice against Socrates, who was neither a heretic nor agnostic as some Sophists undoubtedly were, had persisted from *The Clouds* and was perhaps fostered by the conduct of Alcibiades in the scandalous parody of the Mysteries in 415 BC. But Socrates provoked hostility. Two outbursts of feeling are recorded in court. One was at the mention of Socrates' *daimonion* (hinted at in the charge as a notorious religious innovation), a divine sign apprehended by him alone as a voice from god forbidding a contemplated action. Plato and Xenophon played this feature down, but it was regarded as unique in Socrates (Plato, *Republic* 496c) and was quite distinct from other accepted forms of religious communion. The claim set him dangerously apart from his fellows. The second instance involved the pronouncement of the Delphic oracle to his friend Chaerephon. The oracle said that no man was wiser than Socrates, and Socrates had the audacity to use this as justification of his mission as examiner-extraordinary of the views and conduct of every notable in Athens, claiming that in exposing their false conceit, he proved the god right – he at least knew that he knew nothing. Although this was characteristic Socratic irony – the expression of only half serious suggestions with a curious mixture of humility and presumption – Socrates clearly thought his mission was divinely inspired, and this involved criticism of the received mythology enshrined in the work of the poets and religious experts. In Plato's *Euthyphro* Socrates challenged both popular conceptions of piety and that of the fanatic who preaches strict interpretation of 'scriptural authority'. His logical and moral objections to the confused and scandalous standards of anthropopathic deities were aimed at a truer redefinition of piety. He was no mystic. Religion appears to have been a branch of ethics for him, and conscious right conduct in religious matters he held to be dependent on a rational inquiry into what piety was. Yet, the accounts portray, besides the restless searcher for understanding, a man of sincere practice in traditional cult forms, with a simple faith in the providence of a divinity that was good and without contradiction. It was apparently possible for Socrates to contain his religious purification within the terms of the Olympian pantheon.

## THE PHILOSOPHICAL PERSONALITY

The political and religious attack on Socrates by his enemies, although understandable, conveys an unsatisfactory picture of the intellectual dynamite which released Plato. Socrates' friends and followers placed his contributions in the fields of morals and logic, but they present a philosophical personality, not a philosophical system. The most striking feature of the evidence is that it required the invention of a new literary and philosophical genre, the Socratic dialogue, to convey his influence. The difference between Xenophon and Plato is as much one of form as of content. The shrewd moral confidant of Xenophon's anecdotal account could have been only of local interest; the character of Socrates in the organic dialogues of Plato has stimulated all Western philosophy. In the dialogues the common Socratic element is not quotation of doctrine, which varies, nor the philosophy of Socrates, but Socrates philosophizing.

Socrates philosophized by joining in a discussion with another person who thought he knew what justice, courage, or the like is. Under Socrates' questioning it became clear that neither knew, and they co-operated in a new effort, Socrates making interrogatory suggestions that were accepted or rejected by his friend. They failed to solve the problem but, now conscious of their lack of knowledge, agreed to continue the search whenever possible. These discussions, or 'dialectics', whereby Socrates engaged in his question-and-answer investigations, were, for Plato at least, the very marrow of the Socratic legacy. For those who had not heard Socrates at it, the 'Socratic dialogue' was invented.

Plato revealed the advantages of dialectic by contrasting the method with contemporary Sophistic education typified by the set lecture of dictated information or expounded thesis and the eristic technical exercise of outsmarting opponents. For Socrates knowledge was not acceptance of secondhand opinion which could be handed over for a sum of money like a phonograph record (or encyclopaedia) but a personal achievement gained through continual self-criticism. Philosophy involved not learning the answers but searching for them – a search more hopeful if jointly undertaken by two friends, one perhaps more experienced than the other but both in love with the goal of truth and reality and willing to subject themselves honestly to the critical test of reason alone.

Socrates was the first openly to canvass this conception of the operation of philosophy and is still the best illustration of it. He thought himself uniquely gifted to stimulate the operation in others. He disclaimed authority on his own part, pleading the ignorance of the searcher; this did not prevent him from directing the argument, which is a different matter from feeding information. An intellectual midwife (Plato, *Theaetetus* 149; already in *The Clouds*), he tested the wind eggs of others and assisted fertile production. Wind eggs predominated, and the 'elenchus' (cross-examination) exposing them followed a set pattern: the subject claims knowledge of some matter evidenced in a proposition defining what is usually an ethical term; a series of questions from Socrates elicits a number of other propositions which, when put together, prove the contrary of the original definition. But obstetrics is essentially a personal affair; what is really tested is the person and his false conceit. The premises and argumentation of the elenchus are tailored to each individual, even to the extent, in the case of a hostile witness, of fallacious argument. At this point the establishment of truth is not at stake; the question of whether the person will destroy for himself the main blockage of his thought, his false confidence, is the issue. Socrates' zeal for this demolition work produced such *aporia* (the perplexity of no way out) that he was accused of simply numbing his victims like a sting ray. Plato had to point out, in the illustration with commentary of Socratic elenchus which forms the first half of *Meno*, that false conceit was paralysis, and that Socratic disillusionment was the stimulus, of philosophy. 'The life not tested by criticism is not worth living' (*Apology* 38a).

Even so, the destructive logic could have stifled, sterilized, and offended more than it did had it not been for an element Plato termed *eros*, denoting not only the passionate attachments Socrates inspired but also that quality of passion in the enthusiasm of a great teacher who fires his associates with his own madness. The young especially felt a personal attraction which was not, despite some ribald stories, physical – Socrates was a pop-eyed man with a flattened snub nose and could be compared to a Silenus (Plato, *Symposium* 215) – but for his character and his conversation.

Plato's picture is vivid: of a genial but disturbing personality, a social grace and disreputable appearance; a placidity radiating a calm like that found at the centre of a storm; the puckish humour and wit offsetting the sharpness of mind and clarity of thought and tireless concentration; the freshness and unexpectedness of his arguments, his power of not exhausting a subject but of opening it up; the warmth of his attachments, his eccentricities, mischievousness, simplicity, deviousness, modesty, and presumption; the knack of bringing a gathering or person to life and leaving it exhausted; the practical example of his life and the uncompromising idealism of his death; a man whose talk foreigners came to Athens to hear; whose homely, not to say vulgar, instances could suddenly uncover penetrating and embarrassing truths; talk with which the best brains in Athens literally fell in love, a talk and beauty of inner man, which they took to be the touchstone of truth and right; above all, the affection in Plato's writing – this picture astonishingly still conveys the magnetism of the personality. And Plato would have us believe that Socrates, as the human embodiment of a philosophical attitude directed by a passionate love of truth and knowledge, finally inspired in his associates the love of *sophia* itself. This claim, of course, may still be tested by the reader of Plato's dialogues.

## PHILOSOPHICAL DOCTRINES

Our knowledge of Socratic doctrine is severely limited by his own refusal to formulate his inquiries into a system and by the personal variations of his interpreters. There are indications, however, that the expert skill (*sophia*) for which he so 'lovingly' searched in the operation of 'philosophy' gained a new meaning through him. His version of *sophia*, unlike that in most pre-Socratic thought, was concerned almost exclusively with the ethics of human conduct (this is the evidence of both Aristotle and the Socratics). 'Socrates was the first to call philosophy down from the heavens' (Cicero, *Tusculan Disputations* V. 4, 10). His opposition to the contemporary cult of successful living was based on a new concept of the psyche, to which he assigned for the first time moral and intellectual status, making it the dominant factor in human conduct. The conception was quite different both from popular ideas on the soul and from the psychology of philosophers like Heraclitus (frag. 119) and the Pythagoreans (see Empedocles, frag. 115). Socrates advocated the Delphic motto 'Know thyself' and suggested that introspection showed how man achieves his real personality – the perfectly efficient realization of his being (*aretē*) – when the psyche is in control of the physical, and the intellectual and moral part of the psyche is in control of the rest of it (see *Meno* 88e). Happiness (*eudaimonia*), then, depends not on external or physical goods but on knowingly acting rightly. The proper condition of the psyche is thus of prime importance, and the task of philosophy is its care, training, or doctoring (Plato, *Apology* 29d ff). As there is only one proper condition, being good implies the capacity for any virtue; although different virtues are distinguishable, virtue is a unity and a form of knowledge.

Socrates was a man of essentially practical aims who dismissed physics and theoretical mathematics as useless (Xenophon, *Memorabilia* IV. 7). Through his new interpretation of human fulfilment, he was seeking a way by which *aretē* and right action could be guaranteed. His own character probably suggested the importance of self-control. Only a man in control of himself is in control of his actions; the self-discipline of moral reason frees a man from the slavery of distracting appetites so that he can do what he wishes – that is, pursue true happiness. Above all, only rationally controlled action is not self-defeating. No one voluntarily makes a mistake. By 'voluntarily' he meant consistently with one's true will – that is, to be really happy. Socrates was, of course, familiar with the experience of yielding to temptation, but he explained that in such cases one does not really believe that what one does is bad and does not really know that what is rejected is good. For Socrates 'good' was a term of utility signifying advantage for the doer. Thus, he argued that no one would deliberately choose what will harm him or knowingly reject what will benefit him most. If a wrong choice is made, it must be an intellectual mistake, an error which the man who knows could not make. *Aretē*, according to another Socratic epigram, is (that is, depends on) knowledge. Socrates was thus hunting for a practical science of right conduct which through its rational organization was infallible, predictable, and teachable. It is this search which the earliest Socratic dialogues of Plato are probably testing.

Clearly, the key to such a science is the interpretation of knowledge, and the evidence here displays a confusion over different types of knowing. Socrates is sometimes represented as comparing his moral expert with other experts of practical skills, suggesting the slogan 'Efficiency (*aretē*) is know-how', but he seems to have recognized the moral inadequacy of mere technical expertise. Most frequently, Socrates wanted to know what a thing is (*aretē*, justice, or the like) on the assumption that it is impossible to be good (just, or the like) on purpose unless one first knows what it is. If one knows what it is, one can say what it is (unlike the Sophists, who professed to teach *aretē* but could not coherently state what *aretē* was). Now, since he held that a correct rational account (*logos*) of what good is was not only a necessary, but even a sufficient, condition of being good, the prime practical business of the philosopher involved the examination of moral terms and the attempt to define them. This is the evidence of Aristotle (*Metaphysics* 1078b17 ff) and the main activity of the Socrates in the early Platonic dialogues. ('What is courage, piety, beauty, justice, *aretē*?' he asked in the *Laches*, *Euthyphro*, *Hippias Major*, *Republic I*, *Protagoras*, and *Meno*.) The failure of the attempt is of much interest. The Platonic Socrates rejected as inadequate definition by instance or enumeration and answers which were too narrow or too wide. The equivalence sought appears to be more than mere verbal identification. Above all, Socrates was not seeking the conventional meaning of the word but what the thing really is – the essence of what is denoted by the word. He seems to have been groping for an analytical formula of the type 'Clay is earth mixed with water', which explicates the essential nature or structure of the thing in question. The hope was that if one could recognize for certain with one's mind what was the essential ingredient which made all just acts just, one could recognize any instance and also reproduce an example at will and so act justly. The success of this attempt at real definition was precluded by certain assumptions about the kind of answer and confusion over the type of question involved (see

R. Robinson, *Plato's Earlier Dialectic*, 2nd edn, 1953, Ch. 5); yet even if Socrates had been able to explicate 'justice' to his own satisfaction, the question of how knowledge of its description could prescribe our conduct would have remained. The analogies to which Socrates was addicted tended to obscure the idiosyncrasies of moral terms. Nevertheless, a dialogue like *Euthyphro* is still an excellent introduction to the problem of definition.

In the *Metaphysics* (1078b17 ff) Aristotle qualified Socratic definitions as universal. If Socrates did search (as he did in the early dialogues) for a single ingredient which was the same in all instances and for an explanation of them, he was at least logically committed to a theory of universals, which, however, was probably not systematically investigated until Plato constructed, partly from Socratic 'definitions' his Theory of Forms. Aristotle should be believed when he stated that Socrates did not himself make the universals or definitions exist apart, as the Platonic Socrates did later in the middle dialogues.

Aristotle also said that induction (*epagōgē*) and syllogizing are characteristic of Socrates. Induction probably does not mean the full inductive procedure of the scientist, but merely argument from analogy – by all accounts, one of Socrates' notorious habits, which he most dangerously employed. Syllogizing is 'adding together' premises to discover deductively a conclusion; in the aporetic dialogues it is the method by which Socrates elicited conclusions which destroy as contradictories the originally proposed definitions. But if he did hope to construct a science of living, the syllogisms would have been the necessary arguments developing the premises of the real definitions of 'what-a-thing-is' into a rational system or science.

Socrates' championship of reason took deep root in Greek thought, possibly all the more so because he did not expound a system. He himself was probably concerned simply with continually testing in public the possibility in action of his rationally dominated ethic, but he never really doubted that it was possible. If he overstressed the power of reason in psychology, this may be partly attributed to his own unique strength of character, which conformed his actions to his thinking. It is also attributable to the paradoxical fusion of *eros*-passion with the rational in him. His reason was infused with desire for the end of good and truth, which attracted his mind by its beauty so that he was in love with it. Plato, too, was infected; with rational detachment he demonstrated the

Socratic willingness to 'follow the argument (*logos*) wherever it might lead' in the dialogues. We are also shown how the *logos* led Socrates to a martyrdom which Plato used to canonize him in emotionally moving prose. It must have been the fusion of *logos* and *eros* that was so highly infectious; the Socratic evidence is inexplicable unless it was the gift of the historical Socrates. However, what really matters now is not such a historical supposition, but that the Platonic Socrates' love of *sophia* (philosophy) is still contagious. Yet, the incarnation of philosophy in Plato could not have come so convincingly alive had there not been a man who was regarded by Plato as 'the finest, most intelligent, and moral man of his generation' (Plato, *Phaedo* 118) and who was also the greatest of mental midwives.

## THE SOCRATICS

Socrates established no school. The *logos* led his associates in different directions, and each was critical of the others. Plato cultivated the seeds in ethics, logic, and epistemology that flowered into a rational system. Of the minor Socratics our evidence is sparse. Antisthenes, stressing the self-sufficiency of virtue and its dependence on knowledge, developed the aspect of self-discipline and freedom from convention. His ascetic tendencies were sneered at by the hedonist Aristippus of Cyrene. Socrates' views on pleasure are hard to discover (see, for example, the hedonistic calculus in Plato, *Protagoras* 351b ff), but Aristippus' insistence on the intelligent control of pleasure as distinct from slavish adherence or abstinence does not clash with what we hear of Socrates in Plato's *Symposium*, for example. Euclides of Megara may have fused Socratic and Eleatic elements; his school was notorious for an interest, possibly stimulated by Socrates, in the methodology of argument. Phaedo, who wrote at least one Socratic dialogue (Diogenes Laertius II. 105, and Cicero, *Tusculan Disputations* IV. 37, 80), founded a school in Elis; Simmias and Cebes were active in Thebes; their doctrines are not known. Aeschines of Sphettus (an Athenian deme), probably a contemporary of Plato, wrote dialogues admired by the ancients for their style and for the fidelity of the portrait of Socrates; indeed, a malicious tale accused him of passing off material of Socrates obtained from Xanthippe as his own. The Stoic Panaetius classed his dialogues as 'genuine', together with those of Plato, Xenophon, and Antisthenes.

Aeschines' portrait possibly had the smallest ingredient of originality; it would still be limited by his own capacities and insight. Enough survives of Aeschines' *Alcibiades* and *Aspasia* to give a tantalizing glimpse of these works. Socratic themes briefly appear, but the fragments are too truncated to allow Socrates' personality to emerge, and they are of more historical than philosophical interest. Like Xenophon, Aeschines had no subsequent philosophical influence.

Socrates' influence spread far beyond his contemporaries. The ancients regarded him as the root of most subsequent philosophy. The main stem rose through the Platonic Academy (not least Socratic in its sceptical Middle and New periods), from which Aristotle himself came. From Antisthenes a link (possibly tenuous) was traced through Diogenes to Cynicism. Through Socratic elements in Cynicism and the Platonic Academy, Stoicism tried to graft itself on to the Socratic tradition, although it was later Stoics like Panaetius and Epictetus who expressly admired the influence of Socrates. Even the hedonistic Cyrenaic school stems from Aristippus. It is possible that Socrates' philosophy may still be growing. 'Even now although Socrates is dead the memory of what he did or said while still alive is just as helpful or even more so to men' (Epictetus, *Discourses* IV. 1, 169).

# *ANAMNESIS* IN THE *MENO*

## Gregory Vlastos

## PART ONE: THE DATA OF THE THEORY

In the *Meno* we have a chance, rare in Greek philosophy, to compare a philosophical theory with the data which make up its ostensible evidence. Meno asks if there is any way Socrates can show him that 'learning'[1] is recollecting. Socrates offers to produce the proof on the spot. Meno will see the slave-boy learning, and this will show that he was recollecting. I wish to make the most of this opportunity to examine the presented data before considering the theory. To this I will devote the first and somewhat longer part of the paper, where I will seek by controversial argument to establish the right interpretation of the text.[2] While doing this, it will be convenient to use 'recollection' in quotes, suspending judgement upon its philosophical implications and even withholding attention from its dictionary meaning. Plato says the boy is 'recollecting' and so shall I of this and all other situations which are equivalent to it in a sense which I shall make clear. When a decision has been reached on what exactly is taking place when people are 'recollecting' in this purely nominative sense, it will be time to examine Plato's thesis that this 'recollecting' is recollecting.

In *Plato's Theory of Ideas* (Oxford, 1951) Sir David Ross remarks (p. 18):

> . . . the method by which the slave-boy is got to discover what square has twice the area of that of a given square is *a purely empirical one*; it is *on the evidence of his eyesight* and not of any clearly apprehended relation between universals that he admits that the square on the diagonal of a given square is twice the size of the given square. He admits that certain

triangles have areas equal, each of them, to half of the given square, and that the figure which they make up is itself a square, not because he sees that these things must be so, but *because to the eye they look as if they were.* (my italics)

I dare say that few of those who have read our text will agree with this construction of it – the 'empirical' one, I shall call it for convenience. But why precisely are we entitled to disagree? Not, surely, because 'no mention at all is made of sense-experience either in the dialogue with the slave or in the subsequent discussion of its significance' (N. Gulley, pp. 11–12). This is true, but settles nothing. For it is open to the retort that Plato does not have to mention sense-experience in order to direct attention to it. Is he not doing as much, and more, by dramatic means when he keeps Socrates so busy tracing figures in the sand? Can a process of discovery which leans so heavily on seeing – not in a sublimated sense, but in the literal one – be anything but an empirical process? This is the gist of the argument by which the empirical view would be defended.

In casting about for a reply, one's first impulse is to take a leaf out of the Divided Line. There Plato says quite distinctly that when mathematicians

use visible figures and make their arguments about them, they are not reasoning about *them*, but about those things which these visible figures resemble . . .; they use these [figures] as images, seeking to see those very things which cannot be seen except by the understanding. (*Rep.* 510d–e)

I do think this would be relevant, since Plato is talking here about the common run of mathematicians, not about those enlightened by his philosophy. And since one of his main objects in this passage is to point up the theoretical crudities of these people, we may be reasonably sure that the quoted passage is not Platonic largesse but a straighforward account of the general attitude toward diagrams among practising mathematicians.[3] And if the same attitude could be imputed to Meno's slave, we could safely exonerate him from the charge of getting the answer to a geometrical problem by looking instead of reasoning. But the 'if' in this sentence marks the weakness of this whole argument for the purpose in hand: our opponent could very well say that the subject of the interrogation is no mathematician, but a household slave; the sophisticated use of diagrams by experts in geometry is no index to its probable use by an ignorant boy.

Let us then try an entirely different tack. Since the empirical interpretation rests wholly on the use of the diagrams in the 'recollecting' process, let us ask whether or not they are really indispensable for this purpose. I wish to argue that they are not. Plato could have exhibited this process just as well by using illustrations in which diagrams would have no place – an arithmetical one, for example: The boy, let us suppose, freshly imported from darkest Thrace, has had to be taught even arithmetic, and from the bottom up. His lessons have just started and have only taught him so far to add two numbers at a time and numbers no greater than 10. Socrates now asks him to add 13 to 7, which goes beyond the boy's lessons, and Meno is invited to watch him 'recollect' the answer:

'You can add 10 to 3, can't you?' – 'Yes, that is 13.'
'So 13 = 10 + 3?' – 'Yes.'
'So instead of asking you how much is 13 + 7, I might as well have asked you how much is 10 + 3 + 7?' – 'But what use would that be? I can only add two numbers at a time.'
'That will be enough. How much is 3 + 7?' – '10, of course.'
'So instead of saying "3 + 7," we can always say "10"?' – 'Certainly.'
'Then instead of asking you how much is 10 + 3 + 7, I might have asked you how much is 10 + 10?' – 'Yes, indeed, and the answer to that I know: 20.'
'And we did say that to ask how much is 13 + 7 is the same as asking how much is 10 + 3 + 7. You haven't forgotten that?' – 'Of course not. And since 20 is the sum of 10 + 3 + 7, it is also the sum of 13 + 7.'

I submit that this dialogue, retouched in Plato's style, but unaltered in logical content, could have replaced the interrogation of the boy in the *Meno* for the purpose of Plato's argument. This can be proved by a scissors-and-paste experiment on Plato's text: cut out the whole interrogation from 82b9 to 85b7, paste in the above dialogue in its place, and consider whether any material change will have to be made in what comes before and after. You will find that none will;[4] that the same Platonic theses would be illustrated,[5] and that they would be substantiated to the same degree, so that the meaning and truth-value of the conclusions

Socrates draws from the dialogue at the end will be unaffected. In this fairly stringent sense my arithmetical dialogue could be said to be equivalent to the geometrical one in the *Meno*; and the appeal to sensible objects has been dropped.

I anticipate the following objection: The slave-boy has been learning arithmetic by counting pebbles, it may be said, and has been convinced that, say, $3 + 7 = 10$, not because he has seen 'that these things are so, but because to the eye they look as if they were'; so the boy, who has not mastered a formal *proof* for the addition of natural integers, must be relying on the evidence of his senses, merely transferring what his senses taught him this morning to the solution of the new question Socrates puts to him in the afternoon. I believe that this objection is wholly misconceived. For even if we were to grant that each of the propositions material to the above result

$$(13 = 10 + 3; 3 + 7 = 10; 10 + 10 = 20)$$

were severally established by the purely empirical method of putting $x$ pebbles together with $y$ pebbles and learning the value of $x + y$ by merely counting out the number of the resulting group, the fact would still remain that the answer to the question, 'What is $13 + 7$?' was not obtained by running back for pebbles to find out by counting. Had the boy done anything of this sort, the objection would have had force. But this is precisely what he has *not* done in my example. What happens there has absolutely nothing to do with looking at pebbles or handling them or hearing them dropped clink-clink on a stone nor, be it noted, with remembering results of previous lookings and handlings, nor imagining the results of imagined lookings and handlings: the boy would need to do none of these things to pass from the three propositions I just enumerated to the new proposition that $13 + 7 = 20$. All he would need to do would be to make inferences from these propositions, using nothing but the rule that equals may be substituted for equals and the associative law for arithmetic.[6]

Should the objector remain unsatisfied, the simplest way to proceed would be to shift to still another illustration, fully equivalent in the sense defined to the one in the *Meno*, but so constructed as to block further back the imputation of even indirect reliance on the senses: Let Socrates recite in suitably metrical Greek the familiar conundrum by which a man replies when asked what is his relation to the subject of a portrait:

Brothers and sisters have I none;
But this man's father is my father's son.

Let the slave-boy fail to hit on the solution, as sometimes happens even among the socially elect, and then 'recollect' it under Socrates' prodding. Since this would be to *solve* the puzzle, all that is needed for the 'recollecting' is what is needed for the solution. This calls for no more than just these operations: Noting that 'my father's son' in the second premise of the cryptic jingle must refer to either the speaker himself or to one of his brothers; eliminating the second alternative by the first premise; hence being left with the statement that 'this man's father' must be the speaker himself. In all this there is no recourse to anything other than the logical relations of the concepts *father*, *brother*, and *son*, and the use of the rules of inference. Here there is no occasion for consulting the evidence of the senses or for recalling previous use of such evidence. Had Plato used an example of this sort in the *Meno* no one would have even dreamed of saying that the 'recollecting' process gets results by relying on the evidence of the senses. Even the much weaker claim made earlier by A. E. Taylor that the 'recollecting' discussed in the *Meno* consists of 'the following up by personal effort of the suggestions of sense-experience'[7], would have been ruled out by this kind of example. There is nothing in the process of discovering the answer to the conundrum which can be called, with any plausibility, 'following up the suggestions of sense-experience'. If one tried seeing or imagining fathers and sons, or pictures of them, to get 'suggestions' for the solution, he would be wasting his time.

This is as far as this line of argument will take us. It proceeds on the premise, which could scarcely be questioned, that the 'recollecting' Plato has in mind is in no way restricted to geometry, least of all the sort of geometry done by a tyro, but could be exemplified as well by other cases where sense-experience would be demonstrably immaterial and irrelevant. From this it concludes that reliance on the evidence of the senses is not a *general* feature of the 'recollecting' envisaged by Plato but is, at most, a special feature of the example of it he happened to use in the *Meno*. I say 'at most' for I am not conceding that the empirical view is true of even the example in the *Meno*. Such a concession would be no small matter. For since we have no other clue to what Plato was thinking of as *bona fide* 'recollection' at this time except what he put into his text, it could be argued that those features of the process which are material to its instantiation in the *Meno* were thought by Plato essential for the process itself, even if in fact they are not. This is a reasonable argument, and must be met on its own ground.

Let us then move directly into the text and pick out for inspection a passage where the empirical view should appear to best advantage:

Now does this line going from corner to corner cut each of these squares in half? (84e–85a)

Since Socrates does not proceed to offer proof for the proposition that the diagonal bisects a square or to give any reason whatever, but expects the boy to 'recollect' the answer upon hearing his words and looking at the diagram, would it not follow that, when the boy assents instantly to the equality of the triangles, he does so not because he sees that they are equal but 'because to the eye they look as if they were'? This does *not* follow. To see that it does not, let us construct a case where it would, and see what that would be like. Let Socrates draw an isosceles right-angle triangle and then, without any description of what he is doing or any other comment, let him draw a similar figure of the same dimensions in some relatively distant part of the drawing area; and let him *then* ask the boy to say whether or not the two figures are equal. Here the boy would *have* to rely on the evidence of his eyesight. What else does he have to go by? His only source of information is the sensible figure, and he can only get it by looking. How vastly different is the task which Socrates sets him: The two triangles have not been presented as two independent and undescribed constructions. They are produced by drawing a diagonal across a figure which is known to be a *square*, and is said to be so. Knowing that squares have equal sides and equal angles,[8] the boy could infer that two sides and the included angle of one triangle equal the corresponding items in the other. So he has plenty of clues to the equality of the two figures other than the fact that they look equal. If he followed out those clues, he would see (e.g., by the rudiments of a congruence proof by superposition) that the triangles have to be equal, even if to the eye they looked unequal, as they easily might if the figure were badly drawn.[9] Yet neither does it follow that the boy would make the judgement by merely drawing inferences in total disregard of what he sees. He might have done the latter, had he been gifted mathematically and given the proper instructions. Alternatively, he might have done the very opposite, had his instructions been to go by the look of the figures to the exclusion of any other consideration. The fact is that neither set of instructions has been given him. But looking over the whole course of the interrogation, we see that while it is never even implied that he should decide anything by merely looking, there are several times when it is definitely implied that he should judge merely by thinking – e.g., when asked arithmetical questions ('And how many feet is twice two? Figure it out and tell me', 82d).[10] That the overall effect of the questioning is to set the boy thinking is clear from the boy's mistakes. His two blunders are *miscalculations*, slips of the mind, not of the eye, faulty inferences, not wrong observations: that the desired square must have double the area *if* it has double the sides; that its side must equal 3 *because* it has to be larger than 2 and smaller than 4.

So the boy is reasoning at least as much as looking. Why not then say that his 'recollecting' is a mixture of both, and leave it at that? Because this compromise formula would evade the vital question of the relative importance of the two factors. We could, of course, agree that observation and inference are both occurring, without haggling over the question whether there is more of the one than of the other, if what specially interested us here were the behaviour of just this boy in just this case. But then the relative incidence of the two factors, revealed by our inquiry, would be of no logical consequence; it would have only informed us of the psychological abilities and habits of this particular subject. What does affect the logic of our problem is the relative *dispensability* of either factor to the 'recollecting process', for only so can we determine which of the two factors is logically intrinsic to it. Once we do put the question in this way the answer is clear: The boy's sensory powers may be cut down drastically without impairing 'recollecting' in the least, provided only we suppose his reasoning ability inversely heightened. If, on the other hand, we endowed him with the best hunter's eye imaginable, but deficient in the perception of logical relationships, he would be totally unfitted for 'recollecting'. For the best he could accomplish by superior sensory acuteness would be to collect data of superior accuracy; but unless he could arrange and re-arrange these data in the required logical patterns, they would be of no use, but a burden, for the purpose of answering Socrates' questions. Conversely, the heightening of his intellectual powers would be of the greatest use to him for this purpose, and could so far compensate for sensory defects that he could go through this whole interrogation and in fewer steps even if, for example, he were blind, but had the mathematical talent of a young Pascal; and to think of him as blind is to think of the factor of sensory observation reduced in these circumstances to *zero*.

But would Plato have been aware of this when he wrote the *Meno*? – I think he would. The evidence is indirect, but strong. At the end of the interrogation, when the boy has found the answer to the problem Socrates had set him, we are told that this is as yet no more than a true belief in his mind;[11] but that if 'one were to ask him many times the very same [sort of] questions in many [different] ways . . . he would end up at last with knowledge of such matters no less exact than that possessed by any other person', 85c10–d1. The subject-matter here is geometry.[12] To reach knowledge of it that would be no worse than that of any other person would be to master this science as the firmly deductive discipline it had already become. In that second stage of his inquiry, then, the one that would take the boy from true belief to knowledge, the evidence of his eyesight would be absolutely excluded as a *reason* for any of his assertions.[13] But there is no suggestion that this would involve the slightest change of *method*. Quite the contrary, it is implied that his method would be the same; for if it were going to be different he would have to be subjected to a different sort of question, while, as we have just seen, he would be asked '*the very same* [sort of] *questions*'. In having Socrates say this Plato makes it clear that he thinks of the method of discovery (that of the first stage) and the method of proof (that of the second) to be in principle the same. And this is confirmed in two further remarks: 'To recover knowledge oneself [from] within oneself', says Socrates shortly after (85d6–7), 'is recollection'.[14] Later on, near the end of the dialogue, in a crucial passage where Socrates says that true beliefs become knowledge only when 'bound fast by the calculation of the reason' (αἰτίας λογισμῷ),[15] he adds at once: 'And this, my dear Meno, is recollection, as we agreed earlier' (98a3–8).[16] In neither of these passages does Socrates say that 'recollection' occurs *only* at the second stage of the inquiry. This would have been quite absurd in view of the fact that the first stage – the one the boy traverses in our text – had been laid on specially so Meno could see the boy recollecting.[17] So Plato's reason for speaking only of the second stage when he comes to explain what 'recollection' is, could only be that he takes it for granted that the essential components of the 'recollection'-process as a method of inquiry would be the same at both stages, though they would be so much clearer in the second that it would be sufficient for his purposes to refer only to that. What then are these components?

The language used in the second citation – the 'binding' of true belief by the αἰτίας λογισμός – gives us a good indication of what he thinks they are. The primary sense of λογισμός is arithmetical reckoning. It is used with this sense in the interrogation,[18] as we saw a moment ago. Elsewhere in his works Plato uses it for rational arithmetic, i.e. for number theory, and, still more broadly, for rational thought in contrast to sense-perception and for knowledge reached and justified by formal inference and analysis in emphatic contrast to sensory cognition.[19] The other part of his expression, 'bound fast', would tell the same tale to anyone familiar with the philosophical literature. In Parmenides the 'bonds' and 'fetters' which 'powerful *Ananke*' imposes on Being are the constraints of logical necessity.[20] In Zeno[21] and Melissus[22] *ananke* is the signature of a deductive inference and it is used quasi-adverbially in lieu of 'it follows necessarily that . . .' In the Socratic dialogues too *ananke* occurs with the same force,[23] and the 'binding fast' metaphor caps the long demonstration in the *Gorgias* when Callicles is told that the conclusion that defeats him is 'held fast and bound by arguments of iron and adamant', 508e. Thus to say that knowledge is true belief 'bound' by the αἰτίας λογισμός is to imply that a statement becomes known when it is seen to follow logically from premises sufficient for this purpose: to 'recollect' it, then, would be to see that these premises entail it. But what of the premises? They too could be 'recollected' in the same manner. But how long could this go on? The geometrical model[24] would suggest to Plato, as it did to Aristotle after him, that there must be logically primitive propositions, whose 'binding' could no longer be derived by entailment from yet others, but must lie wholly within themselves. Thus there would be no question of trying to prove that things equal to the same thing are equal to one another. The mathematician's way with this type of proposition would be to list it as a logical primitive in his axiom-set and leave it at that. Plato presumably would go a step further, but only by showing how this and other 'Common Notions' are presupposed in our 'knowledge of Equality', i.e. in our having, using and understanding the concept of equality.[25] Nor would there be any question of proving the *definitions*[26] of this, or any other, concept. We know how prominently these figure among the objects of Socratic search. But though Plato has said so far all too little of the methodology of the 'What is X?' question, it is clear from what he says in the *Meno* itself, that he does not think that the true answer, when found, could be proved by deduction from other premises,[27] or that it needs such proof. Thus if the boy understood what is meant by *square* and also understood what is meant by *equilateral, right-angled,* and *quadrilateral,* he would *see* that the conjunction of the last three concepts is logically equivalent to the first. If he did not, he would be revealing that he had not understood the meaning of one or more of the concepts mentioned in the formula; what would be needed then would be to elicit this understanding in his mind.

Reduced to its simplest terms, then, what Plato means by 'recollection' in the *Meno* is *any advance in understanding which results from the perception of logical relationships.* When these are inter-propositional to 'recollect' a previously unknown proposition is to come to know it by seeing that it is entailed by others already known. Or if the relations are intra-propositional, as in the case of the true answer to the 'What is X', question, then to 'recollect' is to gain insight into the logical structure of a concept so that when faced with its correct definition one will see that each of the concepts mentioned in the *definiens* is analytically connected with the *definiendum.* In either case, we are as far from the empirical discovery and certification of knowledge as we could possibly be. Sensory observation is not excluded in the first stage of incomplete 'recollection' which discovers the looked-for truth, but does not yet know that (or why) it is the truth. But even at that stage the use of the senses is only a contingent factor, wholly unusable in some cases of *bona fide* 'recollection' and in others used only as a crutch to the imagination which must be dropped at the next stage of inquiry in which 'recollection' is brought to full completion.[28]

## PART TWO: THE THEORY

The nearest Plato comes to telling us why the process we have been describing *is* recollection (without quotation marks) is in the two statements that

(a) had the boy continued the 'recollecting' process to the finish he would have 'himself recovered knowledge [from] within himself', 85d4, and

(b) 'recovering by oneself knowledge that is within oneself is recollection', 85d6–7.

These two statements make clear the middle term Plato is offering us between the data and the theory: given, on one hand, the indisputable fact that we do acquire knowledge and, on the other hand, the proposed theory that this takes place *because* the truths we come to know are recollected, the whole burden of convincing us of this 'because' falls on the contention that these truths come from 'within' us. What can be meant by this contention?

Plato talks as though its meaning and truth will be obvious once it is seen that the truths learned by the boy have not been taught him by Socrates or by anyone else. Here 'teaching' is being used, with typical Socratic effrontery, in a wholly untypical way.[29] How very special is this sense becomes clear when we notice that even *telling* the boy the true answer is not allowed to count as teaching it to him! To put a question to someone who has never heard the right answer, and then, noting that he has no inkling of it, to proceed and lay it out before him, saying, 'this *is* the right answer, isn't it?,' is not supposed to be 'teaching'. Why not? – because if Socrates, having said, '*p* is true, isn't it?,' says no more, the judgement that *p is* true must be made on the boy's own responsibility. He cannot shift the responsibility on Socrates *because he cannot cite Socrates' attitude toward p as evidence for its truth.* Socrates makes sure of this both by instructing him, 'Answer just what you think,' 83d2, and also by the more painful method of laying booby-traps for him along the way which teach him that he cannot rely on Socrates to make the right suggestions to him: he cannot adopt toward Socrates the attitude an inexperienced mountain-climber can and does adopt toward an experienced guide. If the climber sees or guesses that his guide wants him to take a certain path, he is entitled to use this as good evidence of its being the right path. By misleading him badly a couple of times, Socrates makes the boy realize that he is not entitled to the same assumption. Thus one avenue along which he might have looked for evidence – that open to the pupil who is only told truths by his teacher and is therefore always in a position to say on empirical grounds, 'this is likely to be true because teacher said so' – is decisively blocked by Socrates' tactics. The reason for any of the propositions cannot, therefore, be sought in the teacher.

Where then is it to be sought? – 'Within oneself,' says Plato. Why so? – Because 'in' one are the already known propositions from which one can derive knowledge of others, hitherto unknown, merely by seeing that they are entailed; and 'in' one are the

familiar concepts whose logical structure one need only understand more clearly in order to come to know axiomatic truths
and correct definitions. This not only brings full lucidity to the
mock-darkness of the claim that Socrates is not 'teaching' but
also lets in some light to the real darkness of the saying that
what the boy is learning 'he himself recovers from within himself'. For 'learning' here is not just a matter of increasing his
stock of true beliefs, but of acquiring *knowledge*, that is to say,
true beliefs logically bound to the reasons for their truth.[30]
Hence the dark saying has *at least* the following sense: new beliefs become knowledge for him when *he* comes to see what is
implied by propositions and concepts which were already in *his*
mind.[31] I say, 'at least' this sense, for to suggest that Plato means
no more than this would be a travesty of his text. But this more
can wait a moment longer while we explore more fully the mini-
mum sense now before us.

The expression 'within oneself', i.e. in one's mind, is significant in
this context only because of the implied contrast with what is *outside*
one's mind. Well, what is 'outside' the boy's mind? Socrates, for one
thing: if he got knowledge from Socrates, this would refute the claim
that he recovered knowledge from 'within' himself. But Socrates is a
small, if energetic, part of this 'outside,' and learning from Socrates
only a local and ephemeral instance of getting knowledge from
'external' sources, if such there were. For the vast majority of men
who have never even heard of Socrates and for the boy himself
through most of his life the only thing seriously worth discussing as
a likely source of knowledge 'outside' the mind would be the whole
of the physical universe as apprehended by the senses. Though the
expression, 'the external world,' had not yet been invented, philosophers had talked and thought in similar terms. Thus Empedocles,
when he spoke of sight, hearing, and taste as 'duct(s) for understanding' (πόρος . . . νοῆσαι, B3, 12), was evidently thinking of the sensible
world as a reservoir of information outside us, whence knowledge
might flow into us through the senses. With this we may compare
the saying of Democritus that 'for all of us belief is inflowing',
(ἐπιρυσμίη ἑκάστοισιν ἡ δόξις B7) and his talk of sensory stimuli as
'coming upon us' (ἐπεισιόντων, B9) and Plato's talk of sensory
impulses 'borne from the outside and falling upon' the soul (ἔξωθεν
αἰσθήσεις φερόμεναι . . . προσπεσοῦσαι, *Timaeus* 44a). With this
conception of sense-experience as a one-way traffic from the world
into the soul familiar to Plato[32] and incorporated, through the

assimilation of its metaphors, into his own thought and speech, his assertion that to acquire knowledge is only to recover what is already 'in' us could not but have the force of an implicit denial that *knowledge can be acquired by sense-experience*.[33] And so far as the acquisition of knowledge here is the securing of evidence for propositions, the implicit part of the minimal sense of Plato's formula is equivalent to the denial that sense-experience can, or need, provide the slightest evidence for propositions known in the special way in which knowledge is here construed: demonstrative knowledge. Thus in this very dialogue and, so far as we can tell from our sources, for the first time in Western thought, deductive knowledge, broadly conceived so as to include all of mathematics and much more besides, is freed completely from evidential dependence on sense-experience.

In saying that this happens for the first time we need not be unmindful of its antecedents nor belittle the achievements of Plato's predecessors in order to exalt his. We need only point out that, while others had prepared the way for Plato's discovery, no one had fully anticipated it. The Greek mathematicians had learned how to construct deductive proofs by the fifth century at the latest, and Plato himself gives them credit, as we saw above, for not counting the sensible properties of their figures evidence for their theorems. But it is one thing to achieve such a working method, quite another to reflect upon it so as to state its rationale and show what this has in common with formal inferences whose subject matter is as different as are the concepts of father and son, justice and virtue, from lines and numbers. A philosophical declaration of independence of rational thought from sense-experience had been made, and in the strongest terms, a hundred years before Plato by Parmenides. But he and his disciples paid a fantastic price for this emancipation. They won it by consigning to illusion not only the whole of the physical universe, but also the whole domain of mathematics[34] – a consequence seldom realized by historians of philosophy who, with unwitting irony, have often cast Zeno in the role of the purifier or even saviour of Greek mathematics.[35] There still remain the Pythagoreans. But before we can say that they anticipated Plato in this doctrine we must have evidence that, at the very least, they held it themselves. And there is no such evidence. Moreover if they had really made such an important discovery it could not have remained unknown to Aristotle who, given his penchant for making historical linkages and comparisons, would have left us some indication, however slight, that Plato borrowed from them the doctrine that learning is recollection. But though he is well acquainted with this doctrine, and turns aside to refute it, he ascribes it to no one but to Plato, and to him directly, referring by title to the *Meno*.[36] So those historians[37] who tell us that Plato derived this doctrine from the Pythagoreans are making excursions into historical romance.

What the Pythagoreans did hold, and not only they but Pythagoras, is the doctrine of transmigration. But the connection of this with Plato's doctrine of recollection is so loose that one can believe in transmigration without believing in anything which includes that minimal sense of recollection I have just been discussing, indeed without having the slightest inkling of it. A doctrine of recollection was a prominent feature of the Pythagorean belief in transmigration, at least to the extent of crediting Pythagoras himself with the power to recover knowledge acquired in previous incarnations. (See Xenophanes B7; Empedocles B129). And if claimed for Pythagoras it might well have also been claimed for other charismatic figures. It is reasonable to assume that Plato knew all this and hence to say that he borrowed *a* doctrine of recollection. But what would this borrowing come to? That some great souls had the marvellous power to recollect what they had learned in former incarnations. Let us magnify this borrowing beyond anything warranted by the evidence and all it still would come to would be this: that every soul had such powers. And this would not even approach Plato's doctrine, unless we were to add that these powers were connected with *learning* in the here and now, and so connected that the acquisition of all new knowledge is recollecting. This doctrine, the only one that would deserve mention in a history of the theory of knowledge, let alone mention as a milestone in this theory, is the product of Plato's genius and of his alone.[38]

In this encounter with Pythagoreanism I have already gone beyond what I have been calling the 'minimal sense' of the Platonic doctrine. To reckon with this doctrine as a whole let me simply itemize the main essential points:

(1)   The full-strength doctrine carries not only the implication that non-empirical knowledge can exist but also, unfortunately, that empirical knowledge cannot exist. This latter thesis could be sugar-coated with the plea that since Plato is willing to admit what we call 'empirical knowledge' under the name of 'true belief',

nothing is changed except the name. But we should give Plato credit for engaging in more serious business than the reallocation of verbal labels. In refusing the term 'knowledge' to propositions of ordinary experience and of the observational sciences Plato is downgrading quite deliberately those truth-seeking and truth-grounding procedures which cannot be assimilated to deductive reasoning and cannot yield formal certainty; and this has enormous implications, theoretical, and also practical ones, as can be seen in the exclusion of disciplines like medicine, biology, and history from the curriculum of higher learning in the *Republic*.

(2) Where $p$, hitherto not known, becomes known through the perception of its entailment by $q$, the full-strength doctrine of recollection holds not only that $q$ is known (*ex hypothesi*), but also that $p$ is similarly 'recovered from within' the soul. This is indeed the whole point of saying that $p$ is recollected (without quotation-marks). And having said this, Plato does not cast about for some way of unsaying it. He does not qualify his claim, as would Leibniz, by making $p$ only *virtually* known at this earlier time. Nor does he try to pass it off by saying, as a modern analytical philosopher might in such a fix, that all he is pleading for is an *extension* to more complex and involved entailments of the admission, common enough for simple and direct entailments from $q$ to $p$, that he who knows $q$ can also be said after a fashion to also know $p$ (as, e.g., if I admit that I know that Lucy is Mary's mother, I would have a hard time convincing a jury I did not know that Lucy is older than Mary). Plato gives no sign of such backing-away tactics. He is excited, not frightened, by the strange landscape to which his imagination has transported him and is more anxious to explore it further than to keep close to escape-routes back to the safety of the old world.

(3) The exploration of the consequences of the full-strength theory of recollection is so closely related to the creation of the Theory of Ideas that it can even be said to determine the main features of this theory. The first question Plato would have to put to himself when he finished writing the *Meno* is the very one raised by Leibniz:[39] to say that we acquire knowledge by recovering knowledge we acquired at some earlier period or periods, no matter how remote, is simply to raise all over again the problem how this earlier knowledge itself was gained. That Plato thinks of

the Theory of Ideas as the answer to this question we know from later dialogues, e.g. the *Phaedrus* (247c–e; 249b–c). And we know of no other answer that occurred to him, or that would have been likely to occur to him at this historical stage of philosophical reflection. Had he emancipated himself completely from the tendency to assimilate understanding to the pattern fixed by the model of sense-perception, and to think of general truths reaching the mind by *vision* (though purely intellectual and intuitive) *of objects* (though purely incorporeal, beyond time and space), he would have assayed other alternatives. But that emancipation was not won even by Aristotle after him, or even by Epicurus. Without it, it seemed a reasonable solution to the problem of the primordial education of the soul to construct suitable objects for the inspection of a discarnate mind. The Platonic Form is built to the specifications of this project. Then, faced with the fact that knowledge thus gained beyond the Cave is so useful when recollected within it that one who has recovered it will be able to 'see a thousand times better' (*Rep.* 520c) in the Cave, once he has got used to its darkness, than those who never left it, Plato solves this problem by postulating, so very reasonably it would seem, that the world seen by the eye is an 'image' of the world seen by the mind, inexact to a degree, but faithful enough to yield physical applications of ideal truths. Thus the requirements of the doctrine of recollection, once satisfied in the Theory of Forms, suggest the broad design of the Platonic cosmology; they do the same for Plato's moral theory and for his interpretation of the experience of love and of the sense of beauty in ways which will suggest themselves to those familiar with the *Republic*, the *Symposium*, and the *Phaedrus*.

(4)  What made this whole doctrine possible for Plato is obviously the belief in reincarnation. Plato marks this as a religious faith on first announcing it in the *Meno* by saying he heard it from 'priests and priestesses who make it their business to be able to give reason for the rites they perform' (81a). Though this does not preclude his having heard it also from Pythagorean philosophers, it makes clear that reincarnation is not for Plato a mere theoretical speculation. He chooses to relate it to rites of worship and invests it with that intense religious feeling that is to pulse through the myth of the *Phaedrus*. Of this faith, just three things:

(a)  It is faith, not dogma, using myth as its favourite vehicle, and feeling free to create and re-create its own myth.

(b) It is a personal faith, maintained in all probability without affiliation with any organized cult, at any rate in Athens.

(c) While derivative at the core it is in important ways a *new* faith, differing from surviving samples of its source in ways which would affect profoundly the substance of its piety. It is wholly free, for instance, of the sensationalism and magic of popular Orphic practices which are denounced in the *Republic* (364b). It appears to good advantage even when compared with the most exalted surviving transcript of the faith in reincarnation, the *Purifications* of Empedocles. The commission of a horrible crime by a god-like soul to start off the cycle of rebirth, hence the conception of human existence as expiation for the delinquency of a prehuman being and the recovery of its supernatural powers – all this is lacking in Plato. Man is created man in the beginning, and is akin to god not in magical power but in his specifically human attributes, his knowledge, his moral sense, his love of beauty.

The theory of recollection in the *Meno* is the work of a profoundly religious spirit united with a powerful philosophical mind. Those who come to our text without sympathy for its religious inspiration are apt to look at this union with annoyance and to think that Plato might have been a great philosopher or, at any rate, a good one, had it not been for his religion. The results of this paper, they may then think, fully confirm this feeling. For do they not come to this: that when the data of the theory are analyzed as they have been here, they exhibit a process of inference and insight which can be described very well by Plato's theory, provided only it be stripped of just those features of it which are directly assignable to its religious provenance? But before we settle on this conclusion, might we not ask ourselves this question: Is there any good reason to think that, without the special perspective of the belief in transmigration, Plato would ever have looked at those data in the particular way which issued in his epochal discovery: that of knowledge which needs no confirmation from sense-experience and admits of no refutation from it? The point is not so much that others, fully familiar with such data, had failed to make this discovery, but that Plato himself had not come within sight of it, though he had been thinking philosophy and writing it for a decade or more by this time according to the received chronology. The faith in reincarnation is not mentioned, or even alluded to, in any dialogue before the *Meno*. If, as seems likely, it is at or near this time that Plato came by this faith, can we reckon it a pure coincidence that the philosophical discovery is presented in the same dialogue and that the form in which it is cast is the doctrine of recollection – the full-strength doctrine of the *Meno*?[40]

## NOTES

1 μανθάνειν, which is being used in this context in the restricted sense of learning which can be articulated in propositional form. The acquisition of inarticulate skills, though well within the scope of the word in ordinary usage, is tacitly excluded.

2 My interpretation has much in common with those offered by the following:

  F. M. Cornford, *Principium Sapientiae* (Cambridge, 1952), Ch. IV, 'Anamnesis.', W. K. C. Guthrie, *Plato: Protagoras and Meno* (London, 1956), pp. 107–14, R. S. Bluck, *Plato's Meno* (Cambridge, 1961), pp. 8–17, N. Gulley, *Plato's Theory of Knowledge* (London, 1962), Ch. I, 'The Theory of Recollection.', I. M. Crombie, *An Examination of Plato's Doctrines*, Vol. II (London, 1963), pp. 50–2, 136–41.

  To each of these works I shall refer hereafter merely by the author's name.

3 Though Greek mathematicians were occasionally misled by their diagrams to assume some proposition not listed in their axiom-set (e.g. a continuity postulate, needed for the proof of I, i, etc. in Euclid: cf. T. L. Heath, *The Thirteen Books of Euclid's Elements*, I, 2nd edn (Oxford, 1925), pp. 235 and 243), they would not dream of citing the sensible properties of a diagram *as a reason* in a proof. One cannot imagine a sentence like, 'This must be true because that is the way it looks (or, measures) in the diagram' in a Greek mathematical text.

4 The *only* required changes would be the substitution of 'figuring' and 'arithmetic' for 'doing geometry' and 'geometry' at 85e.

5 Apart from being so much drier than Plato's example, the main loss resulting from the substitution would be the boy's mistakes; but we could easily make room for these, e.g., by having him make a wrong guess to begin with and then find out by the same method that (and why) his guess was wrong. A graver defect in my example is that it would not show nearly as well as Plato's the gap that may exist between discovery and proof; finding out that $13 + 7 = 20$ by the above method would bring one much closer to seeing *why* this must be so than the slave could have come to seeing the why of the theorem at the end of the interrogation.

6 That $a + (b + c) = (a + b) + c$ was used, without being mentioned, in the example.

7 A. E. Taylor, *Plato, the Man and his Work*, 4th edn (London, 1937)

[hereafter 'Taylor'], p. 137. Taylor then refers to 'the suggestions provided by Socrates' diagrams and *questions*' (my italics), apparently failing to realize that the logical status of suggestions provided by questions is entirely different from that provided by sense-experience. In the *Meno* Plato speaks of recollected opinions as suggested ('awakened') by questions (86a6; cf. *Phaedo* 73a7), not by sense-experience; the latter point is first made in the *Phaedo* (73c6 ff).

8 The equality of the sides was mentioned at the start (82c), that of the angles was not, but would have been admitted right off by the boy: the concept, *equality of angle*, would have been familiar, and Socrates would have had no difficulty in getting the boy to say that all four angles of a square must be equal.

9 It is not unreasonable to assume with Guthrie (p. 110) that the figure would be only 'roughly' drawn, so that the two triangles would be visibly unequal. But nothing is made of this in the interrogation. Socrates has other ways of getting across the idea that the properties of the squares, triangles, etc., he is talking about are those that a figure *would* have *if* it instantiated the concept, *square*. See next note.

10 Subtler suggestions to the same effect are conveyed by the form in which the questions are put almost from the very start: 'Now could not such a figure be either larger or smaller?' (82c3–4) puts the inquiry in the domain of possibility, where it is kept by the next question, 'Now if this side were 2 ft. long and that [side] the same, how many feet would the whole be?', which puts the specification of size in the hypothetical mode and asks what would happen *if* this were the case. The same modalities are signalled by the syntactical form of the sequel: optative with ἄν ('indefinite supposition') in the apodosis at 82c5–6, and imperfect indicative with ἄν (*suppositio irrealis*) at c8 (Cf. E. S. Thompson, *The Meno of Plato* [London, 1901], ad loc.). In the next question (d1–2) the γίγνεται expresses a logical consequence (this is what would result [on the hypothesis] it is 2 ft. long that way too'). The interrogation continues on the hypothetical plane until the second break at 84d: the question remains *what would have to be* the case to satisfy the conditions laid down at 82c5–6 and what would follow *if* we were to suppose with the slave that the required line is 3 or 4 feet long. After the break the syntax is again well stocked with optatives with ἄν to re-establish a framework of inference (exploration of logical consequences) rather than factual observation. The English reader should remember that the modalities and logical connectives do not always come through even in excellent translations. Thus 82b10–c3 becomes in Guthrie, 'It has all these 4 sides equal? . . . And these lines which go through the middle of it are also equal?' Here the οὖν ('in inferences, *then, therefore*', Liddell and Scott, *Lexicon, s. v.* III) has dropped out in the first question; in the second one would miss the fact that a participial form (ἔχον) so links it with the preceding question as to keep it within the field of force of the οὖν. A more literal translation would be: 'Is not a square, then, a figure having all these four sides equal? . . . And having these lines that go through the middle equal also?'

106

11 So it would be obviously wrong to say that the lad 'began by not knowing something and *ended by knowing it*' (Taylor, p. 138, my italics), rather than that he *would have ended* by knowing it.

12 And cf. 85e1–2: the slave-boy 'will do the same thing [as he has done in the preceding interrogation] in the case of the whole of geometry and of all other sciences' ('the same thing', ταὐτὰ ταῦτα, here has the same reference as the same expression at c10–11, where the reference is clearly to his performance in answering Socrates' questions).

13 Cf. n. 3 above.

14 The received translations, down to Guthrie's ('And the spontaneous recovery of *knowledge that is in him* is recollection, isn't it?'), put Plato in the position of saying that the subject already *has* the knowledge he recollects, thus flatly contradicting his earlier assurances that the boy did *not know*, and still does not know, the theorem he has discovered, but has only a true belief of it (85c2–10). Surely all we can get from the wording in 85d6 is that the 'recollected' knowledge is being 'recovered' from inside a person's own mind – not that it is already there *as knowledge*. The commentators frequently represent Plato as holding that what we come to know by 'recollecting' is already present in us in the form of *latent* knowledge. But Plato never uses this expression (or variants of it, like 'potential') in the context of the theory of recollection. He does not picture our souls as being always in a state of 'virtual' omniscience, but as having once 'learned' everything (86a8, where τὸν ἀεὶ χρόνον μεμαθηκυῖα ἔσται ἡ ψυχὴ αὐτοῦ does not mean 'has been for ever in a state of knowledge' [Guthrie], but 'has been for ever in the condition of *having* [once] *acquired* knowledge': cf. μεμαθυκυίας τῆς ψυχῆς, 81d1), and then lost this knowledge (85c6–7; 86b2–3; and cf. especially *Phdo* 75e2, 76b5–c3) while retaining the ability to recover it. By 'the truth of things being always in the soul' (*Meno* 86b1–2) and 'knowledge and right reason being in' us (*Phdo* 73a9–10, αὐτοῖς ἐπιστήμη ἐνοῦσα καὶ ὀρθὸς λόγος) Plato can only mean that all men have (i) some (not, all) knowledge, (ii) the ability to perceive logical relations and, therefore, (iii) the ability to extend their knowledge (by persevering in inquiry) without any preassigned limit (81d2–4).

15 ἕως ἄν τις αὐτὰς δήσῃ αἰτίας λογισμῷ: 'until you tether them by working out the reason' (Guthrie). 'Cause' for *aitia* here (Jowett, Meridier, Bluck) is misleading, since modern philosophical usage reserves the term for relations which instantiate laws of nature, never for purely logical conditions. Thus to speak of the premises of a syllogism as the αἰτία of the conclusion (Aristotle, *Post. An.* 71b22) would be the crudest sort of category-mistake if Aristotle's term did mean what we understand by 'cause'. In some contexts, as in Aristotle's 'four causes', the canonical mistranslation will no doubt have to be perpetuated. But readers of Plato, at least, can be spared some confusion if the mistranslation is avoided when avoidable, as it is certainly in the *Meno*. To tolerate 'chain of causal reasoning' for αἰτίας λογισμός, and illustrate by a mathematical *diorismos* (Gulley, pp. 14–15) which involves no causal reasoning whatever, is disconcerting.

16 Cf. Bluck *ad loc.*: 'No mention has been made earlier, at least in so many words, of an αἰτίας λογισμός, but this reference is clearly to 85c9–d1.'

17 And cf. 82e12–13.

18 In the reference to λογισάμενος εἰπέ, 82d4.

19 Examples in F. Ast, *Lexicon Platonicum, s. v.* λογίζομαι, λογισμός, λογιστικός. When the Theory of Ideas is introduced λογίζομαι, λογισμός, (along with διανοοῦμαι, διάνοια) stand for the mode of their apprehension in sharp opposition to sense-perception: *Phdo* 65c2–3, 79a3, *Phdr.* 249b, *Parm.* 130a, *Soph.* 248a11.

20 H. Diels and W. Kranz, *Die Fragmente der Vorsokratiker*, 5th edn (Berlin, 1934–7), frag. B8, 30–1. (All subsequent references to Presocratic fragments will be to this work.) The same metaphor in lines 14 and 37 of the fragment, with *Dike and Moira* taking the place of *Ananke*, symbolizing the rational appropriateness of the bond, while *Ananke* stands for its inexorable necessity.

21 Frag. B1 (twice), B3.

22 Frag. B7 (twice).

23 Examples in Ast, op. cit.

24 I.e. of an axiomatized science. Though great progress in axiomatization was made in Plato's own life-time, (cf. the references to Leo and Theudius in Proclus, *Comment. in Eucl.* [G. Friedlein (Leipzig, 1873)], p. 66, 19–22 and p. 67, 12–16), there is no reason to think there had been no earlier work along the same lines. The distinction between primitive and derivative propositions in geometry would certainly have been well established by the end of the fifth century.

25 I am extrapolating from the line of argument followed by Socrates in the *Phaedo* (74b4 ff: from certain judgements we have been making since our childhood it is inferred that ἀναγκαῖον . . . ἡμᾶς προειδέναι τὸ ἴσον, 74e9).

26 'Real', not 'nominal', definitions, which are the prime object of Socratic inquiry in many dialogues, including the *Meno*, where Socrates starts by diverting Meno from 'Is virtue teachable?', to 'What is virtue?', as the logically prior one and insists repeatedly that we cannot know any of virtue's properties (ὁποῖον ἔστι or ποῖον ἔστι) until we have come to know its essence (τί ἔστιν): 71b3–8; 86d2–e1; 100b4–6. Cf. R. Robinson, *Plato's Earlier Dialectic*, 2nd edn (Oxford, 1953), pp. 50–1. (For subsequent thoughts on this topic see now my remarks on the 'Socratic Fallacy' in 'Socrates' disavowal of knowledge', *Philosophical Quarterly* 1985, 1 ff, at pp. 23–6.)

27 When someone proposes a false definition there are two ways of disproving it in the Socratic dialogues:
   (1) Find cases which, as he admits, instantiate the *definiens*, but not the *definiendum*, or the latter, but not the former.
   (2) Find propositions known to him which contradict the definition.
   Socrates could not hope to demonstrate the true definition by the same, or analogous, methods:
   (1) He could not go through all the cases of the *definiens* to show they all exemplify the *definiendum*.

(2) A statement of what $X$ is could not be proved by entailment from other statements about $X$ which are known to be true, since in the *Meno* Socrates holds (cf. the preceding note) that if the essence of $X$ is not known nothing else can be known about $X$ (though, of course, there could be many true beliefs about it). Hence, though Plato does not say so, it would follow that, while argument can disprove incorrect answers to the 'What is $X$?' question, it cannot prove the correct one.

28 If one rereads the interrogation in our text in the light of these two paragraphs, one will see how deductive inference and logical insight into concepts are called into play just as far as they can be within the practical limitations of the occasion (dealing with a boy utterly ignorant of the vocabulary and method of geometry, and getting results with a speed consistent with the dramatic tempo of the dialogue). Thus the correction of the two mistakes 83a–e is for all practical purposes a *proof* that the two erroneous propositions (that the side is 4 feet or that it is 3 feet) are inconsistent with the theorem that the area of a square with side $x$ feet long must be $x^2$ square feet. Given more time Socrates could surely have got the boy to grasp a formal proof of this theorem of a sufficiently rigorous sort to pass contemporary mathematical standards. So far from giving this proof, Socrates does not even give a general *statement* of the theorem, and for the simple reason that even to get the boy to *understand* such a statement would take longer than the dramatic time-budget allows. For the same reason he does not take time to dot the $i$'s and cross the $t$'s of items which are matters of conceptual insight. Thus the only feature of a square mentioned at the start is the equality of its sides, this being enough to get the boy's mind moving in the right direction toward the major objective, i.e. to come in view of the concept of superficial (in contradistinction to linear) magnitude, since everything in the sequel will depend on the boy's ability to see the difference between the size of an area, with its two parameters of length and breadth, and that of one-dimensional magnitudes. The boy cannot even *understand* Socrates' question, let alone get into position to attempt its solution, until he gets some inkling of this difference. When the question is first put to him at 82c5–6, 'Now look at it this way: If this line were 2 feet long and that line also 2 feet, how big would be the whole [square, i.e. its area]?,' he is stumped.

29 Untypical not only for common usage (as is obvious), but also for Plato's own: so far from thinking 'teaching' (rightly understood, as dialectic) incompatible with 'learning,' he distinguishes (*Gorg.* 454e) rhetoric from 'teaching' (διδασκαλικῆς, 455a1) as producing respectively 'belief' (πίστις) and 'knowledge' (ἐπιστήμη) and, conversely (*Tm* 51e) *nous* from true belief as produced respectively by 'teaching' (διδαχῆς) and 'persuasion'.

30 Cf. A. E. Taylor's comment on *Tm* 51d3 in *Commentary to Plato's Timaeus* (Oxford, 1928), pp. 338–9.

31 Cf. Leibniz's use of expressions like '*prendre de chez soi*' '*tirer de son propre fonds,*' for our coming to know necessary truths, and of the mind

(or the understanding) as the 'source' of these truths: *Nouveaux essais sur l'entendement humain*, Book I, Ch. I, Sec. 5.

32 Cf. the empiricist theory of the origin of knowledge which is mentioned as a part of the teaching of the natural philosophers in the *Phaedo* (96b).

33 This is precisely what Leibniz takes to be the point of the expressions in n. 31 above, alluding specifically to Platonic *anamnesis*: 'on doit dire que toute l'arithmétique et toute la géométrie sont innées et sont en nous d'une manière virtuelle, en sorte qu'on les y peut trouver en considérant attentivement et rangeant *ce qu'on a déjà dans l'esprit, sans se servir d'aucune vérité apprise par l'expérience ou par la tradition d'autrui*, comme Platon l'a montré [in the interrogation of the slave-boy in the *Meno*],' op. cit., Book I, Ch. I, Sec. 5, my italics.

34 This would follow, regardless of their other doctrines, from their denial of plurality.

35 E.g., Paul Tannery, *Pour l'histoire de la science grecque* (Paris, 1877), p. 254; *La Géométrie grecque* (Paris, 1877), p. 124; H. -G. Zeuthen, 'Sur les livres arithmétiques des Éléments d'Euclide,', *Oversigt det Kongelike Danske Videnskabernes Selskabs*, Forhandlinger, 1910, pp. 395 ff at pp. 432–4; F. M. Cornford, *Plato and Parmenides* (London, 1939), pp. 58–61; H. Hasse and H. Scholz, 'Die Grundlagenkrisis der griechischen Mathematik', *Quellenhandbücher der Philosophie* (Berlin, 1928). Contra: B. L. van der Waerden, 'Zenon und die Grundlagenkrisis der griechischen Mathematik', *Math. Annallen* 117 (1940–1), pp. 141 ff; G. E. L. Owen, 'Zeno and the Mathematicians', *Proc. Arist. Soc.,* 1958, pp. 199 ff. For further references see now my article on Zeno of Elea in *Encyclopedia of Philosophy*, Paul Edwards (ed.) (New York, 1967).

36 *Pr. Anal.* 67a21–2; cf. also *Post. Anal.* 71a1–b8: 99b25–34. Cf. H. Cherniss, *Aristotle's Criticism of Plato and the Academy* (Baltimore, 1944), pp. 69 ff and notes.

37 According to A. E. Taylor it had been 'the mathematician-saint Pythagoras' himself who had converted the theological doctrine of the transmigration of the soul 'into a theory of the *a priori* character of mathematics', *Plato*, 186, n. 2. For a sane discussion of the historical question see L. Robin, 'Sur la doctrine de la reminiscence,' *Rev. des Etudes Grecques* 32 (1919), pp. 451–61; but Robin is confused on the point to which I called attention in n. 11 above: he says that Plato 'suppose que nous naissons avec des connaissances toutes faites . . . les seules qui soient dignes de ce nom.', p. 460.

38 Cf. Gulley, p. 18.

39 *Nouveaux essais sur l'entendement humain*, Book I, Ch. I, para. 5.

40 This essay is in substance one of the John Locke Lectures on 'Mysticism and logic in Greek philosophy' which I delivered in Oxford in 1960. I wish to thank those who have criticized the present version of it, most particularly Yukio Kachi, then a graduate student at Princeton, now Professor of Philosophy at the University of Utah. I have made a few minor corrections, but have made no attempt to incorporate the larger understanding of the topic I achieved some twenty years later when I came to realize how 'recollection' in the *Meno* connects with

the euthanasia of the Socratic elenchus in Plato: see 'The Socratic elenchus' in Julia Annas (ed.), *Oxford Studies in Ancient Philosophy* (1983), pp. 29–58, and 'Afterthoughts on the Socratic elenchus', ibid., pp. 71–4; also Donald Davidson, 'Plato's philosopher', *London Review of Books*, 1 August 1985, pp. 15–16.

# LEARNING AS RECOLLECTION

*Julius Moravcsik*

Important philosophic theses often have the disturbing character of falling somewhere between the areas of *a priori* propositions, empirical theories, and mere metaphors. One such thesis is Plato's proposal, expounded most fully in *Meno* 80d–86c, that learning of a certain kind is recollection. The aim of this paper is to explore both the nature of the problem which this proposal was designed to solve, and the explanatory power of the alleged solution. In what follows no attempt will be made to give a comprehensive interpretation of the passage referred to above; in particular, nothing is said about the relation of this proposal to the Theory of Forms, and about whether the slave-boy has knowledge or mere belief at the end of the demonstration of his learning geometry. Attention is given, however, not only to what Plato actually said, but also to what his statements entail. Thus, for example, part of this investigation explores the type of learning model Plato commits himself to, even though no full account of any model is given in the text.

A few preliminary remarks about the concept of learning should help to clarify Plato's problem. Underlying the puzzles discussed below is the assumption that learning can be distinguished from the more generic concept of acquiring intellectual skills. That is to say, learning something is one, but not the only one, possible mode of acquiring it. Not every way of acquiring a skill will count as a way of learning. It is logically possible that the skill of performing simple arithmetical operations could be acquired by submitting to a certain kind of surgery. Even if this were the case, we would not count it as a case of learning. In order to ascribe to someone the acquisition of a skill, it is sufficient to establish that at some time $t'$ he did not possess that skill, and that at a later time $t''$ he did possess it. In order to ascribe learning to this person, further assumptions

112

have to be made. The defining conditions for what constitutes learning will differ depending on the nature of the subject to be learned. It is not clear that there are any general conditions other than the condition of acquisition that all kinds of learning must meet. In any case, for the purposes of this paper it is sufficient to assume that such conditions can be spelled out with respect to the learning of intellectual skills such as knowing how to do arithmetic, and how to demonstrate geometrical theorems.

If conceptual difficulties surround the concept of learning, the question may arise: 'Is learning possible?' to which the obvious reply would be: 'Why not?' An answer to *this* question leads to our passage in the *Meno*. For the thesis that learning taking the form of inquiry is recollection – proclaimed at 81d4–5 – is given as an answer to an argument designed to show the impossibility of such learning. The argument is expounded in 80d5–e5. It is stated twice, first by Meno and then by Socrates. Socrates' version of the argument proceeds as follows. It is not possible for a man to inquire either into what he knows or into what he does not know. He cannot inquire into that which he knows, since if he knows it there is no room for inquiry. On the other hand, he cannot inquire into that which he does not know, since in that case he does not know what it is that he should be seeking.

As stated, this is a paradox of learning taking the form of inquiry, and not a paradox of learning in general, or a paradox of acquiring information, or a paradox of knowledge. The second half of the paradox depends on the assumption that the projected learning must be given direction by the learner himself. It follows from this that the only kind of learning called into question, and thus the only kind of learning that is explained as recollection, is learning taking the form of inquiry. This is brought out by the Greek words used in the passage. The paradox at 80d–e is stated in terms of *zētēsis* (inquiry) even though in 81e4–5 *mathēsis* (learning) is called recollection. Thus the learning of non-intellectual skills such as riding, or learning by being told, or by imitation, are not included either in the paradox or in its intended solution, since these modes of learning do not involve inquiry in the relevant sense.

The relevant sense of inquiry is itself, of course, in need of clarification. There are reasons to suppose that Plato did not want it to include empirical inquiry. One such reason is that in the case of empirical inquiry the paradox can be resolved by invoking the distinctions between sense and denotation, and between understanding a sentence and knowing which truth value to assign to the proposition expressed by it. For example, the answer to the question: 'Is it cold in Escanaba?' is an empirical proposition. We can describe the inquiry in two stages. The first is the understanding of the sentence 'It is cold in Escanaba,' the second is the process of verifying the proposition expressed by the sentence, involving the gathering of evidence furnished by the senses that leads to the assignment of a truth value to that proposition. The two stages are not only distinct as the stages of understanding and verification, but they also contrast with each other as an internal (understanding) and external (verification) process. Thus the paradox can be resolved for this case by pointing out that in a sense the learner knows what he seeks; i.e. he understands the proposition the truth value of which he attempts to determine. What he does not know at the beginning of the inquiry is the truth value of the proposition in question. This solution leaves us, however, with the unanalysed notion of understanding a sentence. The clarification of this notion leads to a consideration of *a priori* inquiry, since the grasping of meanings of sentences entails knowledge of certain *a priori* propositions.

The distinction between understanding and verification applies also to *a priori* inquiries. In the case of this type of inquiry, however, it is far more difficult to draw a sharp line between the two kinds of processes representing the two stages of inquiry. Not only are verification procedures such as proof, calculation, etc. not matters of gathering external evidence, but they are also not clearly separable from processes that make up understanding. In the case of propositions derived from definitions, such as the one expressed by 'Red is a colour,' verification does not involve anything in addition to understanding, and thus the distinction coalesces. We can see from this that even if the first step toward solving Plato's paradox lies in distinguishing between understanding and verification, further explanations are required to illuminate the notion of understanding in the case of empirical inquiry, and in the case of *a priori* inquiry the processes that make up both understanding and verification.

There are a number of considerations weighing against the hypothesis that Plato understood the paradox within the limits mentioned above. The foremost of these is that he nowhere mentions such a restriction. Another consideration is that the distinction between conditions for truth and conditions for meaning does not emerge in Plato's writings until the *Sophist*, which belongs to the later dialogues. Thirdly, though distinctions like that between the *a priori* and the empirical are often drawn by Plato (though never exactly in such terms or terms coextensive with these), they are not invoked in the passage under consideration. These considerations seem, however, to be outweighed by the evidence in favour of ascribing to Plato the more limited conception of the paradox. The foremost of these are the philosophical considerations mentioned above. For though admittedly some of the technical distinctions required to explicate the restricted nature of the paradox do not appear in this passage or in any of the dialogues written in the same period as the *Meno*, it is intuitively easy to see that one would not be bothered by the paradox except in cases of *a priori* inquiry. Even if one did not have at one's disposal technical notions helping to eliminate the paradox for cases of empirical inquiry, one could be intuitively certain that in these cases the paradox can be resolved in ways other than by invoking the recollection theory. Secondly, nowhere in the passage can one find a mention of empirical investigations.[1] Plato's illustration of the recollection thesis, which in turn is an answer to the paradox, involves the science of geometry, a branch of knowledge regarded by Plato as *a priori* (as evident, e.g., from Bk. VII of the *Republic*). The context of the passage is the search for an answer to the question: 'What is excellence?' and Plato would regard any satisfactory answer to this question as an *a priori* proposition. In 81c7–8 Plato mentions the problem of finding out what excellence is as something falling within the scope of the recollection theory. Further evidence is furnished by the discussion of the recollection theory of learning in *Phaedo* 72e ff, where it is made clear that recollection leads eventually to knowledge and that only *a priori* knowledge is regarded by Plato as genuine knowledge. To sum up, although Plato places no explicit limitations on the paradox, he discusses it and the recollection thesis only in connection with what he takes to be *a priori* inquiries. This, in conjunction with our analysis of the nature of the paradox makes it reasonable to assume that both the paradox and its proposed solution are interpreted by Plato to apply to *a priori* contexts only.

Having considered the nature and scope of the paradox, it is time to consider the ways in which and the extent to which Plato could have regarded the recollection thesis of learning as an answer to it. Some clues are given in the ways in which Socrates' restatement of the paradox differs from Meno's (80d5–8). In Meno's version the paradox is about inquiry into that of which we are *altogether* ignorant. Socrates' restatement omits this strong qualification (*parapan*). The reason for this is presumably that the intended solution covers only those cases in which we in a sense know what we are searching for. The recollection thesis is no answer to a paradox that assumes that the object of inquiry is not known in any way whatsoever at the start of the investigation. The other difference between the two versions is that Meno spells out only the second half of the paradox (we cannot inquire into that which we do not know), and he does this in terms different from those of Socrates. For though Meno too states the difficulty of directing an inquiry toward an unknown object, he adds the question of how one would know that what is found is the information sought initially. This second problem, how does one know that one arrived at the correct solution, is not mentioned by Socrates. The reason for this is presumably that as he interprets the puzzle this question need not arise. If one understands what one investigates, then one will know when an answer is given to the original question. Of course, one might interpret the added question in Meno's version also as raising the problem of how one knows that one knows something. This problem is, however, not dealt with in the *Meno* or in any of the other middle-period dialogues. The difficulty is recognized explicitly only in the *Theaetetus*, which is one of the later dialogues.

These clues confirm our initial suggestion that the recollection thesis is designed to show that in a sense the inquirer does and in a sense does not know that which he is seeking. The distinction between understanding and verification is related to the solution of the paradox in the following way. In the case of inquiries leading to empirical discoveries the initial state of the inquirer is one of knowing (i.e. understanding, which is to be explained by the recollection theory) and of not knowing (i.e. not having evidence to assign the proper truth value to the proposition that serves as the object of inquiry). In the case of inquiries terminating with the knowledge of *a priori* truths, knowing and not knowing cannot be strictly separated as understanding and verification; the recollection theory is supposed to explain both of these.

At least two features that are logically tied to the concept of remembering have also roles in Plato's characterization of *a priori* inquiry. One of these is the historical and the other the entitative aspect of remembering. We can explain the historical aspect by

116

saying that if Jones remembers something at time t″, then there must have been an earlier time t′ such that at that time Jones knew, believed, experienced, etc. that which he remembers at t″. In short, the claim 'Jones remembers p, but at no previous time did he know, believe, experience, etc. p' is self-contradictory. While this historical condition is necessary for remembering, it is not sufficient, else we would have no way of distinguishing between 'Jones remembers p' and 'Jones at one time knew, believed, etc. p, and now he knows, believes, thinks of, etc. p again'. In other words, there is a difference between remembering something from some previous occasion and thinking the same thing twice on two temporally separate occasions. This difference leads us to the entitative feature of remembering. This feature is explained by the statement that there must be an entity or entities contained in a remembering organism, be it mental or physical, such that this or these are related causally both to the event of experience, awareness, etc. at time t′ and to the event of remembering at t″; and that the presence of this element or these elements in the organism distinguishes the remembering mind or organism from one that is merely thinking of something twice.

Our review of the relevant passages will show that both of these features of remembering have roles in Plato's analogy. At this point, however, we should note that by itself the historical feature neither answers the paradox nor gives any explanatory power to the analogy. The entitative feature, however, can even perform both of these functions – given certain qualifications – by itself. This is the feature of the analogy that ties Plato's thesis to what later became known as the innate idea theory. The problem about inquiry is, as we noted earlier, that it seems necessary to suppose that the learner in a sense knows and in a sense does not know what he is seeking. The historical feature of recollection does not help with this problem. For the question: 'How does he know what he is inquiring about?' cannot be answered by saying that he has seen it before in another life. This answer has significance only if we add: 'And he remembers now'. Thus we are relying again on the entitative feature. The explanatory force of the analogy with regard to learning is again carried by the entitative feature. For what is crucial to the explanation of learning geometry is not that one has seen the truths of geometry before in a previous existence, but that these truths are somehow within us, and the task of learning is to bring them to consciousness. Thus the entitative feature allows us to reply to the paradox that in a sense what is to be inquired after is in the mind, and yet in a sense it is not known, i.e. not brought to the surface of consciousness. We can see from this that the claim that we have a set of concepts and beliefs given innately to our minds such that given proper stimulation (and stage of maturation) these can be brought to consciousness, is crucial to the recollection thesis if it is to have any explanatory power at all. Evidence that Plato construed his thesis in this manner is provided by 85c4–5, where Socrates says that recollection involves bringing out in people beliefs that were in a sense in them all along. The theory of innate ideas can be derived from the recollection thesis by dropping the historical feature and modifying the entitative aspect.[2] For the theory thus construed can be understood as the claim that the mind is furnished innately with a set of concepts which it contains in a way analogous to the way in which what is remembered is stored in the mind.

Plato's theory as presented contains two parts. First there is a general account of the processes underlying what we observe as learning, and then an illustration is provided by having Socrates help a slave-boy discover some elementary truths of geometry. The general account can be summarized in the following way. The soul being immortal, previous to our lives we have seen and learned all 'things'. What we call learning is simply recollecting what we once possessed. Furthermore, all things that make up nature are related to each other, and thus if one recollected one part, nothing prevents one from discovering all the rest, provided that sufficient effort is made on the part of the learner.

This account raises several questions. First, what is the force of adding the condition of remembering to the condition of having previously seen all things? Since the latter is equivalent to the historical feature of recollection, we must assume that the addition entails the entitative feature of recollection, else there would be no point in Plato's talking about remembering instead of seeing something twice. Secondly, what are the elements of nature that the soul has 'seen and learned' before? The Greek word used here (*chrēmata* 81c7) is so neutral in meaning that it does not settle the issue. Still, it seems reasonable to suppose that the 'things' cannot be the facts, empirical and otherwise, that make up the history of the world. For example, it is most implausible to suppose that Plato construed human souls as having seen or learned either in Hades or in any of their previous lives the fact that in AD 1966 the Braves would move from Milwaukee to Atlanta. It is far more likely that what Plato supposed to have been seen and learned before are elements of simple *a priori* propositions. Such an interpretation not only makes sense of the passage under consideration but fits well with our previous considerations about the scope of the paradox. The third question is: what is meant by saying that all things making up nature are related, or 'akin'? The phrase 'all [things that make up] nature' could not refer, as Bluck seems to have thought,[3] to everything that exists, since that would imply that all particulars that partake of the Forms are related to each other. 'Nature' in this context must mean 'what is permanent and intelligible,' thus having a meaning related to phrases like 'the nature of a Form' (see, e.g., *Symposium* 210e5). If Plato thinks primarily of concepts as innate in the human mind, rather than propositions, then the claim can be best construed as stating that these concepts form a 'field' of some sort, so that if one has brought one element to consciousness then this will bring with it the ability to bring to consciousness other members of the field as well. In other words, the grasp of one innate idea will facilitate the grasp of the rest, and this is to be accounted for by assuming that these concepts form an interrelated field.

This is not the only possible interpretation. Another interpretation suggests itself according to which recollection and the corresponding sense of 'learning' are to be understood as the intuitive grasp of simple concepts and the drawing of deductive inferences. If this view is correct, then Plato must think of the realm of *a priori* concepts and propositions as constituting a deductive hierarchy. Such a conception of *a priori* knowledge would be surprisingly congenial to empiricists like Hume and surprisingly unlike the conception of a rationalist like Kant. One of the difficulties of this view is that it gives an implausible interpretation of 81c9–d3, where Plato marks off two stages in recollection. As we saw, the first is to recollect one of the elements in the mind, and the second step is to go on and recover all the rest. According to the deductive interpretation Plato commits himself here to saying that if one succeeds in understanding an *a priori* proposition about a Form, then he can deduce from this all of the other *a priori* propositions. Not only is this claim intrinsically implausible, but there is no evidence in the other dialogues that Plato ever held such a view. Another difficulty of this interpretation is that, as we saw, the recollection theory is applicable also to situations in which there is little if any room for deductive arguments such as the discovery of answers to questions like: 'What is excellence?', 'What is learning?' Finally, if recollection is primarily a deductive activity, why would it be necessary for Plato to say that at a previous stage the soul has 'seen all'? There would be no need for this if all *a priori* propositions were deductively related, and if men had innate reasoning ability. None of these objections is decisive, but it is worth noting that the alternative interpretation better fits Plato's general account of recollection.

One point emerging from this discussion is that on any reasonable interpretation Plato holds that the mind contains not only innate abilities such as the ability to reason deductively, but also concepts such as those of geometry and valuation. The term 'innate' does not cause difficulties as long as it is used to characterize abilities. We can contrast innate with acquired abilities by stating that the latter are the result of training or conditioning. It may seem, however, that the notion of an innate idea or concept is less clear. It helps to point out that Plato's claim is not about the slave-boy or Meno in particular, but about the human species of which Meno and the slave-boy are only instances. To say that a concept is given innately to humans is to say that, given proper stimulation and a required stage of maturation, any human will utilize this concept in the interpretation of experience, and that the concept can be shown not to be acquired from experience by abstraction or by any other known process.

Let us now consider the status of the recollection thesis. Was it intended by Plato as an empirical hypothesis or as an *a priori* claim? In order to see this matter more clearly, one must realize that 'learning' is used by Plato in these passages in two senses. For Plato makes the following claim. (i) Learning is, in certain types of cases, recollection. Occasionally this is expressed by (ii) What we call 'learning' is really recollection (81e4–5). At one point, however, during the illustration of the theory, Socrates asks Meno (iii) whether the boy is learning from him or is simply being reminded (82b6–7). It is impossible to assign consistent sense to (i)–(iii) without invoking two senses of 'learn'. 'Learn*' has the ordinary sense of 'learning'; i.e. it has the sense that would allow Plato to use it to cover all cases that would count ordinarily as learning. The sense of 'learning**', on the other hand, is to be contrasted with that of 'recollecting'. 'Learning*' carries no such contrast since it has no implications as to what theory could best account for all cases that fall under it. 'Learning★★' is roughly equivalent to 'acquiring knowledge in such a way that what becomes known is qualitatively identical to what the learner has been exposed to by part of the external environment'. Making use of this distinction we can express Plato's claim as the statement that learning★ *a priori* matters never involves learning★★, but recollection. Thus in (i) and (ii) 'learning' should be interpreted as 'learning★' while in (iii) 'learning★★' is used by Plato. There is no evidence to support the claim that the theory of recollection is used to define either 'learning★' or 'learning★★'. The only plausible candidate for a *definiendum* would be 'learning★ *a priori* matters', but when Plato claims that this can be accounted for only by the recollection theory, he is not claiming this as a matter of definition, based on the meanings of the relevant phrases, or concept containment. If he thought that this was a matter of definition, then there would have been no point to the inclusion of the conversation with the slave-boy.

We might consider the suggestion that Plato intends the thesis as an empirical hypothesis. Some encouragement for this view may be derived from 86b6–7, where some uncertainty is expressed by Socrates with regard to the explanation proposed in the preceding passage. A closer examination of the context shows, however, that Plato expresses reservations only with regard to some of the details of his theory; he has no doubt about the general claim that learning is recollection. There is further evidence in 81e3 ff that tells against this interpretation and supports the claim that for Plato his theory has *a priori* status. For in this passage Meno asks Socrates to teach him that learning is recollection. In reply Socrates points out that on his own view Meno cannot be taught that learning is recollection, he will have to recollect that fact. Meno concludes this interlude by asking Socrates to help him get clear about this matter in any way he can (82a7–b2). This interlude shows that the point of introducing the conversation with the slave-boy is to help Meno to recollect what learning is. Thus recollection takes place on two levels; the slave-boy is recollecting geometry, and Meno is recollecting what learning is. The parallel shows that Plato's theory of learning is meant to be an *a priori* thesis. Since we saw above that the theory is not put forward as something true by definition, its intended status must be that of an *a priori* non-analytic truth.

There are two grounds for Plato's thesis that the learning of *a priori* truths must be recollection. One of these is the resolution of the paradox of inquiry. The recollection thesis enables us to give a consistent and intelligible account of how the inquirer at the outset both knows and does not know what he is seeking. The other ground is the set of general characteristics holding for normal conditions of human inquiry into *a priori* subjects that are illustrated in the conversation with the slave boy. With regard to these conditions Plato's argument seems to take the following form: given that there is successful inquiry into *a priori* matters, and given the nature of such inquiry (illuminated negatively by the learner's paradox) together with certain general facts about human learning conditions, learning within this restricted scope must be like recollection. This structure is very similar to the structure of Kant's transcendental arguments. In those arguments too, certain propositions are shown to be necessary on the basis of the analysis of all pervasive human abilities and their typical manifestations.

In this connection it is also illuminating to compare Plato's treatment of the learner's paradox with the so-called paradox of analysis discussed in twentieth-century analytic philosophy. The paradox of analysis arises in connection with the analysis of the meanings of expressions that have an established use. According to the paradox, such an analysis can only be either trivial and unilluminating or incorrect. For if the *definiens* reflects correctly the established meaning of the *definiendum* then the analysis should not yield anything new and illuminating. If it does yield something new and illuminating, then how could it reflect correctly the established meaning of the *definiendum*?

The learner's paradox is wider in scope. It calls into question any inquiry into those subjects for which the senses can furnish no relevant evidence. The paradox of analysis calls into question only those inquiries the object of which is the establishment of analytic propositions that are true by definition. The paradox of analysis arises only in connection with inquiries whose aim is to establish a proposition of identity one side of which stands for expressions whose meanings must be – *ex hypothesi* – understood at the outset of the inquiry. The recollection theory and the paradox that it resolves carry no such restrictions. The two paradoxes are equivalent only if all *a priori* propositions are analytic and true by definition. Plato certainly would not have accepted this claim about the *a priori*, at least in any form that would construe analyticity in terms of logical truth and stipulative or conventional definitions.

These considerations show the recollection thesis to be an *a priori* non-analytic answer to the question: 'How is inquiry into *a priori* matters possible?' As an answer, the recollection thesis states that inquiry of this type is analogous to recollection. The initial understanding of the object of inquiry is made intelligible by saying that these objects are in our minds in a way analogous to the way in which the content of a recollection is in our minds between the initial experience of what is later remembered and the act of remembering. Finally, the description of recollection suggests that the connections between the concepts given innately are not solely analytic. It is time to test this interpretation on the passage in which the recollection thesis is illustrated.

The illustration (82b–85b) consists of a dialogue between Socrates and a slave-boy, at the end of which the slave-boy has some understanding of certain procedures by which one can construct squares of areas determined with reference to the size of the sides and diagonals of a given square. At the termination of the conversation Meno and Socrates agree that the slave-boy did not acquire his knowledge in the form of information presented by an outside source; he discovered things for himself and his discovery resembled recollection. This agreement cannot rest on empirical grounds, since the inductive basis for the conclusion interpreted as an empirical generalization would be slender indeed. The same consideration shows that the slave boy's knowledge[4] could not be based on empirical evidence, since the group of squares scrawled into the sand by Socrates would hardly furnish adequate grounds for inductive generalization. Nor is there material surrounding the passage in question that would indicate that the conversation is interpreted as a 'crucial experiment' either by Meno or by the slave-boy.

The demonstration is supposed to show that a slave-boy can learn a part of geometry by recollection. The conversation is interrupted twice by Socrates to point out to Meno that the slave-boy is not being instructed, he is only being asked questions (82e4–5; 84c11–d2). How are we to understand this contrast between instruction and questioning, especially in view of the fact that many of the questions require only a yes or no answer? (E.g., 'doubling the size gives us not a double but a fourfold figure? True.' (83b8–c2.) There is apparently, according to Plato, a gap between the question and the response. This unobservable gap is *understanding*. The need for this intervening process is brought out partly by the fact that at one point of the discussion Socrates deceives the slave-boy by leading him to an incorrect conclusion. Thus the slave-boy is forced to see that mere assent to authority will not do. Thus recollection is not the observable event of the slave-boy answering a question, but rather something of which the answering is only a sign. In order to understand the contrast between instruction and questioning we must draw the following fourfold distinction: what the slave-boy is exposed to, the meaning of what the slave-boy is exposed to, the process of understanding, and the response that is the outcome of understanding. Questioning is supposed to serve merely to stimulate the process of understanding. Being instructed would involve information being conveyed to the subject in such a manner that what he comes to know can be identified with what is conveyed to him from the outside source. Under these circumstances understanding could be reduced to simple decoding and would not require the addition of concepts or propositions from within itself.

We can represent the slave-boy as a geometry learning device. The input of this device is what the slave-boy is exposed to, while the output, according to Plato, is understanding. The output is unobservable; the observed event of answering provides merely indirect evidence for understanding. Thus input and output do not correspond to what is observable and unobservable. In this respect too, learning is analogous to recollecting, as the diagrams opposite indicate.

There is no great difference between the nature of the observable input, Socrates' verbal behaviour, and the observable response, the verbal behaviour of the slave-boy. Likewise, there is no great difference in the nature of a reminder and our report of recollection. The difference lies in the nature of the input and the act of understanding as well as between the reminder and the act of remembering. These differences are so great that Plato thinks we must assume, in order to explain the connections, the existence of an independent contribution of the mind that helps to bridge the gaps. The difference between reminder and recollection can be explained only on the assumption that the mind has stored something within it between the time of the experience and the time at which the experience is remembered, and that this element plays a vital role in the act of remembering (this was called above the entitative feature of remembering). According to Plato the difference between the input and the act of understanding can be

Diagram A

| | Input | | Output | Evidence for Output |
|---|---|---|---|---|
| Observable | Questions, Diagrams | | | Replies to Questioning |
| Unobservable | | Mind →|Understanding of Geometry | |

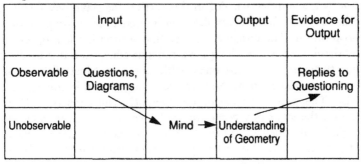

Diagram B

| | Input | | Output | Evidence for Output |
|---|---|---|---|---|
| Observable | Sense Data and Reminders | | | Reports |
| Unobservable | | Mind →| Act of Remembering | |

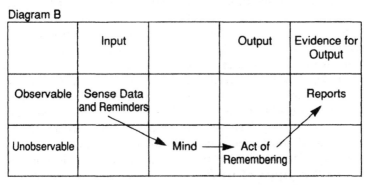

explained only if we assume that the mind contains elements of what is understood in a way analogous to the way in which it contains what enables us to remember, and that these elements in the mind play a vital role in understanding while the role of the input is merely one of stimulation.

It remains to be shown that the illustration contains the recollection of concepts and the recollection of non-analytic connections between these concepts as well as the understanding of analytic connections. The conversation with the slave-boy is divided into three parts: 82b9–e1, 82e14–84a2, and 84d3–85b2. As we saw above, the sections are marked off by brief interludes in which the significance of the illustration is explained by Socrates. The first few lines of the first section (82b9–c5) serve to help the slave-boy to grasp the concept of a square. The slave-boy comes to understand that the square's four sides are all equal, and that its size is irrelevant to its geometrical properties. This section is also a part of the recollecting process, and it provides evidence in support

of the claim that some of what falls under the concept of recollection is non-inferential. For in this section the slave-boy recollects
what a square is; he is not drawing inferences from proposition to
proposition. The remainder of the first section is taken up mainly
by the slave-boy's reaching the erroneous conclusion that by doubling the sides of a square one doubles the area. Most of the second
section is taken up by Socrates' showing that this conclusion is
false. This part of recollection is inferential and deductive. That is
to say, the slave-boy comes to see his error by understanding the
logical consequences of his false belief, as they unfold with the aid
of Socrates. Thus this section provides evidence for saying that the
ability to understand deductive relations between *a priori* propositions is part of the recollection process. In the third section,
however, the boy is helped to understand how to construct a square
with an area twice the size of any given square. This method of
construction is, of course, quite general. But by itself it does not
*prove* deductively any relationship between sides and area. The
diagram shows that a given method of construction *must* always
yield a square with an area of doubled size. This truth is grasped by
the boy intuitively. The construction of an actual diagram and the
counting of squares and lines within the diagram only aid his
intuition. Thus the third section provides us with an illustration of
yet another aspect of recollection; the grasping of non-analytic
connections between concepts.

In order to avoid misunderstanding, the conclusion about the
third section that is proposed in this paper should be restated in the
following way. It is not claimed that Plato distinguished between
analytic and synthetic connections among concepts given innately
and that he consciously included in the demonstration examples of
both types of connection. The claim is, rather, that Plato does not
make an explicit distinction between analytic and synthetic, and
that both his description and his illustration of recollection are such
that not all of it can be characterized adequately as the grasping of
simple concepts and the understanding of deductions and analytic
truths. It is true, of course, that the state of understanding reached
by the slave-boy is regarded as in need of further improvement, but
this improvement is envisioned as the result of further exercises
similar in nature to the ones performed (85 c9–d1). Plato does not
suggest that the slave-boy will have knowledge only if he has
understood geometry in axiomatized form.

Before turning to a final appraisal it is worth while to consider a possible objection to Plato's procedure. It might be argued that the whole discussion is vitiated by Plato's failure to distinguish concepts from propositions. One might argue along these lines that given this distinction Plato's illustration shows only the power of the deductive capacities of the slave-boy. This would hardly show anything about innate ideas or the need for the recollection theory of learning. How we form concepts is one question, requiring an empirical answer; how to explain logical relationships between propositions is another. Plato's recollection theory is perhaps merely a mixture of a dim recognition of the nature of deductive reasoning and bad armchair psychology.

In reply it should be said that though there are important differences between concepts and propositions, there are also important similarities, and that the differences are not relevant to Plato's discussion. The most crucial difference between concept and proposition is that only the latter is true or false. There is, however, corresponding to every sentence expressing a proposition, e.g., 'The cat is on the mat', a subsentential expression derivable by nominalization e.g., 'the cat's being on the mat', and thus a corresponding concept. Thus, as Kant saw, one may talk of necessary connections between concepts (e.g., containment) and necessary links between propositions interchangeably. For Plato's purposes it makes little if any difference whether one admits of concepts or propositions as given innately to the human mind. As for the connections between these, we saw above that not all of them can be construed on Plato's view as analytic.

As a final review, let us return to the point made at the beginning of this paper and ask whether the recollection thesis is best classified as empirical hypothesis, *a priori* truth, or mere metaphor. We saw already that Plato intended the thesis to be an *a priori* truth. He is justified in this interpretation, however, only on the assumption that no alternative explanation of the general facts of learning is possible. This assumption is dubious; Plato might have tried to consider several alternatives to 'being instructed' and recollection.

As a hypothesis about the structure of the mind the recollection thesis seems to fall between being a very general empirical theory and being a metaphor. The reason for this is the inherent vagueness of the thesis. All that Plato can conclude from his analysis is that *something* in addition to deductive reasoning capacity must be given to the mind innately in order to bridge the gap between input and understanding. Plato's argument does not warrant more specific guesses about the structure of the mind. He has certainly no right to suppose that he has shown a need for assuming that all elements of *a priori* propositions are given to the mind innately. Thus the recollection thesis shows only that there must be (in some way not yet clearly specified) concepts and propositions given innately to the human mind if the learning of such subjects as geometry under normal conditions is to be accounted for by the most plausible hypothesis available.

This criticism is not so much a rebuke to Plato as encouragement for the present. The path from metaphor to theory is long and arduous in the history of science as well as in the history of philosophy. The product of Plato's fertile imagination needs to be properly understood in order for it to serve as the basis for the theories of the present.

## NOTES

1 Evidence for this as well as a decisive refutation of the claim that the slave-boy conducts an empirical investigation can be found in G. Vlastos' *'Anamnesis* in the *Meno'*, *Dialogue* 4 (1965), pp. 143–67 [reprinted in this volume pp. 88–111. Ed.]. A bibliography of recent interesting material on this topic is to be found in note 2 of this paper. I am indebted to Professor Vlastos for helpful suggestions concerning this topic, made in personal correspondence.

2 See, e.g., N. Chomsky, *Cartesian Linguistics* (New York, 1966), pp. 63 and 108. For further elaboration see the author's 'Linguistic theory and the philosophy of language', *Foundations of Language* 3 (1967), pp. 209–33.

3 R. D. Bluck, *Plato's Meno* (Cambridge, 1961), p. 288.

4 The term 'knowledge' is used loosely here, leaving it an open question whether at the end of the conversation the slave-boy has knowledge in the Platonic sense, or merely true belief.

# THE FIRST SOCRATIC
# PARADOX

*George Nakhnikian*

The Socratic paradoxes may be regarded as aphorisms that contain
the essentials of the Socratic ethics. There are three Socratic paradoxes. They are: first, that no man desires evil, all men desire the
good; second, that no man who (knows or) believes that an action
is evil does it willingly – on the contrary, all the actions that a man
does willingly he does with a view to achieving some good; and,
third, that it is better to suffer injustice at the hands of others than
to do unjust acts oneself. These paradoxes are related to psychological egoism and to the dictum that virtue is knowledge and vice
is ignorance. In this essay I shall concentrate on the first paradox
and the ways in which it relates to psychological egoism and to the
dictum that virtue is knowledge and vice is ignorance.

The doctrine that Socrates has in mind in connection with the
first paradox can be more fully and less misleadingly stated if we
begin by distinguishing four types of desires and the aversions
corresponding to them:

A type I desire is a desire for something in the mistaken
belief that the thing is good. A type I aversion is an aversion
for, or repugnance to, something in the mistaken belief that
the thing is evil.

A type II desire is a desire for something in the knowledge
or in the true belief that the thing is good. A type II aversion is
an aversion for, or repugnance to, something in the knowledge or in the true belief that the thing is evil.

A type III desire is a desire for something in the knowledge
or in the true belief that the thing is evil. A type III aversion is
an aversion for, or repugnance to, something in the knowledge or in the true belief that the thing is good.

A type IV desire (aversion) is a desire (aversion) for something in the absence of any belief about its goodness or badness.

With the help of these distinctions, we may state the essential content of the first Socratic paradox as follows: in a man all desire for some evil and all aversion to some good is of type I. This is the core of the first paradox. It *is* the first paradox. From this it follows that in a man there is no desire for some evil and no aversion to some good that is of type III or type IV.

I shall formulate all the arguments in the Socratic dialogues that are offered in defence of this paradox. I shall explain what the conceptual and psychological assumptions of these arguments are. We shall then understand what Socrates means by the premises and conclusions of his arguments. This will put us in a position to evaluate the arguments for cogency. When all this is done, we should have a good idea as to how the first paradox is related on the one hand to psychological egoism, and, on the other hand, to the dictum that knowledge is virtue and vice is ignorance.

In the Socratic dialogues there are two passages where Socrates argues for the first paradox. These are at *Meno* 77b–78b, and *Gorgias* 467c–468e. There are other passages, e.g., *Apology* 25c, and *Protagoras* 358c, where Socrates assumes the first paradox to prove one or the other of the remaining paradoxes or some other propositions that are very much like them.

The argument that actually occurs in *Meno* 77b–78b does not clearly state as its conclusion the first paradox as I have formulated it. The argument grants that there are men who desire evils believing them to be goods, and it concludes that there are no men who desire evils knowing them to be evils. The conjunction of these two propositions does not say or imply that all men who desire evils do so on the mistaken belief that what they desire is good. This conclusion, however, is deducible from premises that are explicitly employed or implied or thought to be obvious in 77b–78b. From these typically Socratic premises we can construct three arguments. The conclusion of the first conjoined to the conclusion of the second entails a proposition that is one of the premises of the third argument. The conclusion of the third is the first paradox. I shall first convey what I understand to be the argument in 77b–78b. I shall then formulate and critically examine the three arguments that can be extrapolated from 77b–78b.

130

At 77b Meno defines virtue as the desire for what is fair, lovable, honourable, comely (*kalos*) together with the ability to procure it. Socrates sets out to refute this definition. It is only as part of that refutation that he adduces reasons for the first paradox. Socrates begins his refutation by arguing that all men desire the good, that no men desire evil. If Socrates is right about this, then, no matter how Meno chooses to define wickedness, desire for what is good will not be a criterion for distinguishing good from bad men. From Meno's original definition there thus remains only one purported defining property for being a good man: the ability to procure goods. This, however, cannot be all that there is to being a good man. Therefore Meno's definition is false.

Immediately after his definition Meno asserts two hypotheses. The first says that there are men who desire evils believing them to be goods. The second one says that there are also men who desire evils knowing them to be evils. This includes believing that the desired evils are evil, for knowing entails believing. Socrates has no objections to the first hypothesis. On the contrary, he himself believes it. He sets out to prove that the second hypothesis is false, and necessarily so. Under prodding from Socrates Meno divides the second hypothesis into two parts. The first part states that there are men who desire evils, know that they are evils, and believe that evils do good to those (benefit those) who possess them. The second part states that there are men who desire evils, know that they are evils, and know that evils harm those who possess them. There is a third and a fourth case that Socrates does not mention, but this is not a weakness in his argument. The third concerns men who desire evils, know them to be evils, and believe that evils neither harm nor benefit those who possess them. The fourth postulates that there are men who desire evils, know them to be evils, and know that evils neither harm nor benefit those who possess them. Now the third and fourth suppositions are, like the first part of the second hypothesis, false, if we assume as Socrates does, that knowing that a thing is evil (good) is sufficient for knowing that it harms (benefits) those who possess it. It is, therefore, sufficient for Socrates' purposes that he argue the impossibility of the two parts into which through Meno's mouth he divides the second hypothesis.

His purpose is to discredit the second hypothesis so that he can establish the first paradox. The first part of the second hypothesis Socrates thinks is false, and necessarily so, because it is *conceptually impossible* for a man to know that a thing is evil and at the same time to believe that evils do good to those who possess them. (The third and fourth cases are also conceptually impossible.) Socrates thinks that the second part is false because it is *psychologically impossible* for a man to know that a thing will harm those who possess it yet to desire that thing for himself.

The 'argument' against the first part of the second hypothesis is at 77d–e. I say 'argument' because there really is no explicit argument in this fragment. Socrates gets Meno to admit flatly, as if it were self-evident, that those who believe that the evils that they desire do good to him who possess them do not know that they are evils (77d). The precise sense of this seems to me to be the following: For anything $x$ and any person $y$, it is necessarily true that if $x$ is evil, $y$ desires $x$, and $y$ believes that $x$ benefits those who possess it, then $y$ does not know that $x$ is evil. I think that supporting this proposition there is an unexpressed argument which it is important to formulate if we are to understand the assumptions on which Socrates bases his paradoxes. Besides, without a supporting argument Socrates will not have refuted the first part of the second hypothesis. He will have only denied it flatly and thus begged the question. The argument I think, is this: If a man believes of something which is in fact evil that it will (on the whole) benefit those who possess it, and the man is consistent in his thinking, then he does not believe that the thing will (on the whole) harm those who possess it. Consequently, he does not know that the thing will harm those who possess it. *But if he does not know that the thing will harm those who possess it, then he does not know that it is evil.* This is the crucial assumption. Given this assumption it follows that a man cannot, at the same time, believe of something which is in fact evil that it will benefit those who possess it, and also know that it is evil.

A weaker assumption would be sufficient for the validity of the argument, the assumption, namely, that if a man knows that something is evil, then it is not the case that he believes that the thing in question benefits those who possess it. But this assumption is not strong enough as a premise in Socrates' argument against the second part of the second hypothesis. And, as he does make the stronger assumption in that argument, I think that we are fully justified in attributing it to him in the present instance. The stronger assumption that anyone who knows that a thing is evil knows that it harms those who possess it has a correlative: anyone who knows that a thing is good knows that it benefits those who possess it. There is no reason why if Socrates accepts the one he should reject the other. I shall proceed on the supposition that he does indeed accept both.

I find it both textually supported and illuminating to view these assumptions as if they were intended to convey the idea that there is a conceptual relation between being evil (good) and being harmful (beneficial) to the possessor, a relation like the one that exists between being red and being coloured or between being a cat and being a mammal. One does not know what it is for something to be red if one does not know that nothing can be red and not coloured. In like manner, as Socrates understands things, one does not know what it is for something to be evil if one does not know that nothing can be evil and not harm those who possess it. In other words, we are not thinking of evil if we are not thinking of that which harms its possessor. As I read him, for Socrates 'If $x$ is evil, then $x$ harms those who possess it' and 'If $x$ is good, then $x$ benefits those who possess it' are true in virtue of what it is to *be* good and to *be* evil. However, they are not definitions. They are, so to speak, meaning postulates.

On my interpretation, the necessity of these meaning postulates is conceptual, while the necessity of the proposition, 'Those who know that a thing will harm them do not desire it', is that of a psychological generalization. If the generalization is true, then without exception people do not desire things that they know to be evil. But the truth-value of the generalization cannot be known just by reflecting on what it is to *be* a person or to *be* evil.

I do not mean to suggest that the distinction between these two kinds of necessity is either clear or sharp. Nor do I mean to imply that Socrates (or Plato) deliberately and systematically observes any such distinction. My view is that certain passages may be read in terms of some such distinction, and reading these passages this way seems to give a clearer understanding of some characteristically Socratic conclusions and the reasons he gives in their support.

So far we have seen that from certain Socratic assumptions it follows that no one who is thinking clearly can know that something is evil and also believe that the thing will benefit those who possess it. The opposite is conceptually impossible. This is the Socratic refutation of the first part of the second hypothesis.

The argument against the second part of the second hypothesis is at 77e–78b. The proposition that Socrates means to disprove is that there are men who know that the evils that they desire are evils and that evils are hurtful to the possessor of them (77c–d: Meno admits to believing that there are cases where 'a man knows evils to be evils and desires them notwithstanding and also knows that their presence [the presence of evils] does harm [to whoever possesses them]'). Socrates argues that there are no such men.

Here is the argument. Let $K$ be the class of men who know that something they desire is evil, and who also know that evils are hurtful to the possessor of them. Socrates wants to prove that $K$ cannot have any members.

    (i)  Anyone who is a $K$ knows that the evils that he desires are hurtful to himself (77e).

    (ii)  Anyone who knows that the evils that he desires are hurtful to himself must believe that the more hurt a thing causes us the more miserable it makes us (77e).

    (iii)  To be miserable is to desire evil and to obtain it (78a).[1]

    (iv)  No one desires to be miserable (78a).

    [(v)  If a man believes that obtaining or possessing something will make him obtain or possess something that he desires not to obtain or possess, then he will not desire to possess the former entity.][2]

∴  (vi)  No one who is a $K$ will desire [what he knows to be] evil; and this is logically equivalent to the proposition that there are no $K$'s.

It is not clear why step (iii) is introduced at all. It does not strengthen the argument. In fact it is sufficient to make it unconvincing. I read (iii) as follows: $x$ is miserable = $Df.$ $(\exists y)$ ($y$ is evil, $x$ desires $y$, and $x$ obtains $y$).[2a] Accordingly the argument is that as no one desires to desire evil and to possess it, it follows that no one desires evil. Hence, there is no one who desires evil knowing it to be evil. The proposition that no one desires to desire evil and to obtain it I read as follows: $\sim (\exists x)$ [$x$ desires that $(\exists y)$ ($y$ is evil, $x$ desires $y$, and $x$ obtains $y$)][2b]. This proposition may be construed in two ways. It is not clear which of the two Socrates is asserting. First, $(x)$ [$x$ desires that $(y)$ (if $y$ is evil and $x$ desires to obtain $y$, then $x$ does not obtain $y$)].[2c] In other words, everyone desires that his desires for evil things be unfulfilled. From this it does not follow that no one desires [to obtain] evil. Second, $(x)$ [$x$ desires that $(y)$ (if $y$ is evil, then $x$ neither desires nor obtains $y$)].[2d] In other words, everyone desires that he neither desire nor obtain any evil whatever. Again, it does not follow from this that no one desires [to obtain] evil.

Why does Socrates think otherwise? Perhaps he thinks that the second-order desire to have one's first-order desire for some evil unfulfilled or, as the case may be, the second-order desire neither to desire evil nor to have such a desire fulfilled would not exist if there was no first-order aversion to the evil thing. Socrates may be confusing an aversion to something with thinking that one ought not to have it. These are, of course, not identical. The existence of the second-order desire requires something like the thought that one ought not to have the thing that happens to be the object of the first-order desire. But one can surely believe that one ought not to have something and still desire to have it.

Socrates' definition of misery is defective. Desiring good and obtaining evil is surely a way of being miserable. It might be an improvement to say that to be miserable is to possess evil, regardless of whether or not one desired to possess it. The premise of the Socratic argument would then be that it is false of everyone that he desires the following: that there be an evil thing and that he himself come to possess it. But with such a premise the argument is a *petitio*.

If we ignore the definition of misery, we can construe the argument at 77e–78b as an enthymeme. Eliminate premise (iii). From (iv) and (v) it follows that a man will not desire a thing if he believes that it will bring misery, a thing he does not desire. Hence, by (ii) he will not desire anything that harms him, and, consequently, by (i), he will not desire anything that is evil, if he believes that it is evil. Eliminating (iii), however, does not help. The unexpressed premise (v) is essential to the argument, and (v) is false.

We are now in a position to extrapolate three valid arguments the ultimate conclusion of which is the first paradox. These arguments incorporate all the essential assumptions that Socrates makes in 77b–78b in order to defend the first paradox. Moreover, as compared with the actual argumentation in 77b–78b, these are perspicuous, and, therefore, much easier to appraise.

The first argument can be extrapolated from the one against the second part of the second hypothesis. It incorporates two Socratic premises that are crucial for his defence of the first paradox. That the first of these (namely, that if a man knows that a thing is evil, then he knows that it harms those who possess it) is Socratic is clear if we reflect on the immediately preceding argument against the second part of the second hypothesis. Premise (i) of that argument says that anyone who knows that something that he desires is evil and also knows that evils are hurtful to those who possess them, knows that the evils that he himself desires are hurtful to himself. Socrates and Meno agree that those who know that they will be hurt by the evils that they desire 'must know it' (77e). Moreover, in order to derive the conclusion: 'There are no men who desire a thing knowing that it is evil and also knowing that evils are hurtful to those who possess them', Socrates assumes not that there are no men who know that evils hurt those who possess them but that there are no men who desire to be miserable and ill-fated. We are, therefore, reasonably safe in believing that the proposition 'If a man knows that something is evil, then he knows that it harms those who possess it' is one that Socrates accepts.

The second crucial premise is the psychological generalization that if a man knows that it will harm him to possess a certain thing, then he will not desire [to possess] it. Premises (ii), (iv) and (v) of the argument against the second part of the second hypothesis imply that if a man *believes* that something will harm him, then he will not desire it. But if that is so, then it follows that a man who *knows* that something will harm him will not desire it. The second crucial premise, too, is thus Socratic.

Here then is the first argument that we are extrapolating. I shall refer to it as the first argument.

(1) If a man knows that something is evil, then he knows that the thing will harm those who possess it.

[(1.0) If a man knows that a thing will harm those who possess it, then he knows that it will harm him to possess it.]

(2) If a man knows that it will harm him to possess something, then he does not want to possess it.

(2.0) If a man does not want to possess something, then he does not desire it. (77c–d: 'Desire is of possession', i.e. anyone who desires a thing wants to possess it.)

∴ (3) If a man knows that something is evil, then he does not desire it.

Another valid argument may be obtained by uniformly replacing 'knows' with 'believes'. This I shall call the second argument.

The first premise of the third argument is identical with the conjunction of the conclusions of the first and second arguments. The third argument itself reads as follows:

(1) If a man desires something that is evil, then he neither knows nor believes that it is evil.

(2) If a man who desires something that is evil neither knows nor believes that it is evil, then he believes that it is good (77e).

∴ (3) If a man desires something that is evil, then he believes that the thing is good.

An exactly analogous argument can be constructed to prove that

(4) If a man has an aversion to something that is good, then he believes that it is evil. The conjunction of (3) and (4) is identical with the first paradox.

The second premise of the third argument is at 77e: a man is said to be ignorant of the fact that something that he desires is evil if he does not know and does not believe that the thing is evil but believes that the thing is good. 'Is it not obvious that, those who are ignorant (*agnoountes*) of their nature [the evil nature of the things they desire] do not desire them, but desire what they suppose to be goods although they are really evils; and therefore if in their ignorance they suppose the evils to be goods they really desire goods?'

The statement at 77e clearly indicates that a certain assumption that pervades other dialogues as well is 'obvious' to Socrates. The assumption is that there is a (psychologically) necessary connection between a man's desiring something and his believing that it is good (hence beneficial to himself), and between his having an aversion to something and believing that it is evil (hence harmful to himself). For a man who is in a state either of desiring something or of having an aversion to something is either ignorant or its contrary.[3] Given Socrates' characterization of ignorance it follows that the man who is in the contrary state must be the one who knows (hence believes truly) that the object of his desire is good and that the object of his aversion is evil. Thus both he who has desires or aversions in ignorance as well as he who has them wittingly has beliefs about the goodness or badness of the objects that he desires or abhors. He may not formulate to himself or express to others the proposition that the thing is good (or that it is evil), but, if I am right, Socrates believes that if the man were to ask himself what he thought about the object of his desire, he would find that he believed that it was good. And if he raised questions about the matter and reflected, then his desire would persist if, and only if, reflection did not destroy his belief that the thing was good. I believe that this view is characteristically Socratic. Recognizing that Socrates holds it is essential for understanding the Socratic dictum that knowledge is virtue and vice is a special kind of ignorance (*amathia*). *Amathia* is not absence of belief. It is the presence of false belief about the goodness or badness of things and actions (*Prot.* 358c).[4] A true belief about the value qualities of things and actions is certainly a necessary and perhaps also a sufficient condition of desiring to possess or desiring not to possess them in conformity to virtue. False belief about the value qualities of things and actions is certainly a necessary and perhaps also a sufficient condition of desiring to possess or desiring not to possess them according to the dictates of vice. Thus, all morally criticizable desires, aversions, and actions presuppose belief about the value qualities of the objects of desire or aversion and of the actions themselves.

The first argument has one psychological and two conceptual premises. The psychological premise is (2). The first conceptual assumption is premise (1). If my earlier observations are correct (see p. 133, above), then for Socrates (1) is making a conceptual point, and the point is that evil being what it is, a thing's being evil conceptually necessitates that the thing will harm the one who possesses it. Sometimes by *kakos* (that which is evil, bad) Socrates *means* harmful to the one who possesses it. We have no firm grounds for believing that in the *Meno* this is what *kakos* means. What we are sure of is that from something's being good it follows (conceptually) that that thing is beneficial to its possessor and from something's being evil it follows that that thing is harmful to its possessor. In the *Protagoras* Socrates uses the words *agathos* and *kakos* as having these same implications. None of the arguments for the Socratic paradoxes requires that *kakos* and *agathos mean* respectively harmful and beneficial to the possessor. The implication is all that some of these arguments require. And we can be sure that the implication at least is included in the ways in which Socrates uses the words *agathos* and *kakos* in the *Meno*, and, as we shall see, in the *Protagoras*. It is only when we come to the *Gorgias* that we shall find Socrates using the words in such a way as to suggest that the following biconditionals are conceptual truths: a thing is good

138

if, and only if, it benefits those who possess it; a thing is evil if, and only if, it harms those who possess it. These biconditionals might even be definitions, but that is not beyond doubt.

The second conceptual assumption of the first argument is that to desire a thing at the very least implies wanting to possess it. This is expressed in its premise (2.0). We have to understand this notion of wanting to possess as covering a number of different sorts of things. The first paradox places the emphasis on desire for objects, but presumably Socrates means to be including experiences and states of affairs. Otherwise the paradox would have a much more restricted application than it is intended to have. Now a man may desire a thing such as an apple, and this implies that he wants to possess it in the sense that he wants to appropriate it, own it, make it his own. But a man may also desire the health of his children, and this is something that he cannot possess in the same way. Instead of saying that the man wants to possess something it would be more accurate to say that he wants it to come about that his children are healthy. Wanting to appropriate as well as wanting that such and such be the case, or wanting to experience such and such are to be understood as coming under the Socratic notion of wanting to possess. The first argument does not mention desire for doing this or that. To desire (*epithūmein*) anything is to be understood as implying wanting to possess in the wider sense just explained, and it has to be understood to cover desire to act as well as desire for things, experiences, and states of affairs. The word *epithūmein* is the most widely used word for *to desire* in the Socratic dialogues, and if it is supposed to do the work of our verb 'to desire', it must be understood to have this wide range of application.

We are now ready to undertake a critical assessment of the first argument. Its premise (1) is false under one natural interpretation. Under another interpretation it is tautological. When (1) is tautological, the burden is on (2), the psychological assumption. But (2) is false for obvious reasons that I shall remind the reader of presently.

Premise (1) is false if 'evil' is understood in one of the ways in which it is commonly used. Imagine an incorrigible criminal, a wicked man one who habitually commits irremediable offences. He is the incorrigibly wicked man whom Socrates describes in *Gorgias* 524e–526d. Socrates wants to say that when the appropriate authorities punish such a man they are punishing him justly. The justly punished criminal is the recipient of just punishment.

But surely that which is just is good, insofar as it is just. So to obtain, or to be the recipient of, just punishment is to possess a good. Now by hypothesis punishing an incorrigible man will do him no good at all. His punishment serves only as a deterrent to others. Here, then, is something good that does not benefit its possessor. Or, suppose that the duly constituted authority is remiss in his duty to punish the criminal. This remission brings it about that the criminal obtains unjust reprieve from punishment. The reprieve is evil, insofar as it is unjust. But the criminal who, by obtaining this evil, possesses it, is not harmed by it. Here then is an example in which 'good' and 'evil' do not have the connotation, respectively, of being beneficial and harmful to the possessor. Yet they are being used in an intelligible way to express true propositions. Therefore, premise (1) is not true.

If 'evil' is understood in the special sense that Socrates gives its Greek counterpart, *kakos*, namely, as at least implying harm to its possessor, then (1) is a tautology. As the Greeks used the word *kakos* it may have been a necessary conceptual truth that whatever is *kakos* is harmful to its possessor. Perhaps Socrates is putting a special emphasis on this implicit connotation. Grant this possibility. Then it follows that (1) is a necessary truth, a truth determined by a specific sense of 'evil' which is different from the sense of 'evil' in which '*x* is evil' does not entail that *x* is harmful to its possessor.

Now the burden is entirely on premise (2), and (2) is not true. There are some people who know and others who merely believe that possessing a certain amount of cigarette smoke in their lungs daily over protracted periods is harmful to them. Many such people want, sometimes intensely, sometimes even compulsively, to possess cigarette smoke in their lungs at levels that they know or believe to be dangerous to their health. At *Meno* 77e Socrates asserts that if a man desires something that is in fact evil, then he believes that that thing is good. And because Socrates assumes that a thing is good for someone only if he benefits from possessing it, it follows that if a man desires something that is evil, then he believes (mistakenly) that the thing will benefit him.[5] In other words, in a man all desire for some evil and all aversion for some good is of type I. But the cigarette example disputes this assumption. Those who enjoy the experience of inhaling dangerous amounts of cigarette smoke are justified in believing that the experience is intrinsically good. But inasmuch as the experience leads to suffering, disease, and early death, it is on the whole evil. The experience may be desired as an intrinsic good by those who know or those who merely believe it to be evil in a sense implying harm to him who has it. There are those who are convinced that all things considered smoking is more evil than good. The enjoyment demands an exorbitant price. Many people believe this yet crave to smoke. We must I think conclude that the first argument is unsuccessful against the proposition that people do desire what they know or believe to be harmful to themselves.

An assumption more plausible than premise (2) of the first argument might be that no one desires to be harmed. This is a very difficult proposition to assess. Modern psychological theories make room for 'the death instinct', for unconscious self-destructive wishes, for sadomasochistic syndromes. If these theories are correct, an emendation may be in order to the effect that no man who is psychologically healthy, or no man consciously, desires to be harmed. However, neither in its original nor its emended forms is this assumption a help to Socrates. For it might be true that no one desires to be harmed, yet false that no one desires to possess a thing that will harm him. Indeed, there appear to be clear cases, such as cigarette addiction, that show this to be true. The cigarette addict who does not want to be harmed may, nevertheless, desire to smoke. What is more, he may desire to smoke knowing that smoking is a grave danger to his health. Socrates assumes that a man who knows that something will harm him will not desire it. But this is not entailed by the assumption that no one desires to be harmed, and we have independent evidence that it is false to begin with.

Perhaps the first argument can be saved if we suppose that Socrates equates desiring something with believing that it will benefit you to possess it, and having an aversion to something with believing that it will harm you to possess it. According to this suggestion, (1) and (3) are the same proposition, and it is true by definition. But this definition of desiring something does not express what either Socrates or Plato means by *epithūmein*. Plato says that the desiderative part of the soul, the *epithūmētikon*, is 'irrational' (*Republic*, 439d). He contrasts actions that arise from the calculations of reason with 'the impulses which draw and drag' and 'come from affections and diseases'. The *epithūmētikon* is 'irrational' not in that it is a rational principle gone wrong. It is not a calculating faculty prone to making erroneous calculations. It is

141

not a calculating faculty at all. Inasmuch as to desire is *epithūmein*, and the verb *epithūmein* is clearly associated with the *epithūmētikon*, for Plato desiring something cannot be the same as, or be in part constituted by, believing anything.[6] Nowhere in the Socratic dialogues is Socrates as explicit as Plato about the irrationality of the part of the soul in which we have our desires. In fact, he mentions this part of the soul in *Gorgias*, 493a–b, and says that it 'is liable to be impressionable and persuadable'. This may suggest that it partakes of intelligence. But this is misleading. Elsewhere in the *Gorgias* Socrates speaks of desires in a way that anticipates Plato. 'Now tell me,' he asks Callicles, 'is the life you mean something like feeling hunger and eating when hungry . . . and feeling thirst and drinking when thirsty?' 'Yes,' says Callicles, 'and having all the other desires and being able to satisfy them' (494c). These examples cannot be instances of desire if desiring means believing something. Feeling thirst logically need not be accompanied by the having of beliefs. I earlier emphasized the point that for Socrates there is a necessary connection between a grown man's desiring something and his believing of the object of his desire that it is good. But for Socrates the connection is not one of identity, as the above suggested interpretation would have it. It might be said to be synthetic and necessary, but the necessity is not known *a priori*. It is known *a posteriori*, as a result of familiarity with the workings of the human psyche. It is a psychological generalization, a putative law of human nature. This, I think, is what Socrates would say if he were using post-Kantian terminology.

It is now time to say something about the connection between the first paradox and psychological egoism. The argument in the *Meno* puts the emphasis on *desire for* things, experiences, and states of affairs. But it is easily generalizable to include also *desire to* act. From the generalized versions of premises (2) and (2.0) of the first argument (see p. 136, above) we may infer that a man who knows that performing a certain act is harmful to the agent does not desire to perform it. From the corresponding premises of the second argument we may infer that a man who believes that performing a certain act is harmful to the agent does not desire to perform it. The conjunction of these two conclusions is that a man who knows or believes that performing a certain action is harmful to the agent does not desire to perform it. This is not exactly the same as psychological egoism, but it is very closely related to it. Psychological egoism entails it. Inasmuch as the proposition that is entailed is refuted by our old cigarette example, we have here an argument against psychological egoism that we can add to the catalogue of arguments starting with Butler's well-known critique of psychological egoism.

But there is an even closer tie between psychological egoism and what we find in *Meno* 77b–78b. The root psychological assumption of the three extrapolated arguments is that it is psychologically impossible for a man to desire something and not to believe that it is good. Accordingly, if the object of desire is to do a certain action, then invariably the man who desires to do it believes that it is good. But in the *Meno* if a thing is good then it must be beneficial to its possessor. It follows that a man who has the Socratic concept of good cannot desire to do something unless he believes that it will be to his advantage to do it. From this it follows that a man who acts in the way that he desires to act believes that acting in that way will be of benefit to himself. But to say of a man that he acts in the way that he desires to act is pretty much the same as saying that he acts as he would act if he was not hindered by such things as coercion, lack of tools and materials, sudden paralysis, etc. And this sounds like a fair description of acting voluntarily. If Socrates had this concept of a voluntary act in mind in the *Meno*, then we could say that from assumptions he makes, pychological egoism follows. But in the *Meno* nothing is said to give us a clue as to what Socrates might mean by 'a voluntary act'. So, the most we can say is this. In the *Meno* Socrates makes assumptions that imply psychological egoism, provided that by 'a voluntary act' we understand an act done by a man who acts in the way that he desires to act.

If my reasoning has been correct, then the first argument in the *Meno* in support of the first paradox is unsound. And for basically the same reasons, the second and third arguments are also unsound, though all three are valid deductions. So far, then, the first paradox remains unproved. More than that, I think that what I have said so far shows that the first paradox itself is false. Not all cigarette addicts desire to fill their lungs with dangerous amounts of smoke in the mistaken belief that having a lungful of cigarette smoke is good for you. Some of them know or at least believe strongly that lungfuls of cigarette smoke do no one any good, everything considered.

Much of what I have said so far also vindicates my formulation of the first paradox in terms of the four types of desire and aversion that I distinguished at the beginning of this chapter. The doctrine of *amathia* and its connection with the root psychological assumption that human desires are necessarily accompanied by evaluative beliefs is crucial for understanding the import of the Socratic paradoxes. I stake my rendition of the first Socratic paradox on this crucial point. If to desire something is necessarily accompanied by believing that the thing is good, and if being good necessitates being beneficial to its possessor, then the bare doctrine that no one desires evil and everyone desires what is good is a condensation. What it means is that all human desire for some evil and all human aversion for some good is of type I; and that, therefore, there are no human desires or aversions that are of type III or type IV.

Let us now look at the argument in the *Gorgias* in favor of the first paradox. The argument is at 467c–468e. The argument in the *Meno* is mainly about our desires for things, experiences, and states of affairs. The argument in the *Gorgias* is mainly about our desires to perform actions. I believe that the arguments differ only in emphasis. They have the same import. Socrates wants to prove to us that no one desires any object, experience, or state of affairs that is harmful to him, and no one desires to do anything that is harmful to himself. I was anticipating this point when earlier I suggested that the argument in the *Meno* 77b–78b easily lends itself to being generalized to cover desire to do actions. This is one way of looking at it. Another and equally acceptable view of the matter is this. We can say that the argument in the *Meno* is meant to prove that all human desire for some evil thing, experience, or state of affairs, and all human aversion for some good thing, experience, or state of affairs, is of type I, and that, therefore, there are no human desires and aversions for things, experiences, or states of affairs that are of type III or of type IV. The argument in the *Gorgias* is meant to prove the same to be true of human desires and aversions to do certain actions. Combine these two results and what you get is the first paradox. In both dialogues Socrates is reasonably clear as to what he wants us to believe. Part of his message is that there is a distinction between our misguided desires and our informed desires. A man can misguidedly desire something that is evil, but he cannot informedly desire it. A misguided desire owes its existence to *amathia*. An informed desire is one that persists in the light of knowledge or of true belief about the goodness of the object of desire. Socrates takes it to be a fundamental law of human nature that no man informedly desires to have or to do anything that is harmful to himself.

Here is the argument in the *Gorgias*:

(1)   When a man engages in an action for the sake of something else, it is not the action he desires, but the end and
object of the action (467e).

(2)   Any existing thing is either good, bad, or neither good
nor bad (467e).

(3)   Some actions are neither good nor bad, and by this
is meant that they sometimes partake of the good,
sometimes of the bad, and sometimes of neither
(468a).

(4)   Actions that are neither good nor bad are done for the
sake of the good, i.e., for the sake of benefiting the
agent (468b–c).

∴ (5) We do not desire to perform neutral actions, but we
desire to perform them if they are a means of benefiting
ourselves, and we do not desire to perform them if they
are a means of harming ourselves (468c).

Before we begin to raise doubts about the cogency of this line of
reasoning, we must note certain points. Our English word 'to
desire' admits of a wide range of applications. It is correct to speak
of desiring things and desiring to do this or that action. In the *Meno*
where the arguments place the emphasis on desire for things,
experiences, and states of affairs, the Greek word corresponding to
the verb 'to desire' is *epithūmein*. As a desire for things, *epithūmein*
connotes wanting to possess a number of different sorts of things,
as I tried to explain above. In the *Gorgias* the Greek word is *boulēsis*.
Sometimes this is translated as desire, but more often as *wish*. I
believe that the differences in meaning or nuance between *epithūmein* and *boulēsis* are immaterial to the issue with which I am
immediately concerned. The word 'desire' may be more akin to
*epithūmein* in connoting a stronger craving than does the word
*boulēsis*. But the matter of strength is not the issue. The issue is
whether or not we ever feel some sort of impulsion toward objects,
experiences, states of affairs, and toward actions, that we know or
believe to be hurtful to ourselves.

We ought further to note that by a 'neutral action' Socrates
means something special. He does not mean that the action is in and
of itself neither good nor bad, such as, for example, looking at the
sky at a time when my doing so is purely optional. His meaning is
expressed in line (3) of the argument. But the meaning is not clear.

145

The examples given at 467e of things that are good and their opposites bad are health, wealth, wisdom. One would judge from these examples that a thing is good if, and only if, it is always beneficial to its possessor, or that an action is good if, and only if, its performance on any occasion when one is in a position to do it is a means of benefiting the agent. A neutral thing or action would seem to be one of a kind such that on some occasion possessing such a thing or performing such an action would benefit its possessor or its agent, on other occasions possessing such a thing or performing such an action would harm its possessor or its agent, and on still other occasions would neither benefit nor harm him. If this is a correct reading, then we have in this passage three relational concepts. Something or some action of a certain kind is *good for a person absolutely* if, and only if, on every occasion when one is in a position to possess such a thing or to perform such an action, its possession or performance is beneficial to that person. Something or some action is *good for a person on a certain occasion* if, and only if, on that occasion he benefits from possessing the thing or performing the action. The basic notion is the latter. A thing is good for a person absolutely if, and only if, it is good for him on every occasion when he is in a position to possess the thing or do the action. A thing or action is *neutral for a person* if, and only if, it is good for him on some occasions, bad for him on some other occasions, and neither good for him nor bad for him on still other occasions.

We are now ready to evaluate the argument itself. Some of the premises suggest counter-examples, and this calls for an interpretation of what Socrates means. One may question the first assumption. A man who plays tennis in order to keep fit may also desire to play for the fun of it. One may question (4). This is a restricted form of psychological egoism. According to (4) and the definition of a neutral action that we have elicited from the passage, an action that is neutral would be performed (voluntarily) only on those occasions when the agent believes that the performance will be a means to benefiting him on that occasion. But according to the above definition of a neutral act, looking at the sky might be a neutral action for anyone. Hence, it would on occasion be neither beneficial nor harmful for the person who does the looking. Surely on one such occasion a man may, on impulse and voluntarily, look at the sky without any thought that doing this will be good for him. An interpretation is called for. One is suggested by E. R. Dodds in his book, *Gorgias, A Revised Text with Introduction and Commentary* (Oxford: The Clarendon Press, 1959), p. 235.

(1)   Some activities we pursue as being themselves desired (as ends) and some we pursue only as means to something else. The latter kind of activity is in itself neither good nor bad, but neutral.

(2)   We pursue what is neutral only as a means to what is good. Thus, *all voluntary action is aimed, directly or indirectly, at the presumed good of the agent* (What I have italicized is psychological egoism).

(3)   Therefore, actions which result in harm for the agent do not reflect his will, [are not the actions he desires to perform]. In such cases he does what he thinks best, but not what he desires.

In the terminology that I introduced on p. 144 (3) is saying that actions that result in harm to the agent are prompted by misguided desires. They do not 'reflect' his informed desires.

The crucial difficulty is in line (2). Line (2) in Dodds' interpretation of the argument assumes that psychological egoism is true. But it is in fact a false theory of motivation. The cigarette example proves, to my satisfaction, that not all voluntary action is aimed at the presumed good of the agent. Dodd's interpretation is, I believe, a correct reading of the text, but so interpreted, Socrates' argument is not cogent.

While we are back to the subject of psychological egoism, it is important to note that nowhere in the Socratic dialogues is 'good' used to mean *that which benefits me*. Such a definition would be viciously relativistic. It would make it impossible for anyone but me to mean by the word 'good' what I mean by it. As I pointed out earlier, there are one basic and two derivative relational concepts involving good and bad in the *Gorgias*. None of them is viciously relativistic. It is another kind of difficulty that they create for Socrates. They are factors in his commitment to psychological egoism. The theory of *amathia* and the assumption that being good conceptually necessitates being beneficial to its possessor together entail that no man informedly desires to do anything that is not to his own personal benefit. This is but one step away from psychological egoism. Socrates takes that step explicitly in the *Gorgias* (and by implication in the *Meno* provided that we make a certain assumption about what Socrates means by 'voluntary act') when he says that 'all who do wrong do it against their will' (509e). This amounts to saying that in order to be a voluntary action an action must be done in conformity to one's informed desires. As such desires have for their objective one's own benefit, it follows that all voluntary actions are done with a view to benefiting the agent. This harks back to the argument we have just been examining, the one that starts at 466d. Apparently this is 'the preceding argument' to which Socrates refers at 509e. Socrates seems to think that the earlier argument takes for granted that if we do not desire or wish to perform a certain action, then our performance of it is not voluntary. And he thinks the earlier argument to have proved that we do not desire to perform actions except as they are a means of benefiting ourselves. Thus, it is not just the psychological assumptions of the *Meno* and *Gorgias* that lead to trouble. At least one of the conceptual assumptions (namely, that being good necessitates being beneficial to the one who possesses it) is also unfortunate. For in conjunction with other basic Socratic assumptions it is sufficient to imply psychological egoism. The pervasive psychological egoism of Socrates stands in the way of any sensible qualifications with the help of which the Socratic paradoxes could be acceptably reformulated. There is, thus, in the Socratic dialogues no convincing argument for, and no possibility of sensibly reformulating, the first paradox.

The paradox itself is a bizarre proposition. It sounds incredible. That is why I suppose it and the other Socratic paradoxes are called paradoxes. They are not paradoxes in the technical sense, examples of which are the liar and the Russell paradoxes. They sound incredible, yet they are not 'dead options' in William James' sense. They induce a sort of ambivalence. On the one hand they appear to be plain falsehoods. Everyday experience seems to refute them. On the other hand, it is difficult to believe that a man would decide freely and with open eyes to do something that he knows or believes is harmful to himself, or to desire something that he knows or believes will hurt him. And if that is credible can we really believe that a man would want to be harmed? Surely not, other things being equal. The *ceteris paribus* clause makes all the difference. Its inclusion dispels the air of paradox. There is, however, not the slightest hint that Socrates has any such qualifications in mind. He is definitely committed to the paradox. The facts seem to indicate that people do sometimes desire to be harmed because other things are not equal. We need not invoke abnormal psychology. There appear to be an abundance of instances of people desiring death under torture so as not to give away vital information. One can imagine a man desiring not to have to be in the position of desiring to be tortured to death. But this is a second order desire and its very description presupposes the existence of the first order desire to be harmed.

We cannot avoid the sense of ambivalence by saying that what one wants under one description one does not want under another description. The remedy suggested would have it that a man may desire to prevent the enemy from getting vital information, but that if he described what he desires as wanting to be put to death under torture, it would not be in his nature to desire that. To be sure, the two descriptions are not logically equivalent, but in a given case they may happen to be materially equivalent. In a given set of circumstances a man may be able to prevent the enemy from getting vital information if, and only if, he is killed under torture. Is it psychologically inconceivable that a man may recognize this material equivalence, have so strong a commitment to his cause that he wants to pay the price for safeguarding it, and pay it with no thought of rewards in an afterlife?

But the issue is a bit more complicated. In the Socratic first book of the *Republic* being harmed as a man is equated with being made a worse man than one was before the harm was done. Even so, is it psychologically inconceivable that a man may recognize that in a given situation his cause can be served only by his becoming a worse man, and yet have so strong a commitment to that cause that he wants to serve it by becoming a worse man? A negative answer to this does not seem to be out of order. Other things being equal he does not want to become a worse man. Let us assume that he shares the Socratic conviction that becoming a worse man is inviting personal misfortune. Other things being equal, he certainly does not want to court personal misfortune. But in the case we are imagining other things are not equal.

Again, is it psychologically inconceivable for a man to desire that he should be made a worse man than he is or to remain as bad as he is and thereby invite misery for himself? Can we not imagine circumstances in which a man might desire such a thing? It seems to me that we can. Plato himself provides what appears to be a case in point. In the *Symposium* (215–16) Alcibiades is speaking:

When I heard great orators like Pericles my soul was never

shaken by them, nor was I angry at the thought of my own slavish state. But [Socrates] has often brought me to such a pass that I have felt as if I could not endure the life which I am leading. . . . For he makes me confess that I ought not to live as I do, neglecting the many wants of my own soul and busying myself with the concerns of the Athenians; therefore I hold my ears and tear myself away from him. And he is the only person who ever made me ashamed. . . . For I know that I cannot answer him or say that I ought not to do as he bids, but when I leave his presence the love of popularity gets the better of me.

Here Plato is describing a man who knows better and chooses badly. Alcibiades desires to become a better man and thereby to satisfy 'the many wants of his own soul', but his desire for popularity is stronger. He succumbs to it knowing that he is thereby harming himself. Plato, who often has the clear vision of a great writer, is here depicting a paradigm case of weakness of will – the possibility of which is denied in the Socratic dialogues.

I submit that without a *ceteris paribus* clause the first paradox is a paradox. If we include the *ceteris paribus* clause, it is, I think, a psychological truism. But it is quite evident that it is the paradox and not the truism that Socrates wishes to defend. Given his assumptions that commit him to psychological egoism, the paradox is the only thing that he can consistently defend. If my argument is correct, his defence fails. And it is bound to. There is no defence for falsehoods.[7]

## NOTES

1  The text does not say that (iii) is a definition. But the context suggests that Socrates is thinking of it as a definition.

2  I believe that this is an unexpressed assumption in the argument. It says, in other words, that no one will desire a thing if he believes that it will bring about his possessing something that he does not desire. This is false.

2a  [For readers unfamiliar with symbols of formal logic, a paraphrase of this and the following three formulae may be useful. For this one, understand: ' "$x$ is miserable" is by definition equivalent to "there is something evil which $x$ both desires and obtains" '. Ed.]

2b  ['No one desires that there should be something evil which he both desires and obtains'. Ed.]

2c  ['Everyone desires that, if there is anything evil which he desires, then he should not obtain it'. Ed.]

2d ['Everyone desires that he should neither desire *nor* obtain anything which is evil'. Ed.]

3  We leave out of consideration things that are not ignorant for the reason that they are incapable of cognitive acts. Socrates is talking only about adult human beings in whom cognitions are actualized.

4  We have noted that at *Meno* 77e Socrates speaks of those who are ignorant (*agnoountes*) of the evil in what they desire and in their ignorance believe the evil to be good. Although a word other than *amathia* is being used for ignorance, it is clear that the kind of ignorance Socrates is here talking about is exactly the same as what he calls *amathia* in the *Protagoras*. Incidentally, neither Greek word means exactly what Socrates makes it mean. What is important is to note that he makes them mean the same thing. Moral ignorance is not absence of belief but the presence of false belief about the goodness or badness of things.

5  A thing can benefit a man by (a) benefiting him some ways and harming him in none, (b) benefiting him in some ways and harming him other ways, (i) the benefits outweighing the harm, (ii) the harm outweighing the benefits. It is only this last, namely, (b) (ii), that Socrates would not count as benefiting a man. The idea is that of something benefiting a man *on the whole*, and this can happen only in the manner of (a) or of (b) (i).

6  The desires that are characteristic of the *epithūmētikon* are different from the desires of the rational element in the soul. Reason's desire for the good is rooted in reason's knowledge of the difference between good and evil. The 'impulses which draw and drag' are brute affections whose objects can be evaluated by reason alone. A bodily desire is subject to reason's assessment.

7  I am grateful to my departmental colleagues Thomas Kearns and, especially, Paul Eisenberg for their thoughtful criticisms of an earlier version of this essay. I am indebted to my university colleague, Professor Fred Householder, for his expert opinion on the contours and nuances of key words in Greek.

# INQUIRY

*Nicholas P. White*

## I

As some philosophers know, the paradox about inquiry at 80d–e of Plato's *Meno* is more than a tedious sophism. Plato is one such philosopher.[1] The puzzle is an obstacle to his project of discovering definitions, and is introduced as such (80d1–6). And it is met with an elaborate response: the theory of recollection, explicitly presented as an answer to the obstacle (esp. 81c–e). But then what of the famous conversation in which Socrates coaxes a geometrical theorem from a slave-boy (82bff)? Is the theory not designed to explain the boy's ability to respond to the coaxing? It is, certainly, but that is not its only purpose.[2] The structure of the pasage is this: the theory is there to disarm the paradox, and the conversation is there to support the theory. To see this structure is to understand a notorious and otherwise troubling fact, that Plato is so very quick to take the slave's behaviour – which he might have tried to explain in some other way – to be clear evidence for recollection. The reason why he so takes it is that the paradox has led him to think that only if recollection occurs is fruitful inquiry possible – and he is very anxious indeed to be assured that it *is* possible. He would not have been so enticed by explanations of the boy's behaviour which did not also seem to him to dispose of the puzzle.

Here now is Plato's setting of the paradox:

> *Meno*: But in what way will you inquire after (*zētēseis*) something such that you do not know what it is? What sort of thing, among those things which you do not know, will you set up beforehand as the object of your search? Or to put it otherwise, even if you happen to come right upon it, how will you know that it is that which you did not know?

152

*Socrates*: I understand, Meno, what you mean. Do you see how contentious the argument is which you are introducing, that it is not possible to inquire either after that which one knows or that which one does not know? He would not need to inquire after that which he knows, since he knows it and there is no need of inquiry for such a thing, nor after what he does not know, since he does not know what he is inquiring after.

His exposition is brisk, so we must try to see the nature of the difficulty which he faces.[3] As he presents the problem, we are engaged in an effort to 'know' a thing, and the effort is pictured as, in a fairly literal sense, a search for the thing, i.e. as an attempt to *find* a thing and *recognize* it as what we were searching for.[4] But, we are told, if we do not already 'know' the thing, we shall be unable to recognize it (80d7–8), whereas if we do already 'know' it, then we have nothing further to do. Of course, an obvious reply is that we could be in a position of not yet having found the object, but of nevertheless being able to recognize it when we do. If you like, we might 'know' it in one sense but not (yet) in another. Plato, however, does not take this way out, and we need to see why.

The essential point is that although Plato does think of the effort to 'know' an object as a kind of search for it, that is not the only way in which he thinks of it. He is also thinking of it as an effort to say 'what the object is', i.e., to produce a certain sort of definition or specification of it (esp. 79e5–6, 80d4). It is this sort of attempt that he has in mind when he says that if we can recognize the object, then we already 'know' it. Accordingly, one line of interpretation is to say that Plato has inadvertently conflated two projects: 1) the project of looking for something already specified, and 2) the project of discovering a specification of something. He supposes that we need to find a specified object, but then supposes that the need must have been fulfilled, provided merely that we possess a specification by which we may recognize what we are after. Nor is it impossible that Plato has made such a conflation. For both in early works like the *Meno* and later in the *Republic*, he tends not to mark a clear distinction between – so to put it – gaining a definition of an object (as he thinks of the matter), and getting the object itself somehow into one's 'ken' or mental 'view'.[5] Moreover at 80d7–8, the crucial suggestion, that if you do not already 'know' a thing you will not be able to recognize it, is presented utterly without argument or explanation.[6]

Such a conflation becomes more understandable when one realizes that specifications come in different varieties. Very roughly (cf. n. 10), we can say that some specifications are such that one can tell, simply by examining an object, whether or not it fits the specification. 'The man sitting in the market-place', e.g., might be taken to be such a specification. But other specifications, such as 'my long-lost brother', are presumably not of this roughly demarcated sort. I can obviously initiate an effort 'to see my long-lost brother' even if I do not yet know what he looks like, and have no specification of the former type. What I hope, of course, is that I can subsequently find a description of him by which I *can* recognize him, and that can be shown to be co-referential with the specification, 'my long-lost brother', with which I began. Pretty clearly, however, Plato is leaving this second sort of specification out of account, and if one does so, then it is perhaps not too difficult to fall into thinking that finding an object is not much of a task once one has the specification (especially if the object is thought of as being near at hand or readily 'brought to mind'), and thence into the conflation of search for object and search for specification.

But is Plato subject to this degree of confusion? Perhaps not, since he may have an argument up his sleeve for the crucial move at 80d7–8. Though I shall not attempt to settle the question here (cf. n. 3), the supposition that he does have such an argument gives us more to deal with than a case of mere inadvertence on his part. So let us turn to an interpretation based on that supposition. You are told that if you do not already 'know' the object of your search, you will not be able to recognize it. Why not? Because, the argument goes, you must begin your search with a specification of what you are trying to find, in order to recognize it. But how do you know that the specification accurately describes the object in question? Only, the account continues, by examining the object to see that it does (cf. n. 8). But to do this you must find the object. But for this you need the specification. And so on. (Nor will it help to suppose that you might begin without a complete specification, but with some information constituting part of one; for again the argument says that you must examine the object to check whether the information is correct). So either you must already have examined the object and can describe it, or you will never be able to do either.

Although this argument raises obvious qualms, let us postpone them to consider why we might want to attribute at least a dim awareness of it to Plato. First, it neatly explains, in an obvious way, why recollection might have seemed to Plato such an attractive response to the paradox. Second, it dovetails with other facts about the early dialogues. As I have said, Plato betrays interest both in finding definitions and in 'viewing' or 'looking to' objects which he sometimes calls Forms.[7] But trouble threatens because of the way in which he connects these two projects. Sometimes he says that a purpose of finding a definition is to help us 'look to' such an object (*Euthyphro* 6d–e). At other times (e.g., *Meno* 72c6–d1; cf. *Laches* 190c6), he appears to say that it is by 'looking to' the object that we shall discover the correct definition.[8] Combining these two ideas obviously could lead to saying that we both need to look to the object before we have a reliable definition, and also need to have a reliable definition before we find the object. But this is just the trouble which the paradox, on this account, yields; so perhaps in *Meno* 80d–e Plato is attacking a problem arising out of his own work. Moreover the point can be strengthened by the reflection that the paradox can be seen as an extension of a similar difficulty already touched upon in the *Meno*. At 71b, Plato has distinguished between asking 'what' (*ti*) a thing is and asking 'what it is like' (*poion*), and has maintained that we cannot know what a thing is like until we know what it is – e.g., that we cannot know whether Meno is wealthy until we know who he is. But why not? Why could we not know on good authority (e.g., on Plato's) that Meno is wealthy without in any plausible sense knowing 'who he is'? The answer is that Plato believes that to know that Meno is wealthy we have to find and examine him, so as to see that he is; for otherwise we are simply relying on hearsay, and thus on less than fully 'direct' evidence.[9] But to find him, we need a specification enabling us to recognize him, and in that sense telling us who he is. But if this requirement is applied not only to *poion*-information but also to *ti*-information, then we have our paradox.

## II

In the sort of inquiry concerning us, the inquirer is trying *inter alia* to bring an object into his 'ken', in some sense, and to recognize it. The puzzle arises because he is said to need to examine the object to see whether his specification actually fits it. This need arises because the possibility is left open that his specification may be incorrect. So it is tempting to say right away that when one is seeking a thing in this manner, one's inquiry is, as it were, *defined* by the specification with which one begins, and that one is searching for *whatever* it is that fits that specification. One *could* not, then, be seeking something which does not fit it. This is, I think, the kernel of the solution of the puzzle. But this solution is not gained without a price, and we must see what that price is. I begin by developing this solution, and shall then explain what its cost is.

We must start with an account of what it is for a specification to be, as I shall say, an 'initially usable specification' for the framing of an inquiry or search of our sort. We have seen that one's initial specification may not itself be one by which one can, in any reasonable sense, *recognize* the object when one encounters it. So our account must allow, e.g., for the case in which I begin an effort to see someone with the specification 'my long-lost brother,' unassociated initially with any description of his 'visible' features, and then later discover that that specification picks out the same thing as some other specification which does describe 'visible' features, and which I can use to recognize the thing when I see it. (But notice that the following account will not be limited to efforts to recognize things by sight, or even by sense; cf. n. 10.)

What we must say, I think, is roughly this. A singular term $S$ is an initially usable singular specification for our sort of inquiry if and only if there is a singular term $T$ which we can in some sense find, which denotes something which can be in some sense brought into one's 'ken', and which satisfies the following conditions: $T$ must be such that

(a) we shall be able somehow to tell, upon examination (in the relevant sense) of a given object, whether or not $T$ denotes it,

(b) we shall be able to tell that $T$ is co-referential with $S$.

In supposing, then, that 'my long-lost brother' is an initially usable specification for an inquiry of this sort, we are supposing that somehow we may find a specification which is co-referential with it, and which we can determine to be met, or not to be met, by objects as they present themselves.[10] But there are also many inquiries which must be framed by means of expressions not of the form '*the* so-and-so', but of the form '*a* so–and so', i.e. by a general term. Thus, I can search for 'a long-lost brother of mine', where I do not care which one(s), or how many, I find. By analogy to the foregoing, then, a general term $S$ is an initially usable general specification just in case there is a general term $T$ which we can find, which is true of something which one can bring into one's 'ken', and which satisfies the following conditions: $T$ must be such that

(c) we shall be able somehow to tell, by examining an object, whether or not $T$ is true of it,

(d) we shall be able to tell that $S$ is true of everything of which $T$ is true.

I am well aware that numerous difficulties, requiring discussion all their own, are raised by these conditions, but I think that their basic thrust and motivation are clear.[11]

These conditions are not meant to cover all inquiries. For clearly some inquiries are not naturally construed as efforts to bring objects into one's 'ken'. Thus, many would not think of an effort to, as we say, 'discover a proof' of Goldbach's conjecture as literally an effort somehow to recognize an object which is the proof (cf. n. 10). I am willing to leave such recalcitrant inquiries aside (though remember that Plato allows more of them than others might). But notice that one could hope to claim that all inquiries *are*, or else in some sense, *are 'equivalent to'*, inquiries which fall under the above conditions.[12] Someone might claim, e.g., that the effort to 'discover a proof' of Goldbach's conjecture is, or is equivalent to, an effort to write down and recognize tokens of such a proof, where this effort is framed by the general term 'token of a proof of Goldbach's conjecture'. Of course this presentation is all very informal, but again the motivation and spirit are plain, and I shall not elaborate the idea further here.

Given our contentions (a)–(d), what shall we count as the successful completion of an inquiry? For brevity let me treat only inquiries which are framed by singular terms, since they present the most difficulty. Let us say roughly that the completion of an inquiry is the bringing into one's 'ken' (the 'finding', if you will) of an object denoted by some appropriate singular term $T$ fulfilling conditions (a) and (b), recognizing it as such, and showing that $T$ and one's original specification, $S$, are co-referential. The leading idea is that an inquiry is consummated by the finding of *whatever* object proves, whether directly or indirectly (in the cases, respectively, in which $S$ and $T$ are identical or distinct) to be denoted by one's initial specification. It is this idea which constituted our suggested way of avoiding Plato's puzzle.

## III

But problems arise immediately. The first is best introduced by an example. Suppose that in our current theory of the world we conceive an inquiry framed by a singular term $S$. Perhaps our current theory will itself provide our co-referential term $T$ and allow us to recognize our quarry. But perhaps it will not. We may need what, by some reasonable standard for individuating theories, is a new theory, and indeed we may have good reason at the start to think that we will. Since we must deal with more than one theory, however, we shall then have to face the problems of inter-theoretic translation that Quine has made notorious recently.[13] In order to determine that we have successfully completed our inquiry, we shall have to pass on the co-referentiality of terms in different theories (or, in the case of inquiries framed by general terms, on the overlap of one extension by another). But if Quine is correct that such questions are in a sense indeterminate, and can be answered only relative to a manual – arbitrarily chosen, to some extent – for translating one theory into another, then there will often be an indeterminacy in whether or not a given inquiry has been, or will be, successfully completed.

I would not myself want to claim that practical difficulty will generally arise on this account, though it might occasionally. Nor am I inclined, myself, to see here any crippling theoretical difficulty. For it is not clear to me just what the disadvantage is of being unable to say with utter finality that a certain discovery completes just *that* particular inquiry, and it is not clear that we cannot live with the idea that, in a certain sense, we make up our inquiries as we go along.[14]

But nevertheless the indeterminacy produces a sense of unease. For example, suppose that your inquiry is taken as framed by the phrase 'my spouse,' and that in the course of your search some radical change occurs in your general theory of the world. (You may imagine that the change is quite irrelevant to the search, or else that your spouse has been hidden by a physicist through the means of some ingenious new technology whose secret you must unravel.) Do we really want to say that whether you have found your spouse is indeterminate? Even if there is no practical difficulty, many will feel that even an indeterminacy in principle is undesirable. One might try to escape by denying our supposition that one's initial specification may be different from the one which one finally uses for recognition, but this course seems clearly wrong (and anyway troubles over inter-theoretic translation could still arise). The only course, then, unless one can rebut the relevant claim of indeterminacy, is to pin the blame on the supposition that inquiries are defined by specifications which frame them, and that whatever fulfils the specification is what the inquiry is after.

To deny this supposition is to say that when we search for something we search for, so to speak, *a particular thing*, and not for *whatever* satisfies a certain description. On this view, what defines an inquiry is its connection with a certain *object*, regardless of any specification, so that difficulties of translating specifications can be ignored. The idea can be developed further, too, by means of distinctions like K. Donnellan's between 'referential' and 'attributive' uses of definite descriptions.[15] For him, an attributive use of 'the *F*' is one in which it refers, if at all, to whatever is uniquely *F*, while a referential use of it is one in which it may refer to something else. In this terminology, the notion of inquiry which we are considering says that inquiries are framed by referential uses of descriptions or specifications, and will thus be concerned 'with the thing itself and not just the thing under a certain description'.

But if we adopt this view of our sort of inquiry, then we seem certain to be caught in our paradox again. For this view allows the possibility that an inquirer may not 'know what he is looking for', in the sense that he cannot be sure that his way of framing his inquiry correctly describes what he is allegedly after. But this fact raises the necessity for him (and, equally damaging, for anyone else) somehow to find the object of his search, to examine it, and to see whether or not the specification fits it. But if we need a specification to find the object, then we have our paradox.

Can we avoid trouble by denying that our inquiries must begin with a specification of what they are after? No, for then there would be nothing to distinguish between merely coming across something and finding something *for which one had been searching*, and this consequence could hardly be welcome to one who bridles at the problem of indeterminacy latent in the other view of inquiry. What gives sense to the idea that one has found what one was looking for is, at best, that there was previously a specification governing one's search. This is the reason why, when a person enters a lost-and-found, the manager of the place is well-advised to ask what he is after, rather than simply letting him poke about and claim what he pleases. This is *not* to say that we must always insist that an inquirer be immediately ready to produce a specification. In many situations, where there is no need to be on guard, we may dispense with demanding one,[16] though the more we want to ferret out bogus findings, the more strict we shall be (cf. sec. V). Quite aside, then, from any questions about how we are to *tell* that there is a specification or what it is, the point is simply that somehow there must *be* one if there is to be a genuine inquiry of our sort.[17]

So paradox arises if we try to frame an inquiry with a description which is referentially construed in Donnellan's sense. What, then, about framing inquiries with proper names? Clearly there is no problem if names are construed as 'disguised descriptions', in the manner of Russell and others,[18] so long as those descriptions are not referential in Donnellan's sense. But 'logically proper names', as Russell thought of them,[19] cannot themselves frame an inquiry. For by themselves they provide no way of recognizing what they name, except on one condition, which is that one be in the presence of the object and somehow be told, as it were, '*That* is what the name stands for'. But if one is in this circumstance, then search is pointless.[20] (Thus we have a new way of engendering paradox, by picturing inquiry as beginning with a term whose denotation can supposedly be recognized only by having it somehow pointed out to one – which shows that such terms cannot be used to frame fruitful inquiries.) And of course if there should be anything which can be specified *only* by a proper name, then one could never inquire after it in our sense.[21]

I emphasize, however, that I am not making, here, any general claim about *reference* or *denotation*.[22] Thus, I am not concerned now with the dispute between Russell and Donnellan, e.g., over whether a singular description may refer to something other than whatever may satisfy its encapsulated predicate, nor with the question whether an ordinary proper name like 'Socrates' must be somehow 'backed up' by a singular description.[23] I am simply concerned with what we must have on hand to launch an inquiry or search. I believe, however, that some advocates of construing descriptions roughly as Russell does, or of 'backing up' proper names with descriptions, have been motivated in part by the consideration that it would be *desirable* to be able, in appropriate cases, to search successfully for the denotations of such expressions.[24]

The moral to be drawn, then, is that for inquiries of our sort we must choose between paradox on the one hand and indeterminacy on the other. I see no middle ground. Given these alternatives, the sensible choice seems to me to be the indeterminacy. At least we can then console ourselves with the reflection that the insistence on beginning an inquiry with a specification preserves something of the notion of finding what one was looking for, and I doubt that we can attain more.

## IV

Although I have talked thus far quite generally about efforts to bring objects into one's 'ken' and recognize them, Plato is concerned particularly with a special sort of inquiry, which has to do with objects which he tended to think of as 'Forms'. This concern has been inherited by modern philosophers, in the form of a concern with 'analysis' and the like. One sometimes hears it suggested that certain sorts of analysis or definition are immune to the paradox of the *Meno*, so long as they are cast in the formal mode and are of the form 'Expression *E* means the same as expression *F*' instead of the form '*X* is the same thing as *Y*'. At the same time, however, there is another paradox, the paradox of analysis, which strikes one as similar to the paradox of the *Meno*,[25] but which afflicts analyses which are squarely in the formal mode. A brief comment on this state of affairs will bring issues into clearer focus.

What reason is there for thinking that Plato's paradox is avoided by the move to the formal mode? Simply that whereas Plato's effort to discover what virtue is, say, can be relatively easily construed as an attempt to find and recognize an object, virtue, we have seen that other inquiries are not naturally so regarded (sec. II), and in the view of many modern philosophers the effort to discover 'what the *word* "virtue" *means*' is one such. But as long as we do not view inquiry as a search for an object, then the paradox of the *Meno*, in its fully pristine form, cannot arise.[26]

What, then, of the paradox of analysis? Is it the same problem as our paradox of inquiry? Two factors militate against a straight-forward answer: the fact that there are many versions of the paradox of analysis, and the fact that standards of identity and distinctness for paradoxes are imprecise and probably not worth sharpening. Still, we can make a few observations.

One version of the paradox of analysis argues that a statement of the analysis can mean no more than something of the platitudinous form '*A* is *A*', and goes on to claim that analyses must therefore be trivial, and perhaps be known as soon as the corresponding platitudes are. Another version is directed against a notion of analysis which views its aim as the 'grasping' or 'apprehension' (or otherwise 'bringing into one's ken' and recognizing) of an object which is the meaning of a certain expression, the *analysandum*. Such a version might say that the mere understanding of a request for analysis, or the claim that a particular analysis is needed, requires the very apprehension of that object which the analysis was supposed to provide. These versions involve certain notions, of meaning and understanding, which are absent from our puzzle as it stands, and that in itself is an important point of difference.

Another point of difference might appear at first sight to be the following. The crucial move in our puzzle is to raise an obstacle to our *recognition* of the thing at which, as it were, our inquiry was directed, and it tries to show that if we can *tell* that we are at the end of our search, then the search was unnecessary to begin with. Most versions of the paradox of analysis, on the other hand, have a slightly different structure. For although they usually argue, as does our puzzle, that a certain effort is unnecessary if it is possible, their way of so arguing has not typically invoked a problem about how to *tell* when we have successfully concluded our analysing, but rather a problem about what the conditions must be for the analysing to get started, involving the understanding of the task, or of the meaning of what one must start with, or the like. Still, there can be exceptions, since one may formulate the paradox of analysis by asking how one can tell that a putative analysis is correct, and go on to argue in one way or another that if one can tell this, then one had no need of the analysis in the first place.

## V

Plato believes that his theory of recollection answers his puzzle. Let me now argue that he is wrong. I have two reasons for so doing. First, of the fair number of philosophers with whom I have discussed this issue, sober men all, about half have confessed to some amount of sympathy with Plato's belief. So the point is less uncontroversial than one might think. But, second, Plato's view is of itself an ingenious one, deserving attention, particularly because it helps us to see some important and little noticed facts about both recollection and inquiry.

Plato seems to hold that what ordinarily appears to be successful inquiry is actually successful effort at recollection, i.e. inquiry concerning what we already know.[27] In fact, he goes a little farther, since he apparently believes not merely that all *successful inquiry* is recollection, but also that all *learning* must be so. But it is only the former to which his paradox is relevant. The whole difficulty there has to do with *recognizing* what one comes across to be *what one was after*. Nothing in 80d–e, under any possible interpretation, prevents us from saying that we can learn, or acquire new knowledge.[28] So perhaps Plato has fashioned an answer which is a bit too large for his problem.[29]

But does his answer really meet his problem at all? I have said that I do not think so, but let me make it quite clear what I am maintaining. I am not, I emphasize, quarrelling with the notion of recollection, or even, here, with the idea that we recollect Platonic Forms. For all that it concerns my present point, perhaps we do. But right now I am merely saying that the claim that we recollect, as Plato uses it, cannot, by itself, solve his paradox.

The first step is this: even given Plato's attempted solution, we are confronted with a new puzzle roughly analogous to his, which shows recollection to be no less paradoxical than *de novo* inquiry. Briefly, the problem is as follows:

> You will not of course attempt to recollect what you have already recollected, since you have no need to. But how will you attempt to recollect a thing of which you have merely unrecollected knowledge? What sort of thing, among those things of which you have only unrecollected knowledge, will you set up as the object of your search? Or to put it otherwise, even if you happen to come right upon it, how will you know that it is that of which you had merely unrecollected knowledge?

Not, of course, that this is a serious problem for us, since it rests on analogues of the moves which we have seen to be mistaken. Remember that we had two accounts of Plato's puzzle (sec. I). By analogy to the first, the mistake in this new puzzle would be a conflation of an attempt to recollect a specified object and an attempt to recollect a specification. By analogy to the second, the mistake would be the refusal to allow an attempt to recollect to be defined by the specification which frames it.[30]

The point to grasp is that there is neither more nor less reason to make either of these two mistakes in the case of recollection than there was in the case of *de novo* inquiry. In particular, there is no reason to allow an attempt at recollecting to be defined by a specification while withholding the same privilege from inquiry. But if recollection and inquiry are treated analogously, then either recollection is subject to the new paradox and so cannot be used to avoid the old one, or else there is no difficulty over inquiry which recollection can be invoked to solve. Recollection, therefore, helps to solve no pertinent puzzle. Notice the structure of this argument. It is *not* that we can defend inquiry in such a way that we do not *need* to identify it with recollection. (Thus, it is not analogous in structure to a certain one of Locke's arguments against innate ideas, that they are not necessary to explain the data; see the *Essay Concerning Human Understanding*. I, i, 1 and 3.) Rather, it is that granted the parallelism between recollection and inquiry, *if* recollection is immune to the new paradox, then by parity of reasoning, inquiry is immune to the old paradox, and therefore *there is no* paradox of inquiry for recollection to be called upon to solve.

But *should* we be granted the analogy between recollection and inquiry? According to Plato's defender, we should not. For he says that unlike inquiry, recollection does not require a specification at the start. His reason – and he might, as we shall see, claim that it is supported by the facts of experience – is that in the case of recollection both the object recollected *and* the specification can be recalled simultaneously, as when you cannot remember what you were looking for, but suddenly and simultaneously both come upon what you were seeking and remember that it was what you were seeking. Surely there is no specification here, beyond the plainly quite vacuous 'the thing for which I was looking'. But since you cannot correspondingly go hunting *de novo* for 'the thing for which I *am* looking', therefore we must, the defender concludes, admit an irreducible difference between recollection and *de novo* inquiry, so that the former may be possible even where the latter is not.

This is wrong. There is no justification for such a double standard. We have already seen why inquiry must start with a more or less fixed specification, and the same reasons apply to recollection and serve the same ends: to allow a distinction between purposed and merely adventitious recollection, and between genuine and bogus claims of purposed recollection. (Note that the case of the dishonest visitor to the lost-and-found involves a certain sort of claim of recollection: 'Those are my diamonds – I remember them perfectly!') But the point here is not even that specifications are always required. It is the weaker point that they are required for recollection *neither more nor less than* for inquiry, and that if one does not want a way of distinguishing between genuine and bogus recollection, it would seem overly demanding to insist upon an analogous distinction for *de novo* inquiry.

But the defender's point is perhaps not that we *ought* not to want a single standard for both recollection and inquiry, but rather that applying such a stringent standard to recollection would make it, as we know it, impossible. For specificationless recollection often *seems* to occur. Thus, suppose that you are in the market-place, knowing that you were to meet one of your acquaintances, but not remembering who it was. Thus, it seems, no specification. But suddenly a familiar figure approaches; your mind 'clicks'; and you say to yourself, 'Socrates!' If we insist on an initial specification, are we not in danger of denying that this familiar sort of case is in fact a case of reliable recall?

One point in reply is that this sort of case is not one which Plato could envision as providing an answer to his puzzle. For this case presupposes that a project of inquiry has *previously* been framed, by means of some such specification as 'the snub-nosed philosopher'. This fact was recovered by recollection.   But in Plato's sort of case, there is no earlier specification to be retrieved.[31]

Much more important, however, is that in fact we do *not* in this case start out without a specification. For there are *two* attempts to recollect going on here. In one, which began some time before, the aim is, speaking loosely, Socrates. In the other it is, loosely again, a correct answer to the question 'For whom was I looking?'. Certainly the latter is framed by a specification. Moreover it is what I have called an initially usable specification, which can be determined to be satisfied. For we know from past experience that our sudden feelings or 'clicks' of recollection are usually accurate, especially when accompanied by a memory of the circumstances in which the inquiry was earlier formulated. Moreover our feelings can be confirmed, in those cases in which we have earlier confided our project to another. It is largely thus that we have any faith in this sort of feeling, since we would have lacked faith had people generally said, '*That*'s not what you said you were looking for!' in those cases when the 'click' of recollection occurred. At any rate, once this recollection has been performed, we have recalled the specification framing the other effort, the search for Socrates, that we can proceed to carry out forthwith. And of course it may take no time at all to carry out if he is present (as he will be in the case in which the sight of him helps to cause the recollection of the specification framing the search for him). So no specificationless recollection is required here.

I see one further potential line of defence of Plato's position. It is to say that since recollection is a 'private', 'mental' sort of thing, there is *no point* in requiring a specification in order to distinguish between genuine and bogus efforts at recall. For a person may *say* that he has called up an image of his kindergarten teacher, though he has actually brought to mind an image of, say, John Dewey; and no amount of specifying in advance what he was going to recollect will ever help us to detect the fraud. This fact, says the defender, jibes with the fact that we often, quite without anyone else's corroboration, can be utterly certain that we have correctly remembered a certain face.

But the defence fails. Quite aside from broader issues over the notion of the 'mental' and the 'private', there are two replies. The more limited one is that inquiry too may involve the calling up of something 'private'. Take, for example, a person's attempt to call up a mental image – his first ever – of an octagon, where he has never seen an octagon before, and must extrapolate from what he has seen of hexagons, squares, and the like. There is neither more nor less difficulty in checking up on him here than in the case involving the recollection of the kindergarten teacher, and ordinary standards accord equal right to subjective feelings of certainty in both. So we have here no defence of recollection *per se* as against inquiry *per se*.

Still, the defence makes us realize that there are two types each of recollection and inquiry. In one sense, I can 'recollect Socrates' by calling up a 'mental picture' of him and recognizing it as a mental picture of him; in another sense, I can recollect him by seeing him on the street and recognizing him as Socrates. Likewise, I can try to think what, on the basis of my information, Socrates will look like; or I can go trying to find the man himself.[32]

But even if we say that recollection can involve calling up something 'private', we have a second reply to the defence, which is that in the cases which plainly interest Plato, and which normally interest us, the *object* which we are to recollect is *not* 'private'. In the case involving the kindergarten teacher, the recollection must, if successful, be *accurate*. (Saying what the accuracy consists in, of course, is a general problem about the mentalistic notions which we are employing, and we may leave it aside.) And of course in theory there are checks upon its accuracy, since in theory we could find the teacher, or photographs, or whatnot. But the possibility of checking obviously depends upon the existence of a specification, since it alone can tell *us* what to find to check against what the putative recollector tells us about the image which he has called up. Thus, the specification is still crucial to distinguishing successful attempts to recollect, and both of these from the random flow of memory-images. Of course, the same point applies to inquiries of the analogous sort, since they too aim at accuracy. Once again, recollection and inquiry are on a par. Moreover even if one admits cases in which the object to be recalled *is* a 'private' object (e.g., the mood I was in last Sunday), there are analogous cases of inquiry having to do with equally 'private' objects (e.g., in the case of my attempt to put myself into, and recognize, the most befuddled state I have ever been in).

I therefore see no grounds for treating recollection and inquiry differently from each other, and thus no grounds for thinking that recollection can provide a solution of Plato's puzzle.

## NOTES

1 A mistranslation of '*eristikon*' at 80e2 has helped to foster the idea that Plato does not take the paradox seriously. There is no reason to render the word here by 'sophistical'; it means simply 'contentious' or 'obstructionist' (cf. *Lysis* 211b8, *Sophist* 225c9 with a2). Furthermore when Socrates is made to say at 81a1–3 that the paradox is 'not well taken' (*ou kalōs legetai*), he does not mean that it is sophistical or foolish, but only that it does not establish what it claims to, namely that fruitful inquiry in all senses is impossible.

2 See J. M. E. Moravcsik, 'Learning and recollection', G. Vlastos, (ed.), *Plato I: Metaphysics and Epistemology* (New York, 1971), pp. 53–69 [reprinted in this volume, pp. 112–28. Ed.], esp. pp. 56, 63 [pp. 115, 121–2. Ed.].

3 I shall be unable here to treat the many rival accounts of the paradox and of Plato's theory of recollection – e.g., those of Moravcsik and of

Vlastos, '*Anamnesis* in the *Meno*', *Dialogue* IV (1965), pp. 143–67 [reprinted in this volume, pp. 88–111. Ed.]. Also, the issues raised here are intimately connected with issues arising elsewhere in Plato's works, and to a large extent the present interpretation of the puzzle in the *Meno* cannot be argued for fully here, since much of its support lies in the way in which it links the *Meno* to other Platonic concerns. (I would not deny, moreover, that with varying degrees of exegetical latitude, any number of different puzzles can be read into 80d–e, taken in isolation.) I hope to fill this lacuna and others in this paper with a full-scale account of Plato's epistemology [see now N. White, *Plato on Knowledge and Reality* (Indianapolis, 1976) for further discussion of the *Meno* in this broader context. Ed.].

4 It seems to me that no faithful interpretation can blink at this fact, which is ensured by 80d7–8. I do not think that we can rest content with interpretations, such as Moravcsik's (p. 57) [pp. 115–16 here. Ed.], which suppose that Plato intended a difference between Meno's formulation of the puzzle (d5–8) and Socrates's (e1–5), since this supposition leaves it quite unexplained why he never mentions the fact, and thenceforth acts as though he has only one difficulty to face. What Socrates does is simply to make clear that Meno's puzzle can be cast in the form of a dilemma.

5 See, e.g., R. M. Hare, 'Plato and the mathematicians', R. Bambrough (ed.), *New Essays on Plato and Aristotle* (New York, 1965), pp. 21–38, and Vlastos, p. 165 [p. 103 here. Ed.], and Moravcsik, pp. 68–9 [p. 127 here. Ed.].

6 Or is Plato to be acquitted of the conflation by the reply that Forms are of such a nature that somehow there is *no* distinction to be drawn between acquiring a definition and 'viewing' the corresponding Form? Even if this idea should appear in later works, it plainly does not figure in the *Meno*, and I shall ignore it here (cf. n. 3).

7 'Look to' here renders '*apoblepein (pros)*', as in *Euthyphro* 6e4 and *Meno* 72c8; 'view' represents '*theasthai*', not used in early works, but common in the *Republic* (e.g., 518c10, 526e6; cf. also 511a1, etc.). It has been observed to me by Prof. J. Hintikka that the issues which arise here are connected with matters which he discusses in, e.g., his 'Knowledge by acquaintance – individuation by acquaintance', D. F. Pears (ed.,), *Bertrand Russell: A Collection of Critical Essays* (New York, 1972), pp. 52–79.

8 It is of both historical and philosophical interest that the idea of a need to examine a thing in order to check on the correctness of a putative specification or definition has its roots, as I believe, in the quasi-sceptical attitude apparently adopted by Socrates toward popular or received opinion, and toward any other information which is not gained somehow first hand (see, e.g., *Crito* 47a–d; *Gorgias* 472b–c, 474a–b, 475e–476a; and, perhaps with more fully Platonic material, *Meno* 97b1–2; *Phaedo* 82e3–4, 83a–b). An analogous point applies to what will emerge *infra* concerning the *ti/poion* distinction.

9 This point can be taken to show that Plato views the context 'knows that . . .' as referentially transparent – in the sense discussed by W. V.

Quine, *Word and Object* (New York, 1960), pp. 141 ff, – presumably because Plato is oblivious to the distinction between contexts which are referentially transparent and those which are not. For on this interpretation he is in effect imposing upon statements of the form '*S* knows that *a* is *F*' conditions similar to ones which some would place instead upon statements of the form 'Concerning *a*, *S* knows that it is *F*'.

10 Pressed further, this account would presumably require something like a distinction between observational and non-observational terms (though I am unhappy with this distinction). Note, however, that I have left it *completely* open what counts as 'observation' or 'examination', and have insisted upon no limitation to *sensory* observation. The reason is that for our present exegetical purposes, we need to accommodate inquiries concerning such things as Platonic Forms. (This point prompts the remark that even a quite non-empiricist stance can require some distinction between 'observable' and 'non-observable' features, even though this distinction is generally thought of in connection with sensory observation.)

11 Here are some of the problems. First, we need to know what it is to 'examine' an object, and to 'get it into one's ken'. Next, the account employs modal notions requiring explanation. Third, it turns out on my account that 'the present king of France' and 'unicorn', e.g., are not initially usable specifications. Here, the appearance of problematicality is dispelled, I think, once one realizes that for a specification to fail of initial usability is not for it to be incoherent or meaningless. A fourth problem concerns objects which no longer exist, since my account presumably would not allow 'the greatest philosopher of the fifth century' to be initially usable now, at least on a certain meaning for 'can' in 'can be brought into one's ken'. But perhaps the most serious consequence of the account arises from the indeterminacy which will be discussed shortly. For on certain ways of treating that indeterminacy, it can be indeterminate whether or not a given term is an initially usable specification for a search or inquiry. While I think that *if* this is a problem, then it is an important and serious one, I am not inclined to think that it *is* a problem. But the question whether or not it is a problem *is* a problem, and too large a one to be dealt with here.

12 This claim could be made for various reasons, and with various senses of 'equivalent'. This issue is plainly linked with questions surrounding verificationism, operationism, and related 'isms'.

13 See, e.g., *Word and Object*, Ch. II.

14 Others would see worse consequences here, depending on their views about the relationship between old theories and theories which supersede them. E.g., see P. Feyerabend, 'Explanation, Reduction, and Empiricism', H. Feigl and G. Maxwell (eds), *Minnesota Studies in the Philosophy of Science*, Vol. III (Minneapolis, 1962), pp. 28–97. Notice, too, that a full treatment of these matters would have to deal more meticulously with the various problems and indeterminacies which can afflict inter-theoretic translation.

15 See his 'Reference and definite descriptions,' *Philosophical Review*

LXXV, 3 (July, 1966), pp. 281–304, and 'Putting Humpty Dumpty together again' ibid., LXXVII (April, 1968), pp. 203–15, esp. the former, p. 303.

16 Cf. P. F. Strawson, *Individuals* (London, 1959), p. 85, n. 1, and p. 11.

17 There are obviously further complications, since a person may begin an inquiry with more than one specification, which may perhaps be satisfied by different things, or of which only one may be satisfied at all; or he may begin with a specification, some parts of which are fulfilled by one thing and other parts by another. There are various ways of handling these situations, e.g., by saying that the person does not really have an initially usable specification (cf. n. 11), or by saying that he has more than one and thus is embarked on several different inquiries at once, or by seeing what specification he insists on keeping when his predicament is pointed out to him (this last expedient is similar to one pointed out in another connection by Brian Loar, which he says is similar to one suggested by Christopher Peacocke).

18 See Russell, 'On denoting', *Mind* 14 (1905), pp. 479–93, and Frege, 'On sense and reference', P. Geach and M. Black (eds), *Translations from the Philosophical Writings of Gottlob Frege*, 2nd edn (Oxford, 1960), pp. 56–78.

19 E.g., in 'Knowledge by acquaintance and knowledge by description', *Proc. of the Arist. Soc.*, XI (1910–11), pp. 108–28.

20 This fact is reflected in Russell's view, ibid., that identity-statements linking two logically proper names are 'tautologies' along with the idea that 'that' is a logically proper name.

21 Whether Russell or Plato thought that there are such things is too large a question to be pursued here (cf.n. 3).

22 Nor have I said anything directly about how to construe the 'logical form' of such sentences as 'Terpsion is searching for Euclides' or 'Diogenes is searching for an honest man', or about whether the context produced by 'is searching for' is transparent or opaque (cf. n. 9). I have also left aside issues arising out of the views on reference of Donnellan, 'Proper Names and identifying descriptions', *Synthese* 21 (1970), pp. 335–58, and of S. Kripke, 'Naming and necessity', D. Davidson and G. Harman (eds), *Semantics and Natural Language* (Dordrecht, 1972), pp. 253–355. I do not believe that those views can be adapted to yield a satisfactory account of the framing of inquiry.

23 See Donnellan and Kripke, op. cit., as against Russell, 'On Denoting', and Frege, op. cit.

24 For possible signs of this motivation, see e.g., Strawson, pp. 3–19, and possibly Frege, p. 58, n. 1.

25 See Moravcsik, pp. 63–4 [p. 122 here. Ed.], and G. Nakhnikian, 'Elenctic definitions', G. L. Vlastos (ed.), *Socrates: A Collection of Critical Essays* (New York, 1971), p. 129.

26 Notice that further complications arise if we capitalize on an earlier suggestion (sec. II), and decide somehow to construe the effort to say what a certain word means as the effort to bring into one's 'ken' and recognize some object which is a token of an expression giving the meaning of that word.

27 That it is what we already know is apparently disputed by Vlastos, p. 153, n. 14 (though cp. p. 164 [pp. 107, 102 here. Ed.]), but I do not agree with him in taking so lightly the wording of 86d6 (and of 86d9, 12, which he does not there mention), or in thinking that 86b1 'can only mean' something less than that we already know. His invocation of '*memathēkuia*(s)' in 81d1 and 86a8 does not seem to help him, since it does not matter to the point in question whether the soul once learned things, so long as it learned them before its present incarnation. In saying earlier (e.g., at 84a) that the slave-boy does not 'know', Socrates is obviously speaking in accordance with ordinary usage, since he has not yet fully established his right to say that the boy is recollecting. Later on, when Socrates says that the boy only *believes* but does not yet *know* (98a), he is marking a new contrast, with a new use of 'know', between the state in which the boy would be able to keep the geometrical theorem and its proof ready at hand, and the state in which he is liable to lose his grip on it (cf. 97e5–98a2); but there is no reason to take him to be going back on 86d. If we do so, then we cut the explicitly forged link between recollection and the paradox.

28 Cf. Moravcsik, p. 54 [p. 113 here. Ed.]. It is not certain, however, that Plato has gone so far as to deny the possibility of learning, particularly since 81d4–5 and 84c4–5 are phrased guardedly, and 85d12–13 and 86a1 *might*, in spite of 86b1–2, be an admission that knowledge can be acquired.

29 Following most earlier commentators, both Vlastos and Moravcsik believe that for Plato, recollection has to do exclusively with *a priori* knowledge. Now this view may well be correct, but it is noteworthy that Plato does not say so in the *Meno*. Why not? Because he is primarily using recollection to solve the paradox, and can thus say merely that we recollect *whatever* we might be said to be able to come to know (through inquiry, *if* n. 28 is right). If he thinks that we can know only what we can know *a priori*, as he certainly believed later, then of course he must think that we can recollect only what we know *a priori*. But he need not pause here to say so (it would have involved a considerable digression), and the present interpretation allows us to see why he did not.

30 It may be objected that on this interpretation, Plato fails to tailor the conversation with the slave-boy to the paradox, since the conversation, unlike the paradox as here pictured, seems to have to do with 'propositional' knowledge rather than knowledge 'of' an object. But we have also seen that Plato slurs over this distinction elsewhere (n. 5). Moreover in 84a4–6 and 84c5 he writes in such a way as to suggest explicitly that he thinks that there is indeed an object of the boy's inquiry, namely '*the side* of the eight-foot square'.

31 This is because *ex hypothesi* the inquiry was not yet launched at any earlier time. But if it had been, then we can pick the time at which it was, and reinstate the paradox at that point.

32 Though I cannot develop the point here, Plato does not always make clear which sort of inquiry or recollection he has in mind; see, e.g., *Phaedrus* 254b5–7.

# SOCRATIC DEFINITION

## I. M. Crombie

### INTRODUCTORY

It is a commonplace (derived from Aristotle) that Socrates sought definitions; and it is a related, but logically distinct, commonplace, that he is to be seen seeking, or pretending to seek, them in many of Plato's earlier dialogues. It is my argument in this paper that this latter commonplace is more misleading than illuminating, in that 'definitions' is not without question an apt description of what Socrates means to be after in those dialogues, such as the *Euthyphro*, *Laches*, *Charmides* or *Meno*.

'Definition' has of course no one fully determinate meaning. This is a notoriously large subject; to be wantonly brief about it we can introduce a crude trichotomy: definitions can be linguistic, or they can be conceptual, or they can be real. The basis of this crude trichotomy is: what is it that is unknown? (And the basis of its crudity is that more than one thing may be unknown, and that a decision on one unknown may be involved in that on another). I offer a linguistic definition if I say how a word is, or stipulate how it is to be, used. I am doing something useful in doing this if both there is some uncertainty as to what the word means (or is to mean) in the sense that there is some uncertainty as to what other expressions are (are to be) fair synonyms, and also if the recipient of the definition sufficiently understands the synonymous expressions constituting the definition for the offer of them to remove the uncertainty by which he was or might have been irked.

I am offering a conceptual definition when what is unknown, or not clearly enough grasped, is the conceptual environment of some concept. The concept under consideration will be identified by the use of some expression or expressions which can be used as its vehicle. Thus it is, I suppose, a correct piece of linguistic definition if I say that 'speed' has a sense in which it means the same as 'quickness', '*celeritas*' or '*tachutēs*'; there is then a concept of which all these, and many others, are vehicles. If I do not see clearly enough with what other concepts this concept is related, I may see a bit more clearly if you tell me that a process has been a quick one if more of it than is the norm for a process of that kind has been accomplished in a given time. This gives me a little more insight into what we are doing when we predicate 'fast' and 'slow'; it shows me, what I must of course be implicitly aware of, that the questions 'How much was accomplished?' and 'How long did it take?' come into it, and that some kind of notion of a standard relation between the answers to those questions for a performance of the appropriate kind (for example, the locomotion of a tortoise, or of an animal in general) is also involved. The utility of a conceptual definition is the essentially philosophical utility, that a portion of the conceptual map is drawn by it, and that we thereby see better the interrelationships between various propositions, or the questions to which these are answers. Since the distinction between the three members of our crude trichotomy is based on what is unknown, it is clear that it will often be impossible to say whether a given performance is to be construed as a linguistic or as a conceptual definition; the answer that supplies somebody with a synonym for a word that he does not know the meaning of might also be used to help somebody else to get a clearer grasp of a concept. Thus 'brother of a parent' might tell somebody the meaning of the word 'uncle', or it might be used to clear the mind of somebody who thought that an uncle might be an only child.

I offer a real definition if I attempt to say what some *res* or thing is. What is paradoxical about the notion of real definition is that, for it to be the case that we are talking about what some *res* is, the *res* in question must have been to some extent and in some manner identified; otherwise it is not the case that we are talking about *that*. And this seems to mean that, when we ask for a real definition of what $X$ is, we must already know what $X$ is! Thus when we ask what *the mammal* is, we must be able to pick out the mammal from the rest of the world, so that it is determinate what it is that our question is about. There seem to be two ways in which we might know what $X$ is, and yet find it useful to seek, for the case of $X$, something that could count as a real definition of it. On the one hand we might feel that some set of objects constituted a really distinct kind, that there held between them an important common feature, by the possession of which they were importantly differentiated from everything else; and our purpose might be to identify this common feature. The topic of our investigation would be identified as: the feature common to and distinctive of some determinate set of objects. In the case of the mammal the objects would be those ordinarily thought of as mammals, or the bulk of those (for we might allow that a few of those ordinarily regarded as mammals might turn out to be interlopers, belonging to a radically distinct kind); and the object of the investigation would be to find out what it is that makes the creatures, thus identified, a really distinct kind. The difference between a real definition of the mammal and a conceptual definition would be that in the latter case we should be interested in getting clearer about the criterion by which we *do* distinguish mammals from non-mammals, whereas in the former case we should be interested in the criterion by which we *should* do this (and might of course find that no such criterion existed – that mammals were not a really distinct kind). It might illustrate this difference to observe that we might seek a conceptual definition *of the witch*, but that only believers in witches could seek a real definition.

Alternatively the topic of our investigation might be identified as: that which possesses a certain property; and the object of the investigation would then be to discover what thing or things this is. Normative properties (such as the property of being conduct owed by us to the divine) provide the easiest and most numerous examples of investigations which move in this direction – that is, from the intension of the term which identifies the topic to its extension – but other examples can be found. *The cause of cancer*, for instance, is presumably a property which characterizes something (perhaps some disjunctive set of things); and in seeking to identify that which has this property we might be described as trying to define the cause of cancer.

This has been a very rough and crude account of definition. No more is claimed for it. But let us ask this question: if Socrates is correctly described as seeking definitions in such dialogues as the *Euthyphro*, *Laches* or *Meno*, can we allot the kind of definition he is seeking to any of the kinds we have distinguished? The argument of this paper is that it is not particularly useful to do so. A very brief summary of how the argument will go is as follows. Nobody suggests that Socrates is interested in linguistic definition. There are a number of indications that he is interested in conceptual definition, but a greater number of indications that he is not; perhaps he thinks that this is what he wants, but perhaps it is not what he really wants. Is he then interested in real definition? And if so is he interested in the kind where we seek a cap to fit a head (where we move from extension to intension), or in the kind where se seek a head to fit a cap (where we move from intension to extension)? Our answer will be that he is to some extent interested in both these things. We can say that, in the *Laches* for example, he both wants to know what it is that makes courageous behaviour (this being identified as that behaviour of which the paradigms we would ordinarily offer are paradigms) a really distinct kind of behaviour, and also wants to be able to tell what pieces of behaviour deserve the description 'courage'. This involves a *prima facie* odd kind of two-way movement. Starting with what would ordinarily be thought of as instances of courage, one asks what it is that is really common to them; and one then proceeds to ask in what this common factor is really present. Plainly the common factor which we discovered is either common and peculiar to the instances we started with, or we failed to find the factor common and peculiar to *them*. Equally plainly the explanation of this apparently strange position is that we feel intuitively that there is something common to the instances that we start with, and expect to find that this intuition may be partly but will not be wholly at fault. When we find something which explains our feeling that the instances we started with are instances of laudable behaviour[1] then we shall be free to perceive that some few of our initial instances may have had only a spurious resemblance to the others, and that further instances, which we had not included, were really much more homogeneous with the majority of our initial instances than were some few which we had included. This is how we can ask 'What is the common factor which marks off *these*?', and yet be willing to accept as the answer a common factor which marks off not precisely these.

We can say, then, that in the *Laches* (to continue with this example) Socrates seeks a real definition of courage; and that he wants to know both what the common factor is which marks off courage from non-courage, and also what precisely it is that this factor really marks off. But though we can say this, it hardly seems to do justice to the way the conversation goes. By the end of the dialogue we seem to be concerned, rather, with the question under what conditions a man will be a brave man (the suggested conditions being: if he knows what things are truly terrible, and what are not). In one way there is nothing wrong with this. Given that courage is that by virtue of which a man acts bravely, then courage may be said to be identical with the conditions under which he can be relied upon to do so (and so virtue is knowledge of something, if that knowledge is the necessary and sufficient condition of virtuous conduct). But for the conversation to terminate on the question whether courage is a certain kind of knowledge is for it to have got rather a long way away from where we would have expected it to get, if we expected it to be concerned to discover the factor common and peculiar to what is truly courage. In this sense it is rather unilluminating to say that the *Laches* is concerned with the definition of courage; and similar remarks apply to other dialogues. My contention, then, will be that there is no one kind of definition such that it is both correct and illuminating to say that Socrates, in such dialogues, is interested in achieving that. If one wants one thing that he is interested in, it is the basis of the distinction between the good life and the bad, with a view to the identification of the former. Let us proceed to try to make this out.

## SOCRATIC QUESTIONS

If I asked you to say what justice is, you might think that I wanted your views on disputable questions about what is fair and unfair, and you might illustrate your views by giving me examples of what you thought to be fair. But if I said that I wanted you to *define* justice, rather than to say what you thought it consisted in, I think you would soon be telling me that justice involves an equal respect for the rights of those concerned in some transaction, and perhaps adding that the apportionment of receipts to deserts is a special case of this. It seems very obvious that an equal respect for rights is essential to what we have in mind when we use words of the 'just'-family. If I went on to ask you whether a just community was just in the same sort of way as a man, I think you might say that it was, but that, when we called a society just, we might be thinking of it distributively or collectively. We might mean, that is, that its institutions respected, so far as institutions can, the requirement that equal rights be equally regarded as between its members, or groups of its members; or we might mean that as a community it behaved justly towards other communities. And you would add that it was only when 'just' was predicated of a society collectively that it was predicated in exactly the same way as when it was predicated of an individual, since we do not predicate it distributively of an individual. If I suggested that a man would behave justly only if there were fair do's between certain of his drives or impulses, you would retort that that might be so, but that that this condition was fulfilled was not what we *meant* when we called an individual just.

Notoriously this is not what happens when Plato makes Socrates ask, in the *Republic*, what *dikaiosunē* is. It may be true that '*dikaiosunē*' is not a very good equivalent of 'justice'; but it is not such a bad equivalent that this explains the whole difference between what Plato does in this dialogue, and what you would do if I asked you to define justice. It might be said that a further part of the explanation is that Plato could not, at that primitive stage of political theory, have been happy to speak of *equal respect for rights* as the core of justice, since he would no doubt hold that justice and egalitarianism were not the same. This is true, but it leaves unexplained why it is that Plato leaves unmentioned the obvious and vital fact that justice is essentially concerned with relationships – why he left it to Aristotle to bring '*pros heteron*' explicitly into the story. (Had he made the point that justice essentially concerns relationships, he would surely have had to attend to the question which he so signally ignores, namely whether in speaking on some occasion of a just city we have in mind relations between its members, or between the city itself and other cities).

'Socratic definition' is being used in this paper to stand for Socrates' asking what something is (what justice is, what piety is, what courage is, and the like); and my contention is that the 'What is X?' of Socratic definition should not be generally thought of as an invitation to define X. But I must indicate how this contention is to be taken. I do not, then, mean that if you found some Greek word or phrase which seemed to you to come near in meaning to 'definition', and then asked Plato whether the *Laches* (say) was concerned with the definition of courage, he would have said that it was not. I mean, rather, this. A question is a request for a performance. The kind of performance which is accepted, or judged to be on the right road, indicates how the questioner intended the interrogative sentence with which he posed his question to be taken. An answer, therefore, can be apposite or inapposite, and it can be correct or incorrect. For example, if I said to a

German 'What is the time?', and he, putting this word for word into his own language ('*Was ist die Zeit?*'), gave me a philosophical account of the nature of time, his answer would be inapposite, however philosophically profound. If, on the other hand, he said 'Six o'clock', when it was in fact five, his answer would be apposite, but incorrect. Now it is perhaps the case that we ought not to say that Plato offers us any answers to Socratic *What-is-X?* questions (henceforth 'Socratic questions') which he is confident are correct, but I think he certainly does offer us answers which he thinks are apposite, and some which he thinks are on the road to being correct. I think he thought that 'Courage is the knowledge of what is really terrible' was on the right road towards the answer to the Socratic question posed in the *Laches*, and that '*aretē* is knowledge' and '*aretē* is right belief' were apposite answers to the Socratic question in the *Meno*. 'Justice is the rule of reason, with the aid of spirit, over appetite', I think he thought an apposite, and pretty much a correct, answer to the Socratic question in the *Republic*. My contention is that, in the light of the answers to Socratic questions which Plato regards as apposite, it is not entirely useful to say that Socratic questions are intended to elicit anything that we would be inclined to call a definition. Vague as we no doubt are about what exactly counts as defining, there are certain things some or all of which we expect to find in a definition; and these are not the things which we find in the apposite answers to Socratic questions. (I shall in future use 'Socratic definitions' to refer to those answers to Socratic questions which Plato seems to regard as apposite; something is a Socratic definition, by this use, if it has a claim to be regarded as an apposite answer to a Socratic question).

This, having been said, should be immediately qualified. We have three sources from which we can learn how a Socratic question is to be taken; we have so far used one of them, in that we have asked what kind of answers seem to be taken as apposite to the Socratic questions which constitute the theme (or a theme) of certain dialogues. But the instructions which Socrates sometimes offers as to how his questions are to be taken, and the illustrative examples that he gives, provide other sources; and I shall concede that, if we focus our attention on these latter sources, we shall be much less inclined to deny that a Socratic question is a request for a definition. Socrates' instructions and examples being, from my point of view, hostile witnesses, I shall proceed to cross-examine them. We shall look chiefly at the *Euthyphro*, *Laches* and *Meno*.

178

# THE EVIDENCE OF THE *EUTHYPHRO*

First the *Euthyphro*. The Socratic question here is 'What is *to hosion?*' (There is no good English equivalent of 'hosion'; 'pious' is less bad than 'holy'). In the dialogues in general, as we have seen, we get three sorts of evidence as to the kind of performance a Socratic question is meant to elicit. First Socrates sometimes tells us what he expects of the answer to a Socratic question; second he sometimes illustrates this by asking, and himself answering, what is presumably intended to be another question of the same kind; and third we have the answers with which Socrates shows at least some sympathy, and which he therefore presumably accepts as apposite. In the *Euthyphro* Socrates tells Euthyphro what kind of answer he wants, but he does not illustrate this by offering a paradigm. Nor does he show much tendency to sympathise with any answer given in the dialogue. He is totally destructive, and gives us no indication of what he himself takes piety to be. He does, however, in 7a, say, of Euthyphro's answer, that it is 'just the kind I wanted, though I don't yet know whether it is right (*alēthes*)'. So in this guarded commendation of Euthyphro's performance he gives us some idea, at any rate, of what an apposite answer is like.

But what he mainly offers in this dialogue is instructions, and I shall briefly summarise what these are. (They are to be found in 5c–d and in 6d–e; there are a number of points of controversial detail which I shall ride rough-shod over). There is a common quality in every pious action (likewise in every impious action). This common quality or character is that by virtue of which whatever is pious is pious. Socrates wants to know what this character is, so that he may refer to it, and use it as a *paradeigma* in order to tell whether any act alleged to be pious really is so.

Let us ignore the question what metaphysical status, if any in particular, Socrates believes this *eidos, idea* or common character to possess. He attributes to it a role in relation to actions and our assessment of them – it is that by virtue of which pious actions are pious, and it is that by looking to which we can tell which these are – and we will content ourselves with trying to identify these roles. We should be helped to do so if we knew what a *paradeigma* was. Unfortunately we do not; Plato uses the word in a number of ways. (The one thing that is fairly clear is that Socrates does not want a paradigm case of a pious action; Euthyphro offers him that in 5d, and Socrates makes it clear that he wants an explicit account of the

179

common character, and not an exemplary instance of it). Nor of course can we get any very clear indication out of the dative case which I have represented by 'by virtue of'; the Greek dative is a versatile tool.

Still, it may seem as if Socrates wants to be given something like the criteria for application of '*hosion*'; he wants something which he can refer to ('look away at') in order to tell what actions 'hosion' can be predicated of. It is of course the case that *a, b* and *c* are pious actions if and only if they satisfy the criteria for application of 'pious'; and their satisfying these criteria is therefore that by virtue of which they are pious actions. So let us suppose that the sort of answer Socrates wants will give the criteria for application of '*hosion*' (it may also tell us something about the Platonic Form of *to hosion*; but that is a question we are not going into).

However Socrates does not want nothing more than some criteria which will tell him where to apply the predicate '*hosion*'. For the answer that Euthyphro gives him in 7a (and which is 'just the kind he wanted' though he 'doesn't yet know whether it is right') may, for all that is shown to the contrary, do that well enough. Or rather, the amended version of this answer which is arrived at in 9d may do that well enough. This amended version is that the pious is what is congenial to all the gods (and the impious what is uncongenial to them all). This answer is faulted in the well-known passage 10a–11b. The essential point of this rather tangled piece of argument seems to be: 1) that we cannot say both (a) that pious actions are pious because they are congenial to the gods, and (b) that pious actions are congenial to the gods because they are pious; and 2) that since Euthyphro wants to say (b) (10d4–5), he cannot say (a). But what does this show? It does not in itself show that 'Is it congenial to all the gods?' may not be a perfectly effective criterion of application for '*hosion*'. If we have some way of telling what is congenial to all the gods, other than determining what is *hosion*, then it would be an effective criterion and might seem likely to pick out the right things; for we surely cannot suggest that an act congenial to all the gods might be impious, or even indifferent. The point is, rather, that we have not penetrated deep enough into the nature of piety if we do not discover what it is that makes congenial acts congenial. Therefore what Socrates is after, if we judge by what he rejects, is a criterion for application of '*hosion*' which does not just tell us what to apply it to and what to withhold it from, but which also gives us some insight into what we are doing when we apply or withhold it.

But what kind of insight could this be? To sketch an answer to this question I shall touch briefly on what I shall have more to say about later. If I call some action pious I commit myself to the proposition that we ought to act thus with reference to the gods. We should have some insight into what we are doing in calling conduct pious if we had some understanding of how we come to have obligations with respect to the gods, and of the nature of these obligations. Now I think it is fair comment that Socrates rejects 'what is congenial to all the gods' as an account of the being *(ousia)* of piety for the reason that it fails to tell us what it is that the gods find to like in the conduct that they find congenial; and I think it is also fair comment that Socrates would not accept that he could with confidence agree that he had diagnosed what the gods find to like in such conduct unless he had found something that *deserved* to be liked. Therefore what he wants an account of (that which makes certain kinds of conduct congenial to the divine nature) is pretty much the same thing as that which explains why such conduct is incumbent upon us. Therefore what Socrates wants Euthyphro to do for him is: to show him that conduct really can be (and not just conventionally is) sorted into pious and impious (and, presumably, neutral), for the reason that some conduct with respect to divine beings has an intelligible rightness about it, and other conduct an intelligible wrongness.

This feat is, of course, well beyond Euthyphro's powers, and Socrates only pretends that he thinks that Euthyphro can accomplish it. Still it is the feat that he wants accomplished. Had it been achieved, would it be an apt comment to say that we had been given a definition of piety? Plainly not a linguistic definition. Perhaps a conceptual definition?

It may be suggested, first that it is not too clear what should count as a conceptual definition of a concept which has evaluative elements, and secondly that Plato is in general not interested in concepts. The first point I shall concede, and say no more about now. The second point has some substance. In this dialogue, for example, Plato is plainly interested in what our duties are with respect to the gods, and not in how we think of these duties. He is not interested in our concept of piety. More generally, it is far from clear that he has any word or phrase which means the same as our 'concept'. There is therefore something anachronistic in the suggestion that he is interested in conceptual analysis or definition. However, too much should not be made of this. Plato would no doubt accept that we have some system (though we probably cannot say what it is) in our application of such predicates as '*hosion*'. At one time he seems to have believed that our systems for applying predicates are some sort of memory of a pre-natal vision of the property whose presence we are alleging when we apply the predicate. But however we come to have such systems, the fact remains that we have them (we do not apply predicates at random); and we could no doubt persuade Plato to allow us to describe as *A's* concept of piety the system in accordance with which *A* ascribes and withholds the predicate 'pious'. It would therefore not be too anachronistic to say that what is sought for in the *Euthyphro* is a conceptual analysis of piety.

But would it be correct? Surely, not very. To say that it was would be to suggest that Socrates conducted the investigation by eliciting such points as that a pious action is one that we ought to do, and one that owes its obligatoriness to some relation to the divine. Not only are such platitudes not what Socrates is aiming at discovering; he also does not much seem to think that it would be helpful to the search if they were brought out and made explicit. These points are taken for granted. Questions connected with them do indeed arise, as they must; the course of any piece of philosophical thinking is partly determined by the structure of the concepts involved in it. (For example, the question how we can have any obligations towards the gods arises from 12e onwards under the guise of the difficulty that we cannot benefit them.) But it is not suggested that it would help us to see what piety is if we explicitly set out what is involved in the concept. And yet the course of the discussion is governed by an implicit grasp of this. It is true that, if we succeeded in doing what Socrates wants Euthyphro to do for him, we should in one way have a new (or at any rate a deepened) concept of piety, in that we should understand how it is that we have obligations towards the gods, and therefore the nature of these obligations. But this new concept would still be a concept of piety; we should then be understanding better what that reality is which we intend to speak of when we apply the predicates 'pious' and 'impious'. And the reason why this is so, and therefore the reason why what we have is a deepened concept of piety, is that it is still a correct conceptual analysis of what we intend by 'the pious' that this expression stands for our obligations (whatever these are, and however we come to have any) towards the divine. What would persist from the beginning to the successful end of the investigation would be that these obligations are its topic; and this is what would make it right to say at the end that we had found what we were looking for at the beginning, and that it was our understanding of piety that had been deepened. But what we had *found* would not be the correct analysis of the concept of piety; on the contrary, a grasp, explicit or implicit, of that analysis would have been what steered the investigation, and made it right to say that it was the investigation of one thing, and specifically of piety, however startling its results might be with respect to what things are pious and impious (even if, in the limiting case, it turned out that nothing was either). Analysis of the concept of piety is not the goal of the investigation; rather, it is its guide.

(On the question how it is that a grasp of what 'piety' means guides the investigation, I am expressing no view. What I am saying is open between such possibilities as (a) that in some discarnate state we clearly perceived that property, the presence of which in pious conduct makes that conduct obligatory, and that a 'memory' of this clear perception determines our thoughts; and (b) that, as we consider the various possibilities, we simply make up our minds what it is that we owe to the gods. For my part I see no reason to think that Plato had as yet any hard view on such issues; but at any rate no view upon them is implicit in what I have so far claimed. All we are so far committed to is the modest claim that it may help us to decide what obligations we have towards the gods if we explicitly observe that the application of the predicate 'pious' implies that we have some.)

Is it then the case that what Euthyphro would have achieved, if he had achieved what Socrates wanted, is a real definition of piety? The answer, surely, is that a real definition would have been achieved, but that it would have been achieved as a part only of a much larger result. We are imagining, it must be remembered, a larger and more constructive *Euthyphro*, in which Socrates and Euthyphro manage to do what Socrates seems to ask Euthyphro to do for him, namely to show that conduct really can be (and not just conventionally is) sorted into pious and impious (and, presumably, neutral) for the reason that some conduct with respect to divine beings has about it an intelligible rightness, and other conduct an intelligible wrongness. In this imaginary dialogue we should have an account both of a cap, and of a head that fits it; we should have, that is, an understanding of the nature of the obligation which we have towards the divine, and we should be able to derive from this an identification of the conduct by which this obligation is acknowledged. But it is inconceivable that this result could have been achieved except in the context of a very wide-ranging investigation of moral and theological topics. Perhaps, then, it is fair comment on the (actual rather than the imaginary) *Euthyphro* that what it really aims to do is to show that our inability to say what piety is points to the need for this wide-ranging investigation, and gives some hints as to what questions will arise in its course. This seems an apter comment than that the dialogue is an unsuccessful search for a real definition.

## THE EVIDENCE OF THE *LACHES*

The Socratic question in the *Laches* (posed in 190d) is 'What is *andreia* (manliness or courage)?' Socrates gives no special instructions as to how his question should be answered, except that he makes (in 191e) the obvious point that he wants to learn about the identical feature in all brave men of whatever kind – those who are brave about pleasures and appetites, as much as those who are brave about pains and fears. But to illustrate the generality of the desired account, Socrates gives Laches a paradigm example. One can do many things quickly: what then is the general account of quickness? To this Socrates' answer is 'The power of accomplishing much in little time'. It is also the case that in the *Laches* we get an example of an answer with which Socrates obviously has some sympathy. It is true that the formula 'Courage is the knowledge of what is and is not fearful' (194e) is thrown out at the end of the dialogue on the ground that it would not leave courage as a distinct part of *aretē*, or virtue (as it has been agreed that courage is), but would collapse it into *aretē* in general. But the contemporary reader, to whom it was probably notorious that Socrates maintained the thesis that virtue is a unitary thing, and does not have distinct parts, would not have taken this rejection very seriously. And nor need we. We should notice that Socrates treats this formula as if it deserved careful attention, spending, for example, some time and care in distinguishing the tenable interpretation of it from untenable misinterpretations (as that to be brave is to be an expert in doing something which is risky if attempted by a non-expert), and in drawing out corollaries (as that animals cannot be

strictly speaking brave). Nor does he ever suggest that the answer
is inapposite. The formal conclusion of the dialogue is that the
answer must be incorrect if courage is indeed a distinct part of *aretē*;
but there is no suggestion at all that any misunderstanding of the
force of the Socratic 'What is . . .?' is involved in giving this
answer.

That, then, is the evidence of the *Laches* about the significance of
a Socratic question. Where does it point? The answer is that it
seems to point in two different directions. Socrates' model answer
to the question 'What is speed?' is precisely a definition, and in
particular a conceptual analysis. It is also, of course, a real definition
in that it is an account of a general feature of a world of process,
namely that feature which we are attending to when we predicate
'slow' and 'fast' of things done – a feature of which our concept of
speed is a correct appreciation. It is true that instances of some
kinds of process have, as one of the ways in which they can be
compared with each other, the way which derives from asking the
yoked questions 'How much was accomplished?' and 'How long
did it take?'; and it is true that it is this comparison between
instances of digging or running or reading that we are making
when we say that *A* dug, ran or read fast. It is an incomplete
conceptual analysis, since it leaves out the point that what counts as
fast (or what counts as *much* done in a given time) is determined in
relation to a standard for that kind of performance or for that kind
of performer. This is how a slow hare can cover more ground in a
minute than a fast tortoise, or how Klemperer can be a slow
conductor, although a *presto* conducted by him can get through
more bars in a minute than a *molto adagio* at the hand of some faster
conductor. Therefore one might say that Socrates' model answer is
a somewhat defective conceptual analysis, and that he might have
repaired the deficiency if he had attended less to the question 'What
is the real difference which we are attending to when we speak of
fast and slow?', and more to the question 'What are our procedures
for applying these predicates?' (And this might have prevented
Plato from making certain well-known mistakes that he is alleged
to have made in connection with middle-period arguments for the
Theory of Forms.[2]) But the model answer can be called a piece of
conceptual analysis none the less.

It is hardly so with Nicias' formula that courage is the knowledge
of what is and is not fearful. It is not the case a man will get a better
grasp of what he is doing when he predicates 'brave' and 'cowardly'

of men or actions if he attends to this formula. It is conceivable that he might get a better grasp of what he *should* be doing; yet even this must be said with considerable qualification. If the man thinks that you manifest courage in the way in which you manifest knowledge, and that you manifest knowing that $p$ by thinking and speaking in certain ways, then he may think that you manifest courage in what you think and say and not in what you do (which is presumably why Laches says, in 195a, that Nicias' formula is unplausible nonsense).

'Love is chemistry'. The man who says this is not, despite appearances, telling us what it *is* for one person to love another; that is, he is not telling us what is involved in this relationship, he is not telling us what we believe we have detected as between $A$ and $B$ when we say that $A$ loves $B$. Rather he is telling us how it comes about that $A$ loves $B$; his belief is that love arises between two people when and only when their physiological make-up is suitable. 'Courage is the knowledge of . . .' is akin to 'Love is chemistry'. Based on the Socratic beliefs that a man will never choose what he judges the more disagreeable of two courses, and that the actions characteristic of the coward have very disagreeable effects upon us, it claims that a man will act as the brave man acts if and only if he knows about how things affect us for weal or woe; such a man will know what things are to be dreaded – namely the actions characteristic of the coward – and will dread and flee such things. It is therefore a diagnosis of how it comes about that a man acts bravely; but this diagnosis is of no use to us until we have cleared our minds as to what it is to act bravely. Any account of courage which fails to say that courage is a disposition, that it is manifested in actions, and in particular in actions of certain kinds determined by the compresence of something obligatory or noble and something arduous – any such account of courage can hardly claim to be a conceptual analysis. Being cautious, therefore, we can nevertheless say that in the *Laches* Socrates fails to castigate as an inapposite answer to a Socratic question an account of courage which cannot claim to be a conceptual definition. If we were incautious, we could say that what he seems to want is an account of courage which diagnoses its psychological roots. In the *Laches*, therefore, what Socrates seems to be looking for is not in agreement with the model that he lays down for Laches' guidance.

An answer that was in agreement with that model would render explicit the point that to be brave is to face what is arduous in an admirable manner. This point having been rendered explicit, one would expect the further question to be asked: 'And what is that manner? What must a man do for it to be right to say that he has faced something arduous in an admirable manner?' A conceivable answer to this further question is: 'He has faced it in the manner in which it would be faced by a man who knows what things are goods, and what things are evils; there is no more specific formulation that can be given.' *If* Socrates holds that this answer may be correct, then he could think that Nicias' proposed answer to the question what courage is does all that can be done to give one a criterion with which to recognize brave men and brave acts. In that case 'Courage is the knowledge of what is truly terrible' would be the best one could do in order to give a real definition of this virtuous disposition; it would be incorrect to say that Nicias was ignoring the question what it is and answering the question under what conditions it arises. But *unless* we hold that Nicias and Socrates believe that no other criterion can be given (that there is nothing else that makes the admirable disposition that we call courage really one distinct thing), then we have to say that they allow the conversation to drift away from the real definition of courage to the discussion of the necessary and sufficient conditions of its arising. I have no particular objection to saying that Nicias and Socrates do (obscurely) hold this theory; but it is important to stress that we *have* to say this if we say without qualification that the *Laches* is concerned with the real definition of courage.

We shall get not dissimilar results if we look at the *Meno*, as we shall now do.

## THE EVIDENCE OF THE *MENO*

We come then to the *Meno*. The Socratic question in this dialogue is 'What is *aretē*?'. (We shall have to consider what this word means later on; for the moment let 'virtue' be our translation, bad one though it is.) In this dialogue we get each of the three kinds of evidence that we distinguished; Socrates gives instructions; he provides model answers to parallel questions; and certain suggestions are taken seriously enough to make it hard to say that they are regarded as inapposite. We also get a number of other things which are relevant to our purpose, one of which is the great stress laid on the proposition that, until you have answered the Socratic question about $X$, you are not in a position to say whether it is $F$ (for any '$F$' other than one which says 'what $X$ is').

The instructions Socrates gives are not identical with those he gives in the *Euthyphro*, but do not differ very much for our purposes. Their upshot is that it will have been said what $X$ is when we have specified the factor which is common to all $X$ things and is that through which they are $X$ things; and values of '$X$' which Socrates offers, apart from '*aretē*', are 'the bee' and 'shape', with 'colour' as an afterthought.

The model answers that Socrates provides to parallel questions are interesting. They are (a) (for shape) 'the sole invariable concomitant upon colour', and then, when Meno objects to that on the ground that somebody might not know what colour is, (b) 'the boundary of a solid'; and finally (c) (for colour) 'an efflux of shapes which is commensurable with sight and perceptible'. What is interesting about these is that they seem to be of three distinct kinds. What (a) does for shape is to identify it. It would hardly, indeed, do so for somebody who lacked the idea of comparing things in point of shape – for such a person would be at a loss to find just one thing which is invariably concomitant upon colour. But in that (a) is, let us suppose, true of shape and of nothing else, it is rather like Euthyphro's 'what is congenial to all the gods' for piety. Neither this nor (a) advances one's understanding of the matter in hand; the most it does is to identify it, by holding of it and of nothing else. (b) on the other hand is an analysis of what we have in mind when we speak of shape; in relating the notion of shape to the notion of a solid and its boundary, it draws a small part of the conceptual map. We are inclined to think, therefore, that (b) is better than (a) for Socrates' purposes; but he himself seems to express disagreement (75c–d). Finally what (c) seems to do for colour comes close to what 'the knowledge of what is and is not fearful' does for courage; that is, it tells us what it is for something to be of some colour only in the sense that it refers to a theory as to how colour vision comes about. Since, however, Socrates seems not to think well of (c) as an answer to 'What is colour?' (76e), we must not make too much of this. But with that proviso, it seems fair comment that the models Socrates offers suggest that he is not too clear what he wants as an answer to a Socratic question. All that is common to (a), (b) and (c) is that each (it is hoped) applies to all of its $X$, and to nothing else.

We can say also that (b) is the model which nobody in the

dialogue criticizes, and that (b) is a straight case of definition by conceptual analysis. (b) does not attempt to tell us how it comes about that there are shapes, nor does it content itself with identifying shape, no matter in how unilluminating a way. Perhaps, then, what Socrates says he wants for virtue is a conceptual analysis.

But this is not at all how things look when we see some of the suggestions he seems to treat as apposite – that virtue is the knowledge of something, and that it is right belief about something.[3] For here we are plainly back at the business of diagnosing how virtue comes about, what are its roots. We want to say that we have completely lost sight of the question what it *is*. And I do not only mean that we are not explicitly told. We really do not know whether that which may perhaps be knowledge of something, or right belief about something, so far as its psychological roots are concerned, is in itself a matter of living so as to get the best out of life, or so as to be of use to one's fellows, or so as to be an object of admiration to our capacity for moral appraisal. All of these are possible accounts of what *aretē* is (and so is the conjunction of two or more of them); and, while I think we can be reasonably confident what selection from these and other possibilities the Socrates of this dialogue would have made, it is all very much a matter of inference, so far is Socrates from pressing for any conceptual analysis, or definition in that sense, of *aretē*. Nor, again does he give any indication as to what might be the subject of the knowledge, or of the right beliefs, the identification of which with virtue is contemplated. Is the subject how the individual may get the best out of life? Or how he may contribute most to it? Or what is demanded of him by his fellows? Or what is needed by his fellows? It might of course be quite correctly said that these are subsequent questions which arise after it has been established that virtue must be in some way a matter of outlook or belief; and that it is unreasonable to complain that they are not answered in a short dialogue. But this would be to miss the point. The point is that in a very real sense we do not know what this thing is that may perhaps be identical with some kind of knowledge or right belief, and that whereas we might have derived an identification of this thing from the account of what it is knowledge of (for example, if it were said to be knowledge of how to be useful to one's fellows, it would be a fair guess that *aretē* consisted in such usefulness), in fact we are not even given this kind of clue. But this means that Socrates has transgressed the principle which he laid down at the beginning of

189

the dialogue, and repeated during its course, namely that we cannot consider whether $X$ is $F$ until we know what $X$ is (for any '$F$' which does not constitute an answer to that question). For it is being suggested that something or other is identical with some kind of knowledge or belief. Is this *something or other* living so as to maximize one's happiness? Is it living so as to maximize one's utility? Or so as to command admiration? Is it living in accordance with human nature? And if we had had any kind of definition of virtue, how could these questions arise? Surely we should know *what* we were talking about?

We often wonder whether it is correct to say that the Greek outlook on morality was fundamentally egoistic. Was it, we ask, their assumption that each man may and must pursue his own good, and that any attention that he ought to give to the good of others is due solely because the giving of it is a necessary condition of his attaining his own good? Was *aretē* the attainment of one's own true good (this involving some attention to the good of others)? Or was the concept of *aretē* the concept of something altogether more disinterested? Plato was aware of this question; his formulation of it might be 'Is *aretē* an *oikeion agathon*?' In a dialogue the ostensible subject of which is 'What is *aretē*?' we expect to get light directly shed on this question. Some light is indirectly shed here and there in the course of the dialogue, and much might have been shed had we been given an indication of the subject of the knowledge or right beliefs which *aretē* may perhaps consist in. We are given *some* indication; it is fair to infer that the knowledge in question is knowledge how to use potential goods. But how to use them to what end? To our own good or that of others? Such questions are almost ostentatiously ignored. The suggestion, therefore, that virtue is knowledge of something is the suggestion that one unknown is another unknown.

It is not just that we do not know what *aretē* consists in, in the sense that we do not know what relatively concrete pattern of conduct manifests it. It might be said that there is a great difference between the things on which Socrates offers model answers (speed, shape and colour), and the things which these are models for answering questions about (piety, courage, *aretē*). For we can attach no clear sense to a distinction between what speed or shape consist in and what they are. But we can draw this distinction in the case of evaluative concepts. Let us suppose that we all agree that to have *aretē* is to live well, to live in that manner in which it is right

190

and reasonable to try to live. It is perfectly clear that we can go on to disagree (as Socrates and Meno plainly do disagree) as to what manner of life that is. Therefore it is not at all the case that a conceptual analysis of *aretē* – the kind of thing we were desiderating in the last paragraph – would determine what *aretē* consists in. This is perfectly correct. It is also perfectly correct that it emerges explicitly enough in the *Meno* that *aretē* is a good thing, and that it involves living well; and these are truisms that might seem to correspond reasonably well to the truism that shape is the boundary of a solid. But firstly these truisms are not offered as answers to the question what *aretē* is, but apparently leave that question still posed. And secondly this is quite right in that these truistic points about *aretē* constitute a very defective conceptual analysis, not because they fail to settle the subsequent question what life-style manifests *aretē*, but because they fail to scratch the prior question, from the answer to which questions about life-styles must be derived, the question namely whether living well is a matter of achieving one's own true good, or of something else.

Socrates says that we must determine what $X$ is before we can profitably attack any other questions about it. We may have understood this instruction in this manner: we must analyse what is involved in the concept of $X$, and we must then look to see what distinct reality there is of which this concept is a, perhaps imperfect, representation. It is only when we have done this that we can turn our minds to any question not already answered in the course of this prior inquiry. If this way of understanding Socrates' instruction is correct, it seems we have to say that he himself ignores it in that he allows himself to consider whether virtue may perhaps be knowledge at a stage at which it is quite unclear, not only what lifestyle we are referring to as '*aretē*', but also what the criterion is for determining this.

It might, however, be suggested that Socrates is aware of this. In his concluding remarks (100b) he says that we shall not know clearly how *aretē* comes to be in human beings unless we postpone that question until after we have tried to discover what it is in itself. It might be thought that this comes near to a recognition on Socrates' part that a proposition such as '*Aretē* is the knowledge of the right use of potential goods' would not amount to an answer to the question what it is in itself; for he has treated the bi-conditional 'If it is knowledge it can be implanted by teaching, and *vice versa*' as pretty indisputable, so that we could almost read his concluding comment quoted above as implying that we shall not know for sure that it is knowledge until we know *what it is in itself*. But I think it much more likely that his line of thought is: 'If it is knowledge it is indeed teachable; but we shall not be sure whether it is teachable until we know *whether it is knowledge.*' But that means that he is treating 'It is knowledge of . . .' as an answer to the question what it is in itself; and that seems to mean that an answer to the question what it is in itself might leave us in real doubt as to the identity of the thing.

The provisional conclusion is that we must say that the *Meno* contains no tolerably adequate definition or analysis of the concept of *aretē* (and that the truisms offered under this head are not offered as answers to the question what *aretē* is). Can we say that it offers us, tentatively, any real definitions – that is, can 'It is knowledge' or 'It is right belief' be regarded as real definitions? They obviously cannot be regarded as adequately achieved definitions; but could they be regarded as first steps in a real definition? Only, surely, if it were the belief that nothing underlies the distinction we draw between living well and living badly except the distinction between living as those who are in possession of certain truths will live, and living otherwise. If that is the only distinction that underlies, and renders more than conventional, the sorting of lives into good and bad, then a start has been made on identifying that real thing which the word '*aretē*' represents when we have said that it involves the possession of certain truths. Otherwise we are talking, surely, not about what *aretē* is in itself, but rather about the conditions under which it (so far something undetermined) arises. So, as with the *Laches*, the comment that the answers that are accepted as apposite in the *Meno* are so accepted because it is thought that they might be the first steps in a real definition – this comment commits us to imputing to Socrates the (no doubt implicit) holding of a wide-ranging theory about the moral life and the nature of moral discourse. If there were some factor common and peculiar to all instances of living well which was more proximate or less abstract than that they are all instances of living as those who are in possession of certain truths will live, then in an important way so long as we have not discovered this less abstract common factor we would not know what *aretē* is, but only what it results from.

# MENO'S DILEMMA, AND WHAT IT TEACHES US

To take the discussion further it will be useful to introduce a new point, namely the one which Meno throws at Socrates at 80d. In the form in which Meno offers it, it is a dilemma argument against the proposition that we can usefully ask what something is. If you know, there is no point in asking: and if you do not know, you will not be able to tell whether any proffered answer is right. Socrates calls this argument eristic; and indeed in this form it is a smart-Alec version of what is, nevertheless, a real point. This is that in any determinate investigation the topic of the investigation must have been somehow determined; and that this makes it problematical how there can be an investigation into what something is. For we must be able to identify that which is the topic of the investigation; and if we can do that, we already have something that would count as an answer to the question we are asking.

It is difficult to be confident how far Plato is explicitly aware of the implications of this. His own reply to Meno's point is the story about reincarnation and *anamnēsis*, as to the truth of which Socrates expressly denies he is certain (86b). But let us ask what the implications in fact are.

Consider such phenomena as phototropism, symbiosis or osmosis, and imagine a man who holds that he, or that the scientific community, does not sufficiently understand one of these (i.e. he wants a real definition of it). He might express this by 'We do not know what phototropism is'. But this would be the statement with respect to some determinate phenomenon that we do not sufficiently understand it only if the speaker knew what 'phototropism' means. I must know that phototropism is the movement of plants in relation to light before I can say, using the word 'phototropism', that we do not know what it is. To put it in Latin, we must know *quid investigemus* if we are to ask *quid sit id quod investigamus*.

This means that in attempting to answer a Socratic question such as 'What is piety?' there must come into the story somewhere the sort of truisms which do for piety what 'Much accomplished in little time' does for speed. Either these truisms must be wanted as answers to the question (and Socrates' paradigms suggest that this is the position); or, if a real definition is being sought, it must be these truisms that serve to identify the thing that is to be defined; and either they must be explicitly spelt out and used as guides, or they must be taken for granted. On the whole we have seen that they are taken for granted; they are certainly not treated as the answers that are being sought. Socrates and Euthyphro take for granted (and, by virtue of the meaning of the word used to identify their topic, must take for granted) that pious conduct is that conduct which is incumbent upon us with respect to the gods; Socrates, Laches and Nicias likewise do and must agree that brave conduct is that endurance which is part of living well. Without these truistic agreements, it would be indeterminate what was being investigated.

Likewise Socrates and Meno take for granted that *aretē* is a matter of living well. As we have seen, this agreement is a very open one. It may be that a close inspection of the dialogue will show that they are in agreement on something a good deal less open than this. It may be that they take for granted that the man of complete *aretē* is the man from whom nothing is lacking of those things that are both within a man's power to achieve, and also such that any man of sense and spirit will want to achieve them (and that their obvious disagreements are subsequent to this, namely over the question what these things are, for example whether they include moderation of bodily appetites). But however this may be, there must be some things, which would count as answers of a kind to the question what *aretē* is, and which Socrates and Meno hold in common; otherwise they are not talking about the same thing. At the very least each of them must accept some answers of this kind, or there will not be any determinate thing that he intends by '*aretē*'.

Therefore in all the three dialogues that we have looked at it seems that certain truisms (which do for the topic of the dialogue roughly what Socrates' model answers do for speed and shape) are taken for granted, and not thought of as the answers demanded by the Socratic question. In this way Socrates' models are bad models. It is fairly clear also that this holds of the *Republic*, that is of the one dialogue in which a Socratic question gets an answer which is treated not only as apposite, but also as probably more or less correct. In the *Republic* also conceptual definition is not the target, but the guide. It would take too long to work this out in detail, but in the briefest outline it is surely clear that every participant in the dialogue takes it for granted that justice is a matter of not taking advantage of others, and of complying with the social rules which have it as their effect that such taking of advantage is prevented. (Indeed it is by this criterion that Socrates tests, in 442–3, the answer to his question that he has arrived at). What is in dispute between the parties is how conduct which conforms to this criterion is related to our objectives in life. Does such conduct mean our being hoodwinked by the rulers into behaving conformably with their interests? Is it a matter of abiding by a social contract, whereby we all stand to gain from the compliance of others? Or is it a matter of keeping one's appetites to their biological function, and not allowing them to usurp the functions of spirit and reason, nor the former to usurp the function of the latter? What, therefore, is the relation of such conduct to a man's pursuit of his true good? Does the former impede the latter, as Thrasymachus thinks? Or is it, with Glaucon, that it would do so had we not been able to secure mutual advantage by a Hobbesian compact? Or is it, with Socrates, that the former is an essential part of the latter? Clearly what is disputed, if it comes under the head of definition at all, comes under the head of real definition; what comes under the head of conceptual definition is taken for granted, and is used only to guide the dispute and to check its results.

On the whole, then, the analysis of that concept which represents the thing the Socratic question is about is not taken to be the answer to the Socratic question. Rather, an implicit agreement as to a rough sketch of that analysis is what serves to identify the thing about which the question what it is is being asked. It might be suggested that this would have to be the case, on the ground that the analysis of concepts is merely a somewhat mechanical preliminary to the attack upon a philosophical problem – that there is not enough meat in a conceptual definition to occupy the space of even a short Platonic dialogue. But on reflection this is obviously wrong. We often cannot clearly formulate what we take for granted with regard to something like, say, justice. I suggested earlier that, if asked what justice is, you might well say that it was a matter of equal respect for rights, no matter whose. But if I then asked you how that applied to just reward or just punishment, you might well have an intuitive feeling that the answer was not outside your grasp, but that you could not explicitly provide it. And if you tried to do so, the history of philosophical attempts at doing that sort of thing shows that your offering would probably not be impeccable. Conceptual analysis is a large and difficult matter, and might well have been that which a Socratic question was an invitation to embark on.

How does it come about that it is not, and yet that Socrates tends to suggest (by his model answers) that it is? Part of the answer to this plainly is that what Socrates always wants to do is to get a plainer view of some reality – that, namely, which is identified as that which is more or less well represented by the concept which occurs in the framing of the Socratic question. Very naturally he uses the form of words, 'What is X?' to express this desire for a plainer view. Now, given that we sufficiently understand the meaning of the word which goes in the place of 'X' for the interrogative sentence to constitute a determinate question, the uncertainties which can lurk behind the form of words 'What is X?' will vary with what the value of 'X' is. With 'speed' or 'shape' in the place of 'X' there really is very little that the question can be seeking apart from conceptual analysis. There is, for example, hardly a question what speed consists in which is distinct from the question what it is. There is, perhaps, a distinct question how speed comes about; but this question is so distinct that it would hardly present itself as one way of understanding the question what speed is. With 'colour' as the value of 'X' there is perhaps more room to treat, as what may be intended by the question what colour is, something that could be better expressed as the question how it comes about that we see things differently coloured. But when 'aretē' is the value of 'X' there are a number of distinct things, a desire to settle which may be what provoked the question. There is the analysis of the concept, and this, as we have seen, is no light matter. There is also the question what aretē consists in, what manner of life the man of true aretē follows. In so far as our conceptual analysis of aretē has displayed it as a matter of being disposed to behave in certain ways, or to pursue certain ends, there is also the question what is the ground of the disposition, the psychological conditions of its arising.

What is brittleness? Is it the tendency to break under shock (whatever this depends on)? Or is it a certain physical constitution (from which it results that things so constituted break under shock)? Philosophers tend to regard the former answer as more correct, plain men the latter answer as more illuminating. Clearly the question what is the ground of the disposition to pursue certain ends could be taken to be the question which the interrogative sentence 'What is aretē?' is posing, given that some identification of these ends had been accomplished by an explicit or implicit analysis of the concept of aretē. Therefore part of the answer to the question posed at the head of the last paragraph is that the reason why we tend to think that Socrates wants a conceptual analysis is that he selects, as the questions to which he offers model answers, questions that are relatively easy and uncontroversial, and that in these cases there is little but a conceptual analysis that can plausibly be provided by way of answer. In the difficult cases, however, for which the models are models, there is a good deal more that comes very plausibly within the ambit of 'What is $X$?', and what Socrates wants is part of this good deal more.

Is it correct to say that, where the value of '$X$' is some virtue-word, what Socrates wants is the ground of the disposition identified by the virtue-word? And if that is what he wants, under what conditions would he be strictly correct in using the form of words 'What *is* $X$?' to elicit it?

Taking the first question first, there is some ground for an affirmative answer. It seems to me that in the *Laches* and the *Republic* the Socratic definition toyed with or accepted is an answer that gives the psychic ground of the disposition identified by an implicit conceptual analysis (it is as if they specify the molecular constitution of brittle things, it being taken for granted that these are those which break under shock). In the case of the *Euthyphro* we have to conjecture what would have satisfied Socrates, but we thought that what he wanted was an account of how we come to have obligations with respect to the divine. Having obligations is not the same thing as acknowledging them. But '*hosiotēs*' is ambiguous between the feature common to pious actions, and the disposition to perform such actions; and on Socratic assumptions I have an obligation only if it is in my true interest to do what is obligatory, so that there is no gap between acknowledging an obligation and being disposed to discharge it. Therefore in our imaginary extended and constructive *Euthyphro* one can readily suppose that the question how we come to have obligations towards the gods might have merged into the question what is the ground of the disposition to discharge them; and 'Piety is the knowledge of . . .' seems a promising beginning to a Socratic answer to the question 'What is piety?'

The question with regard to the *Meno* (that is, the question 'Does Socrates want the ground of the general disposition to live well? Is that how he understands "What is *aretē*?" ') – this question is a little more complex. Clearly 'Perhaps it's knowledge', 'Perhaps it's right belief' suggest that this is what he wants. But on the other hand there is some reason for thinking that in the *Meno* concrete

197

misidentification of *aretē* – the identification of it with the wrong life-style – is intended to be a case of not knowing what virtue is, with the corollary that the correct concrete identification of *aretē* would be an essential part of knowing what it is. There is, in other words, some ground for thinking that 'If you suppose it is living like *that*, then of course you will be wrong about how it arises in men' is an important part of how Socrates means to apply his principle that until you know what *X* is you will not know whether it is *F*. The risk of identifying the wrong thing is an important theme of the dialogue.

This starts with the analogy with which Socrates supports (71b) the principle I have just stated. He says that if he does not know who Meno is he cannot say whether he is, for example, rich. This suggests: if I pick on the wrong man, I am in danger of ascribing the wrong properties. The analogue to this is: if I pick on the wrong life-style for the role of *aretē*, I shall ascribe to *aretē* the wrong properties. This might be just a bad analogy, but there is some support for the view that it is not, and that Plato really does intend this analogue.

First, one needs to read only a little below the surface of the dialogue to see that it is one of its themes that Meno does not and will not understand what *didachē* (teaching) is. That is, what it consists in; for Meno is no doubt sound on the truism that to teach *X* to *A* is to get *A* to understand and know *X*. But Socrates shows Meno, in the exhibition with the slave, that to teach is to elicit the pupil's understanding, and that to learn is to have one's understanding elicited. But Meno fails to take the point, and makes no protest when Socrates assumes that Sophists, and ordinary parents, can be said to try to teach *aretē*. It needs no great penetration, no exaggerated emphasis on Plato's ironical method of making his points, to say that we ought to see that there is no real argument in the dialogue for the proposition that virtue cannot be taught, and that such argument as there is rests on the misidentification of teaching with laying down the law, or the like. But if one mistake made in the surface reasoning of the dialogue rests on a misidentification of teaching, this ought to alert us to the possibility that another rests on the misidentification of *aretē* as that quality which enabled prominent fifth-century Athenians to become effective leaders.

Next one notices that it is in conversation with Anytus that Socrates takes Themistocles and Pericles as paradigms of *aretē*. If

one remembers the disparaging attitude taken towards these statesmen in the *Gorgias*, and puts this together with the fact that Anytus
was one of Socrates' two accusers at his trial, suspicion is further
aroused. One wonders whether it is not reasonable to say that a
further theme, which we are meant to read, just a little below the
surface of the dialogue, is: if you identify *aretē* with those properties
that enabled men like Pericles to make the somewhat dubious
contribution that they made to Athens, then you will come to the
conclusion that *aretē* cannot be purveyed by any kind of teaching
(and certainly not by the 'teaching' that they presumably tried to
give to their sons); and then you will come to think that the
explanation of how they came to have such merit as they had is that
by some divine dispensation they happened to have right opinions
of certain matters.

Thirdly one cannot help seeing that the ostensible psychic-
ground conclusion of the dialogue (that *aretē* is certain right beliefs)
is not credible. Socrates does indeed, in the *Republic*, maintain that
under certain conditions right belief about moral matters could be
rendered stable; but in the *Meno* it is stressed that right beliefs are
unstable, and guide us rightly only when they are present, as they
cannot be relied on to be. We can believe that Socrates thought that
moral goodness was at bottom a matter of clearly understanding
something (say the destiny and true interests of the soul); we cannot
believe that he thought it was at bottom a matter of happening to
be right about how to use one's natural advantages. Therefore,
though Socrates does not say 'Oh dear, this conclusion will never
do; we must have made some mistake. What was it?', who can
doubt that Plato expected the reader to ask just this? If he does ask
it, the answer ready to hand is: 'Why, that we accepted that *aretē* is
to be identified with that which made Themistocles and Pericles
men of renown.'

Therefore, when Socrates insists that we cannot ask whether *aretē*
can be taught until we know what it is, part of what is covered by
'not knowing what it is' is not knowing in what way of living it
consists. Yet, in so far as 'It is knowledge of something' and 'It is
right belief about something' are accepted as apposite answers, the
question 'What is it?' is not to be taken as the question what it
consists in. We have, therefore, this troublesome situation in the
dialogue: (i) When Socrates illustrates how a 'what is *X*?' question
is to be answered he suggests that what he wants is a conceptual
analysis. But he is offered none; and the truisms that stand to *aretē*

as 'boundary of a solid' stands to shape are taken for granted as that which determines what the thing is which we are inquiring into. (ii) A large part of the discussion must provoke in the reader's mind the thought that the misidentification of *aretē* which Socrates foists upon Meno is responsible for the paradoxical conclusion, and that this is a practical demonstration of the truth that we cannot profitably ask whether *aretē* is teachable so long as we do not know (and therefore may be wrong about) what it is. Yet (iii), the formulas that are put forward as accounts of what *aretē* is offer neither the equivalent, for *aretē*, of 'the boundary of the solid', nor an account of the way of life in which *aretē* consists. They seem to be concerned with the ground of the general disposition to live well.

Clearly this might be the most important question. It might be that we could not determine which way of life is the right one until we had cleared our minds on this. But I gave notice some while ago that I would raise the question whether, if what Socrates wants is the ground of the disposition indicated by the virtue-word which occupies the place of '*X*', he can be said to be strictly correct in using the form of words 'What is *X*?' to elicit this (and we can be strictly correct in saying that he is after a real definition). We must now try to answer this question.

Why (where '*M*' is some description of a physical structure) do some of us feel that 'Brittleness is *M*' is not strictly speaking an account of what brittleness essentially is? I suppose it is because it is thought that a statement of the form '*A* is essentially *B*' is a statement of identity, and that a true statement of identity cannot be contingently true. In some possible world the propensity to break under shock might be dissociated from the property *M*; it is not dissociated in the actual world, but this means that brittleness and *M* are correlated in the actual world, not that the one *is* the other.

Many philosophers – for example many mind-brain-identity theorists – will find this reasoning misguided. But whether it is or not, the point I want to make is that the case (if there is one) for denying that brittleness actually *is* *M* rests on the fact that this proposition is at best contingent, and this in turn on the fact that we can tell whether a thing is brittle independently of telling whether it is *M*. If we say that it is on Socrates' part a pardonable confusion, but none the less strictly speaking a confusion, to use 'What is *X*?' in order to elicit the ground for the disposition indicated by '$X$' rather than the disposition itself, then we are implying that the disposition can be identified independently of the identification of what we are calling its ground. To most of us it seems quite evident that moral excellence can be identified quite independently of any kind of knowledge, and that therefore nothing along the lines of 'Virtue is knowledge' can be quite strictly described as a real definition of virtue. But on the other hand it has to be admitted that Plato may have thought quite otherwise. If he did, then it might be quite right to say that for him something along the lines of 'Virtue is knowledge' would be the real definition of virtue. If he did not, it would not be quite right. It is partly because the aptness of the description hinges on whether this condition is satisfied that I say it is not very helpful to describe a Socratic question as an invitation to produce a real definition. This description may commit those who offer it to more than they want.

One of our problems has been that a Socratic investigation tends to go thus: Socrates suggests that he wants some criterion by the use of which he can tell whether an allegedly $X$ thing really is $X$, and that he therefore wants to know what it is that is common and peculiar to every instance of $X$. After some time, however, (in the *Laches, Meno, Republic,* and, we might add, *Charmides*) we seem to have got away from this and to be considering something that might be the ground of the disposition under investigation, but that hardly looks like what Socrates wanted – a criterion with which to tell genuine from spurious instances of the exercise of the disposition. The ground of the disposition is identified in such a way that the disposition itself, we feel, is no more identified than it had to be at the beginning of the conversation if that conversation was to have a determinate topic. We no more know at the end of the fourth book of the *Republic* what kind of conduct ought to be described as justice than we know at the beginning of the dialogue.

But we have already seen that this seemingly rather odd structure of a Socratic investigation might not be due to a certain (understandable) confusion on the part of the author. It is possible that there *is* no feature common and peculiar to all instances of courage except that each is what would be done, in the particular situation in which he is, by the man who knows what things are truly terrible. It is possible that certain rules of thumb – tell the truth, pay debts, respect property – hold well enough in the case of justice; but (since not every debt-paying, for example, is a just action) that none of them, nor any group of them, gives us the

factor common and peculiar to all instances of justice; and it may be
that there *is* no such common factor other than that each just action
is the action that would be done by the man in whom reason rules
appetite with the aid of spirit (or stands in some close relationship
to that condition of soul). It is possible that there is nothing
common to every exercise of *aretē* except that each is the action
dictated in the situation by a knowledge of something – perhaps of
the nature of one's true good. If these possibilities were the case,
then in fact there would be no account of what courage, justice or
*aretē* is which was independent of what we have been calling the
ground of the disposition; it would not be true that the identification of the disposition with its ground would be a contingent
identification. There would remain, of course, a logical distinction
between possessing certain knowledge, or having a certain spiritual
structure, on the one hand, and acting, on the other hand, as the
man who possesses that knowledge, or has that structure, acts. But
the ground for saying, so to speak, that in some possible world the
disposition to act bravely might be dissociated from the knowledge
of what is truly terrible would have been cut away (and so with the
other dispositions). In no possible world can we *dissociate* acting as
the man who knows that *p* would act from knowing that *p*.

To say this is of course to presuppose that there exists such a
thing as: acting as the man who knows that *p* would act. It is to
presuppose that there is such a thing as, for example, acting
as the man who knows what things are truly terrible would
act. Notoriously we are inclined to think that there is no one such
way. Notoriously we are inclined to think that a man may know
that *A* is more truly harmful than *B*, but that, if *B* is more
superficially alarming, may embrace *A* in order to escape from *B*.
But if for some reason or other we were to decide that this is not
the case – if we were to decide that no man ever deliberately
embraces what he regards as the more harmful of two options[4] –
then it would follow that there was such a thing as the way in
which the man who knew what things were truly terrible would
act. And it might be the case that nothing was common and
peculiar to all instances of bravery but that they were cases of
acting in such a way. A reference to this knowledge would
then be essential to the real definition of courage. It might
be the case that nothing was common and peculiar to all instances of justice but that each was a case of acting as a man
would act in whom inordinate appetites did not impede his

appreciation of his true good. It might be the case that nothing was common and peculiar in all instances of *aretē* except that each was a case of acting as the man who knows something (perhaps what goals are worth pursuing) would act.

If we impute to Plato the belief that these possibilities do in fact obtain, then the apparently erratic structure of the dialogues we have looked at is no longer really erratic; and it would incidentally be correct to characterize as real definitions the answers at which Socrates seems to aim. How reasonable is it to impute such beliefs to him, not perhaps as fully explicit and articulated doctrines, but as part of what he took for granted in his approach to morality? I think that it is very reasonable to impute to Plato the belief, in this sense, that the moral life is a unity, and that the point of entry into the understanding of it is a grasp of what things are truly rewarding to the man whose spiritual constitution approximates, as closely as that of an embodied soul can approximate, to the true nature of the soul. In that case it will be the pursuit of those things that will deserve the title 'living well', and no more concrete account of living well, can, in face of the variability and complexity of the human predicament, be given; that pursuit, and nothing but that pursuit will be *aretē*. Along these lines it is fully intelligible why Plato should think that 'It is knowledge of what is truly terrible' does better the same thing that is done worse by Laches' first offering at 190e, 'It is staying at your post and keeping the enemy off, not running away'; the former gives us the only mark by which we can certainly tell a truly brave act from a counterfeit. It is a sketch of the real definition. (It will be no more than a sketch until it is filled in how we are to determine what is truly terrible.)

## TWO FURTHER QUESTIONS

Of the many questions that remain we will pay some attention to two. The first is this. If Plato really believed all this, how did it come about that he had difficulty (as the *Protagoras*, for example, suggests he did have) with the thesis that *aretē* is a unitary thing? For the doctrine of the unity of virtue seems to flow pretty smoothly from the beliefs we have imputed to him. What we intend by 'courage' is the handling of arduous matters as the man of *aretē* will handle them, what we intend by '*sophrosunē*' is the handling of things that appeal to appetite as that man would handle them, and so on. The virtues differ from each other primarily with regard to the field of exercise which is implied in the distinct virtue-concepts. Why does Plato seem not to have seen this? The short answer is that he assumed that, since 'courage' and 'justice' are not synonyms, they must stand for distinct things. But the question remains why he did not query this assumption, since he clearly did not like the conclusion.

No doubt some primitive semantical assumptions were involved. But from our point of view it seems a just comment that his neglect of conceptual analysis was partly to blame. We want to tell him that his unity thesis will be easy to state (and highly convincing) once he makes it explicit that there are in life many different predicaments that the good man has to face, and more than one angle from which we can assess his performance, and that, in consequence, we have many non-synonymous expressions which convey moral praise but also something else (as, for example, that the praiseworthy action involved the facing of a dangerous situation, or that it involved the recognition of a number of legitimate claims). We want, in fact, to urge him to spend more time on defining and analysing the concept of $X$ before pressing the Socratic question what $X$ is. Had he done this, some of his problems might have seemed simpler; but he might have become, like Aristotle, who did follow this course, a clearer but a less interesting moral philosopher.

The second question is this. What is Plato's answer to the question how it is that real definition is both possible, but also difficult? Why is it that, if we can identify the thing that we are trying to define, this does not allow us to read off the definition? We have in effect answered this question already; but I shall restate the answer with the aid of the doctrine of *anamnēsis*.

This doctrine is offered in the *Meno* as an explanation of how something can be possible which Socrates fervently believes is possible – namely that in such matters as the nature of *aretē*, as in geometrical matters, we can by mere discussion get rid of false beliefs and come to see the truth. Now, leaving aside the questions whether *anamnēsis* could explain this, and how it is meant to do so, the thing to be explained has certain implications. If we can by mere discussion get rid of false beliefs and supplant them with true ones, then the ideas with which we conduct the discussion cannot be totally false, however many false beliefs we may have derived from putting two and two together and making five, or failing to put two and two together to make four. Therefore the *basic* distinctions that we draw in thinking about the world must correspond to realities (the *anamnēsis* explanation being that they are traces of a clear perception of these realities had in a discarnate condition). Among these basic distinctions are those between living well and living badly, with its special cases such as living well with respect to what is arduous, or with respect to what excites appetite, or with respect to not overriding the claims of others. The task of the philosopher is to try to see how it is that there is such a distinction to be drawn. If he succeeded in that task, he would see why it is that there exists a style of life which is worthy of admiration and emulation, and others which are worthy to be rejected; and he would surely also see, *pari passu*, the broad outlines of the style of life which is admirable. Therefore to come to see what *aretē* is is at the same time to see what it consists in. It is to come to understand what it is of which moral approval and disapproval are the confused recognition. Just as it is obvious (to Meno's slave) that you double the area of a square by doubling its side, so it is obvious (to Meno) that you do not deserve much respect unless you can achieve a pretty effective and prominent place in your society. This is a terribly confused recognition of what the good is. But, since by mere discussion, Meno can (the faith is) be got to abjure such false opinions, he must retain a buried recollection of the elements, out of which the truth can be put together. Therefore when he comes to see what *aretē* is, he will be seeing what he 'knew all along', in the sense in which the slave knew all along that the square on the diagonal of a given square is double the area of the given square. Philosophy, or dialectic, is the recovery of what we knew all along.

But Meno is right to say that we cannot ask what *aretē* is, or what piety is, or courage is, unless we actually know (and not just 'know all along'), *some* kind of answer to these questions; the topic of our investigation must be somehow pinned down, or we are discoursing of something, we know not what. It seems that the topic is pinned down, in a Platonic dialogue devoted to the search for a Socratic definition, by the acceptance by all parties of the truistic explication of the *X* of which a real definition is sought. It is pinned down, in other words, by the crude beginnings of a conceptual definition. What makes real definition possible in moral matters is that the concepts with which we operate do not totally misrepresent reality – for whatever reason this may be, whether because we retain some 'memory' of a clearer vision, or otherwise. Therefore when we speak of piety, intending by this what we owe to the divine, even Euthyphro's monstrous misrepresentations are not total and irretrievable; he can be made to focus on what the divine nature must be, what obligation must be, and so he can be brought, step by step like Meno's slave, to a perception of the truth. Via the analysis of the concept, we can work round to the perception of the reality. That is what makes real definition possible – namely the fact that the reality sought is identified as that clearly intelligible thing which fits the specification provided by the analysis of the concept. What makes it difficult is, of course, the fact that our many misapprehensions as to what does fit that specification have first to be cleared away, and that, when that has been done, two and two must still be pieced together, and four made of them.

## SUMMARY

Briefly to summarize our conclusions, they are these. A Socratic question does not seek a linguistic definition. Nor does it seek a conceptual definition, though Socrates seems to suggest that it does. But in truth little space is devoted to conceptual analysis. Conceptual analysis does, however, play an important, but surreptitious, role in determining how the investigation proceeds; and in some cases it might have done it better had it been rendered explicit. We can say that what is sought by a Socratic question (of the kind we have been considering) is a real definition if we are prepared to attribute to Plato a certain theory of the moral life. Otherwise we should strictly say that what is sought is the ground of the relevant disposition, and not the definition of the disposition itself.

## NOTES

1 The search for the real definition being thus guided by a (perhaps implicit) grasp of the conceptual definition, which would bring out, of course, that courage is a virtue.
2 I refer to the alleged argument-pattern: physical processes can be both fast and slow, physical things both heavy and light; therefore physical instances of properties both are and are not instances; therefore it is not the case that physical instances fully are.
3 'Of something', 'about something'. The justification of these additions is: that the Greek words for 'knowledge' and for 'belief' readily take the

plural (as 'belief' does, and 'knowledge' does not); that there is no indefinite article in Greek; and that therefore 'X is *epistēmē*' can mean (even without the addition of '*tis*') 'X is an *epistēmē*', or '. . . a knowledge'.

4 Here I am, of course, almost quoting *Protagoras* 359d.

# CONCLUSIONS IN THE *MENO*

*Kathleen V. Wilkes*

## I

At 86c7 Meno reiterates the question with which he had opened the dialogue: Can *aretē*★ be taught? With the renewal of this query the *Meno* takes a most puzzling turn. There are at least five oddities in the ensuing chunk of dialogue; these merit close examination.

The first oddity comes with the introduction of the two 'hypotheses',[1] (a) that *aretē* is knowledge (*epistēmē*) (87c5), and (b), that *aretē* is good (*agathon*) (87d3). What is odd here is not the fact that, for the first time in Plato's writings, we find him using the so-called 'Hypothetical Method'; he had to begin sometime. It is rather the content of the hypotheses themselves that is curious. Hypothesis (a) is noteworthy because we know that it expresses Socrates' own view, the view that *aretē* is knowledge or wisdom (*epistēmē, phronēsis*). Hypothesis (b) is no less interesting. It seems more like a tautology than something we would call 'hypothetical'; no Greek would dream of denying it, even if he were an 'amoralist' like Callicles or Thrasymachus; all would agree that *aretē* was good, even if they disagreed about what did, and what did not, count as falling within the scope of the term *aretē*.[2]

The second oddity also concerns the hypotheses. The answer to Meno's question that the dialogue ostensibly reaches is that *aretē* cannot be taught. The argument for this conclusion (89d3–96c10) runs: if *aretē* were teachable (*didakton*), there would be teachers and learners of it; but there are none; hence it is not

★ '*Aretē*' is typically translated 'virtue'. This is misleading, since the set of *aretai* includes many qualities that are not specifically 'moral'. A less misleading translation might be 'excellence'; least misleading of all, though, to leave it (and similarly the plural *aretai*) in transliterated form.

teachable. Neither hypothesis is used in this argument, so given 89d3 to 96c10 the elaborate introduction of the hypotheses seems unnecessary. This somewhat blank observation leads to the third oddity. The argument from hypotheses (a) and (b) reaches a conclusion that directly contradicts the subsequent 'unteachable' finding; for if *aretē* is knowledge it must be teachable, and it is knowledge.

The contradiction is apparently resolved by an argument that gives us the fourth oddity of this part of the dialogue. Socrates returns to examine the argument that led from hypothesis (b), that *aretē* is good, to hypothesis (a), that *aretē* is knowledge, and concludes that it was fallacious. Whatever is good is beneficial, but it is not invariably knowledge that guides men right; right belief (*orthē doxa*) can as well. Thus from the premise that *aretē* is good, one cannot conclude that it is knowledge; it might be either knowledge or right belief. Since there are no teachers or learners of *aretē*, *aretē* cannot be knowledge, which would be teachable – it must be right belief. Now this conclusion we should find extremely puzzling. *Aretē*, as the excellence of the soul (*psūchē*) stands to the soul as health does to the body; it must be a stable state, and the best possible state of the soul. But beliefs 'run away from a person's soul, so they aren't worth much until one ties them down by reasoning out the explanation' (*aitiās logismos*) (98a2–4), in other words, until one converts them into knowledge. Whatever else *aretē* may be, we cannot seriously suppose that either Socrates or Plato would degrade it to the status of true belief.

The final and most striking oddity of all these arguments is the context in which they appear. Immediately before Meno's question at 86c7 comes the description and discussion of recollection (*anamnēsis*) (81a5–86c2). Meno accepts the theory of recollection; but to accept it means that one accepts also a redefinition of 'knowledge' as 'recollection', of 'teaching' as 'reminding' – prompting the rememberer with questions, parallels and objections – and of 'learning' as, again, 'recollecting'. Moreover, in his speech in reply to Meno's question at 86c7 Socrates explicitly reminds Meno of these redefinitions: 'teachable' now means 'recollectable' (*anamnēston*). Given, then, the revised understanding of what 'teaching' and 'learning' are, the only way to give relevant sense to Meno's question is to suppose him to be asking whether or not *aretē* is something which one can recollect, something of which one man can remind another. But if the question is indeed taken in this sense, then the entire argument from the absence of (orthodox) teachers and learners of *aretē* (89d3–96c10) becomes wholly irrelevant.

## II

To resolve these puzzles, it is necessary to go over some of the main points of the theory of recollection as presented in the *Meno*.[3] If it is stripped of myth and metaphor, and if the religious doctrine of reincarnation and any (possible) reference to the Theory of Forms are ignored,[4] then what is left is, simply, dialectic. This is put beyond all doubt by Socrates' interrogation of the slave. Up to 84a the inquisition has followed the familiar path of the elenchus: two false beliefs have been disproved, and the slave has reached a state of *aporia*, bafflement. Thus far, as Socrates points out to Meno at 83a3–c9, the reactions of Meno and the slave have been precisely analogous – each floored by the elenctic method. After 84d the question-and-answer method leads to a positive and true conclusion at 85b, and in this respect differs from any other elenchus found in earlier dialogues; but this is due rather to the nature of the subject (geometry, not ethical definitions) than to any departure from the elenctic method. Still, we need not and should not equate the method of recollection with the elenchus; but we could equate it with dialectic generally.

To recollect something, then, is to follow through a dialectical inquiry, aiming to discover the presuppositions and implications of certain propositions, to discover which beliefs lead eventually to contradiction or refutation by counter-example and must hence be rejected, to discover the consequences of analysing a concept in a certain way. It is a purely *a priori* method of inquiry, even though sensible prompts (sticks, stones, drawings in sand) may be employed to aid the investigations; no empirical truths can be learnt by this method.

The next critical point to notice about recollection is that it may lead *both* to true belief and to knowledge. This Socrates makes clear at the end of his interrogation of the slave. He gets Meno to agree (85c6–8) that the slave has proved to have within him true beliefs about things of which he had, *and as yet has*, no knowledge; the experiment has given the slave true beliefs about squares and their areas, beliefs that are now 'as in a dream' (*hōsper onar* 85c9). But he continues by asserting (85c10–d1) that if the slave were to undergo similar questioning many times, he would end up with knowledge of these matters as precise as anyone's. By persisting with the method of recollection one can convert true *a priori* beliefs into knowledge, as one provides the beliefs in question with an *aitiās logismos* – the sufficient reasons that prove the belief true. In other words, recollection is a means both of discovering, and of proving, true *a priori* beliefs. This is indeed what we should expect. The method may take as starting point anything at all – a belief, a hypothesis, a drawing in the sand and a question – which puts both parties to the debate into a certain area of inquiry, such as geometry or the analysis of moral concepts; within this area each true belief will entail, be entailed by, and be consistent with, other true beliefs in the same area. Hence the longer one spends in that conceptual field, the more often one explores it, hunting out implications, entailments, and presuppositions, and looking for contradictions, counter-arguments, or counter-examples, the firmer will become the hold upon each true belief until it is thoroughly 'tied down' and can be counted as knowledge. The difference between right belief and knowledge, understood in this light, will be simply a matter of the degree of thoroughness with which the area has been explored.

After this brief outline of the method of recollection we can return to reconsider Meno's question at 86c7. 'Can *aretē* be taught?' may be taken in either of two ways, depending on our view of Meno's acuity. The first and less interesting interpretation of his demand supposes that Meno is not only undisciplined in argument (we know he is that)[5] but also stupid; that he has enjoyed the passage with the slave as a kind of sideshow, which he dismisses in order to return to his original question about *orthodox* teaching and learning. The more interesting interpretation of the challenge is to suppose that Meno has fully realized the difference that the redefinition of 'teaching' and 'learning' has made to his inquiry, and to credit him with a laudable scepticism about whether *aretē* is as suitable a subject for recollection as is geometry. This would be an excellent question, and one in which Plato would have been much interested. For if the method of recollection is simply dialectic, and if it proves to be merely elenctic dialectic at that (no hint of any new method has appeared by 86c), then one must remember that all the dialogues preceding the *Meno* that have inquired into one or all of the *aretai* have ended in *aporia*, bafflement; false beliefs may indeed have been unearthed and

rejected, but rarely are true or positive beliefs discovered to supplant them. It may well seem – to Meno and to Plato – that the
truth about *aretē* somehow eludes the elenchus, and if the method
of recollection is simply the elenchus all over again, it will elude
that too. There is another reason for finding Meno's revised query
interesting. Recollection is an *a priori* philosophical method of
inquiry. What reason is there to suppose that success at this intellectual enterprise will ensure that the inquirer has 'learned *aretē*' in the
sense that he has learned to become a man of *aretē*? Certainly this
question should appeal to us today; there seems no good reason to
suppose (for example) that a thoroughly evil man could not write a
brilliant and enlightening article entitled 'The Good'. Our sym-
pathies may lie rather with the suggestion put forward by both
Anytus (92e3–6) and Theognis (95d4–e1), that the best way of
acquiring *aretē* is to spend time in the company of 'fine and good'
men – the *kaloi kāgathoi*.

Unfortunately it seems clear that Meno did intend his question in
the unrevised and boring sense, and has failed to grasp the difference that the discussion of recollection has made to the problem.
He asks Socrates to consider 'the question I first asked' (86c8), just
as he had posed it before; yet it would have been simple for him to
have altered the wording to ask if *aretē* were something of which
one man could remind another. Moreover, Socrates' reply to the
reiterated question (his speech from 86d3 to 87c3) begins by chid-
ing him for his lack of discipline in argument – a criticism that
suggests that Meno is carelessly or wilfully ignoring the relevance
of the recent discussion and is dropping that in order to return to
the beginning again. Finally, although Socrates explicitly reminds
Meno (further on in the same speech, at 87b7–8) that the doctrine of
recollection has changed the interpretation of the question, pointing out that 'teachable' must now be taken as 'recollectable', Meno
must have forgotten this by 89d. For it is only if Meno were still
thinking of *orthodox* teaching and learning, ignoring Socrates'
reminders, that he could be taken in by the argument of 89d3–
96c10; this argument moves from the absence of orthodox teachers
and learners of *aretē* to its unteachability. It is, of course, wholly
irrelevant to a query about whether *aretē* is something of which one
man can remind another through dialectic. We can only conclude
that Meno has failed entirely to see the bearing of the theory
of recollection on his original question. Equally clearly, though,
we can see that Plato was fully aware of it, and intended his

readers to be so too. Thus there are two problems to solve: Meno's old one, and Socrates' new one.

The new question is whether or not *aretē* is recollectable. The simplest, most elegant and convincing answer to this problem would be, of course, to recollect what *aretē* is, thereby illustrating its teachability-through-recollection and also going some way towards answering Socrates' primary question: what is *aretē*? And this – if the above interpretation of 86c7–87c1 is correct, and if we are right to see the essence of the method of recollection as being dialectic – is precisely what Socrates does from 87c to 89c. I suggest, in other words, that 87c to 89c is a second exercise in recollection with Meno instead of the slave as the pupil, and the subject *aretē* instead of geometry. All endeavours to recollect need some starting point. With the slave, Socrates began with a drawing in the sand and a question about it; the parallel exercise with Meno takes a hypothesis as the jumping-off point. The hypothesis is, of course, that *aretē* is knowledge; and one immediate entailment of this is that *aretē* must be teachable. And 'teachable', given the explicit reminder of 87b7–8 means 'recollectable'. A second entailment of this first hypothesis is not here picked up overtly, but we cannot suppose either that Plato has overlooked it, or that he intended the reader to neglect it. 'Knowledge', like 'teaching' and 'learning', has been given a revised interpretation by the discussion of recollection; to know is to recollect. What is known is precisely what one has recollected, so long as the process of recollection has gone far enough for the rediscovered true beliefs to have been tied down as knowledge by an *aitiās logismos*. So knowledge is recollection; and if *aretē* is knowledge, it too is recollection. We shall discuss this entailment shortly.

Socrates does not stress this second implication of his first hypothesis; instead, he looks for a proposition that might entail the hypothesis itself, so that there may be some *aitiās logismos* to confirm or at least strengthen it. He finds such a proposition in the second hypothesis, that *aretē* is good.[6] If he can prove from this that *aretē* is knowledge, the first hypothesis will indeed be well supported; for the proposition that *aretē* is good is, as we have seen, indubitable and undeniable. The argument from the second to the first hypothesis, although it has its puzzling elements,[7] is clear enough: whatever is good is beneficial. But nothing at all is invariably beneficial unless it is controlled by wisdom. A concealed premise that Socrates does not bother with is that the man of wisdom is the man with knowledge – for the purposes of this argument, wisdom (*phronēsis*) just is knowledge (*epistēmē*).[8] Hence knowledge or wisdom is the only truly beneficial thing, and must be *aretē*.

Meno has followed all this, and concludes without hesitation that *aretē* must be teachable. However if it is right to regard 87c–89c as a second exercise in recollection parallel to the interrogation of the slave, then we should expect that what was true of the slave at the end of his inquisition is no less true of Meno now, at the close of this experiment in recollection; 'at present it's as though in a dream that these opinions have just been aroused in him. But if someone questions him many times and in many ways about the same things as now, you may be sure he'll end up knowing them as precisely as anyone does' (85c9–d1). Meno has now no more than a true belief about *aretē*, and true beliefs are not stable but shift around like the statues of Daedalus (97d–98a). Where the subject is as important as *aretē* (cf. *Apology* 29e–30b), and where the pupil is someone as unstable as Meno – always at the mercy of a plausible sounding argument and unlikely to have the patience to submit to answering 'the same questions put to him on many occasions and in different ways' – he cannot be left in complacent possession of a half-understood argument. Socrates therefore proceeds to shake Meno's belief; he 'refutes' the conclusion that *aretē* is knowledge and hence teachable by an argument so irrelevant that Meno could not have failed to dismiss it if he had really followed and understood the discussion since the introduction of the theory of recollection. Meno, who as we have seen almost certainly intended his question at 86c7 in the original 'unrevised' sense, sees nothing odd when Socrates reverts without warning to talk of 'teaching' and 'learning' in their orthodox senses and points out that there are no teachers and learners of *aretē*. Meno grants the dubious premise that the absence of teachers and learners shows a subject to be unteachable. But if this is so, then *aretē* cannot be knowledge, since whatever is knowledge is teachable. Thus the conclusion of 89c – a conclusion that we have excellent reason to believe that Socrates held true – is overturned. This tactic of Socrates, refuting a view that he himself holds when it is adopted by someone who fails to grasp its import, has been seen before, in the *Laches*. There Nicias, in order to avoid the humiliating refutation that befell his friend Laches, adopted what he knew to be Socrates' own view about what courage was (*Laches*

194d1ff). But since he did not himself understand adequately the definition that he was parroting, Socrates refuted him easily (*Laches* 194d–200a), despite the fact that it was his own view that was being 'disproved'. The use of this tactic in the *Meno* has, however, an extra element of irony: the 'irrelevant' argument from the absence of (orthodox) teachers and learners of *aretē* does in fact provide a sensible answer – an answer that Plato probably thought valid – to the question of the teachability of *aretē as Meno intended it: aretē* cannot be taught by orthodox means.

In this rebuttal of the former conclusion by the 'irrelevant argument' we see Plato illustrating the distinction he is soon to draw (97d–98d) between right belief and knowledge. Knowledge is tied down by sufficient reasons, beliefs can fluctuate; being inadequately based, a true belief can be made to look false. Meno's beliefs, whether true or false, will always be vulnerable to this sort of refutation, since he is idle and too impatient: concerned only with conclusions, he is too little concerned with the adequacy and merit of the arguments by which they are reached. It is not for nothing that Socrates has stressed the need to become active and energetic in the search for truth (81d–e, 86b–c). If one persists in the endeavour to recollect, then one becomes better, and braver, and more active; in other words, one gets more *aretē*. Yet to persist in this way means that one's true beliefs will become tied down and will turn into knowledge. So we see again, from a different angle, how *aretē* is indeed a matter of knowledge and recollection.

Surprisingly enough Socrates' resolution of the contradiction – namely that one argument has led to the conclusion that *aretē* is knowledge and hence teachable, and that another has led to the conclusion that it is unteachable and hence not knowledge – does not, as one might expect, resolve it by pointing out the irrelevancy of the second argument.[9] Instead, he locates the fault in the first. It is not after all knowledge alone that guides men right, for right belief can do so too. If so, *aretē* may be either knowledge or right belief; and given the absence of teachers and learners, it must be right belief rather than knowledge, unless perhaps a true statesman one day appears, a man who is capable of teaching *aretē* to another. But until such a man is found, *aretē* must be merely right belief. This argument is surely most unexpected. For it is impossible to think that either Socrates or Plato[10] would endorse the conclusion, holding the view that they do about the pre-eminence that *aretē* must have. True belief is a second-best and is inferior to knowledge, but *aretē* cannot be inferior to anything; for it is to the soul what health is to the body, a stable state of excellence. True beliefs are not stable (cf. the Daedalus passage, 97d–98a). Above all, the man who merely believes something without knowing it will, evidently, not know whether his belief is true or false; hence, if he is honest with himself, he will not know whether or not it is a belief upon which he should act. (Meno has a glimmering that there is something wrong with the idea that right belief is as good a guide to right action as is knowledge at 97c6–8; but unfortunately he muddles his point.) Right belief seems a most unpromising candidate for identification with *aretē*.

Nevertheless there is good reason to stress a connection between *aretē* and right belief at this point of the dialogue. We have already heard and seen many true beliefs in action, and they have played various roles. First, the true beliefs of the slave provided a starting point for Socrates' interrogation. Second, what the slave reached as a result of the experiment was, again, true belief; but a true belief different from any of those with which he began. Third, we have been told that true beliefs can be converted into knowledge by persistence with recollection – persistence that works to ground the beliefs in the *aitiās logismos* that turns them into knowledge proper. We saw that both right belief and knowledge of *a priori* matters may be attained through the method of recollection and that the difference between them lay in degree rather than kind: the degree of thoroughness with which the subject matter in question had been explored. In sum, the stage of believing truly is required if one is to attain to knowledge; it is part of the process that leads to knowledge and hence to *aretē*.

But it is even more than that. For *aretē* is not solely, and perhaps not even primarily, something that one 'attains', it is certainly not something that is attained if one thinks of 'attainment' as a once-and-for-all achievement. The least inadequate translation of *aretē*, as already commented (see footnote on p. 208 above], is probably 'excellence'. As such, it cannot be something that one either has *simpliciter* or does not have. To 'have' *aretē* is not a matter of resting on one's moral laurels; it is rather a matter of a steady determination to attain new laurels. In 86b–c Socrates affirms that men become better, braver, and more active by looking to discover what they do not yet know; *aretē* is not only the product, it is also the process, of inquiry. This is a note that resounds throughout the

*Apology*: the chief demand made by *aretē* is that one must search unceasingly for it. *Aretē* is thus 'recollection' even more than it is 'what is recollected'. But in order to recollect, one needs must begin with belief, and one's first achievements will themselves be beliefs too; however, as what one is doing is searching for *aretē*, one will be displaying and acquiring it by the very search, even when one is merely at the stage of gaining and rejecting beliefs. What one must not do with beliefs, true or false, is to rest content with them and leave them unexamined: the demand to persist and either convert them into knowledge or dismiss them as false is a demand imposed by *aretē* itself.

The successful statesmen of 93c–94e and 99b–d have indeed true beliefs; however they do not treat them as mere stages on the route to knowledge, but instead rest content with them and leave them unexamined. Thus they can have no guarantee that their beliefs are true rather than false, and they cannot have the *aretē* that is, simply, the determination to discover it. That these Daedalus-like beliefs do in fact lead these men to correct action is nothing but lucky chance – a chance so unexpected and remarkable that it is practically miraculous and should be thought of as coming by 'divine dispensation' (*theia moira*). This is the shadow of the substance that is *aretē*; it is the image of the genuine reality that is possessed by the man who has knowledge, and who is capable of teaching others true *aretē*.[11]

The identity of the statesman of 100a1–2 who can indeed make others like himself and teach them *aretē* is now no mystery. He has been seen in action already, giving Meno his introductory lesson. Moreover, there is the striking testimony of the *Gorgias*, a dialogue probably written only a short time before the *Meno*.[12] Socrates is winding up his argument with Callicles: 'I think I am one of a few Athenians – not to say the only one – who undertake the real political craft and practise politics – the only one among people now' (*Gorgias* 521d6–8, trans T. Irwin, Oxford 1979). The context of this passage confirms the parallel with the *Meno*. In each dialogue Socrates has either agreed or suggested that a primary duty of the statesman is to teach men *aretē*; moreover, as in the *Meno*, the *Gorgias* passage follows a discussion of the inadequacy at this task of Athenian statesmen past and present. It is impossible to believe that Plato did not intend his readers to put these two dialogues together, and realize that it is the dialectician who alone can teach *aretē*.

217

## III

The *Meno*'s conclusions are self-referential, or perhaps self-reflecting. Once the theory of recollection is set out, then 'knowledge', 'teaching', and 'learning' are all redefined in terms of recollection and reminding. Thus to try to find out what *aretē* is, and whether or not it is teachable, means trying to recollect the answers to these questions, for they are *a priori* matters. The argument from 87c to 89c is ostensibly an argument to the conclusion that *aretē* is teachable. In fact it proves that *aretē* is knowledge and hence is recollection by constituting the recollection that it is so; and it proves also that *aretē* is teachable not only by entailment from '*aretē* is knowledge' to '*aretē* is teachable', but also by itself constituting a lesson in *aretē*, the lesson that should have succeeded in teaching Meno what *aretē* is. However, a further implication of the identification of *aretē* with recollection via its identification with knowledge is that the attempt to recollect is as critical as is the product of recollection; one aims not merely to get conclusions, but to discover further arguments for those conclusions, and to use the conclusions themselves as steps towards further discoveries. Unless one is willing to do this, the conclusions reached, however glossy in appearance, will remain on the level of beliefs – unstable and liable to overthrow. This point too is illustrated in the *Meno*, by Meno. The true belief that he has reached by 89c is 'disproved' by the irrelevant argument from the absence of orthodox teachers and learners; he loses the truth he has gained because he lacked the readiness – indeed lacked the *aretē* – to persist in the attempt to examine and support further the arguments that led him and Socrates to the conclusion that *aretē* was knowledge and hence teachable. Since he will not ponder over the highly satisfactory conclusion reached at 89c, it is better that he be left with a conclusion that he is bound to find unsatisfactory, and which he is more likely to examine for flaws. If indeed *aretē* is the attempt to scrutinize the beliefs one holds in order to arrive at better ones, then, paradoxically enough, Meno is more likely to learn *aretē* if he is left with an unsatisfactory false belief than if he were left with a true belief that he mistakes for knowledge.

## NOTES

1 Although 'hypothesis' can be an unsatisfactory translation of the Greek *'hupothesis'* (see n. 2), I shall follow the convention used by most commentators and retain it as a translation. Hence the scare-quotes used here will not be repeated.

2 To call (b) a 'hypothesis' is therefore misleading; it has puzzled many that a truism like (b) is 'hypothesized'. R. S. Bluck, in his edition *Plato's Meno* (Cambridge, 1961), p. 88, gets round the problem by arguing that it is *not* a truism, and *can* be called a 'hypothesis', because 'good' is intended in the sense of 'beneficial' (*ōphelimon*) and *'aretē* is beneficial' is a genuine hypothesis. But this explanation will not suffice, as there is a separate move from *'aretē* is good' to *'aretē* is beneficial' at 87e1–2, a move for which Meno's agreement is asked and secured, and whose validity it was open to him to deny. The problem, however, is not a real one. As R. Robinson points out (*Plato's Earlier Dialectic* (Oxford, 1953) Ch. VII), the Greek term *'hupothesis'* can, and often does, mean simply 'premise', 'proposition', or 'something laid down' (to serve as a basis for further inquiry); as such a tautology, or even a falsehood, would serve quite as well as a genuine 'hypothesis'. Possibly, too, Socrates is using these 'hypotheses' to play a role analogous to the two sketches he drew for the slave; starting points to jog the recollector's memory. Notice, too, that 'hypothesis' (b) is implicitly or explicitly used elsewhere in the dialogue; e.g., at 77b4–78c1, and at 98e10–12. (I am grateful to Professor Wagner, and an anonymous reader of the *Archiv für Geschichte der Philosophie*, for some of these points.)

3 For a full and illuminating discussion of the theory of recollection see G. Vlastos, *'Anamnesis* in the *Meno', Dialogue* IV (1965), pp. 143–67 [reprinted in this volume, pp. 88–111. Ed.].

4 For the purposes of this paper, the doctrine of reincarnation is best ignored; so also the question of whether or not Plato is here presupposing the existence of Forms. The doctrine of recollection is not yet in its full-blown form, and it would be risky and unnecessary to read too much of the *Phaedo* back into the *Meno*. For a full treatment of the theory of recollection in the *Meno* and in later dialogues see T. Irwin, 'Recollection and Plato's moral theory', *Review of Metaphysics* XXVII (1973), pp. 752–72.

5 Cf. 75b1–3; 76a9–c2; 80d5–81a3; 86c7–e1.

6 See n. 2.

7 The most puzzling part of this argument is that Socrates claims that courage, temperance, quickness of mind, and presumably all the other *aretai* (except *sophia?*) may be harmful unless their possessor governs their exercise with *phronēsis*. Elsewhere (cf. *Protagoras*) he argues that to have such *aretai* is, precisely, to have wisdom.

8 We need not bother with this concealed premise either. Socrates here uses *epistēmē, phronēsis, nous* (88b5, 99c7, 100a1), and *sophia* (99b4) more or less interchangeably, and substitution of *epistēmē* for all these others would not materially affect the argument.

9 Hardly ever in the early dialogues – that is, in all the dialogues preceding the *Meno* – does Socrates explain to his interlocutor any mistake that the latter has made. His ambition is rather to get the other to find out for himself what beliefs he should and should not hold; we never find him imparting information directly. See G. Vlastos, 'The paradox of Socrates', in Vlastos (ed.) *The Philosophy of Socrates* (New York and London, 1971), especially pp. 12–15.

10 Socrates certainly would never endorse this conclusion; and Plato, although he allows in the *Phaedo* and the *Republic* (cf. 430b) that the vulgar, the slavish, and the non-philosopher may have a version of *aretē* that does not rest upon knowledge, would never agree that genuine or philosophic *aretē* could be true belief. It is important to remember that this dialogue is a dialogue between philosophers about the true nature of *aretē*; to the extent that they are talking about a second-best kind of *aretē* they have changed the subject.

11 It is instructive to compare the position of the statesmen who have the shadow of *aretē* by 'divine dispensation' with that of the prisoners in the cave at *Republic* VII; cf. 515c1–2.

12 Bluck argues (op. cit., pp. 108–20) that the Gorgias was probably written in about 387 and that the *Meno* is Plato's next work, written in 386/5.

# MENO'S PARADOX AND
# SOCRATES AS A TEACHER

*Alexander Nehamas*

Meno has always been considered as one of the least gifted and co-operative characters in Plato's dialogues. Commentators have disdained him generally, but their greatest disdain is reserved for the argument he introduces to the effect that all learning is impossible at *Meno* 80d5–8. Shorey, who had no patience for the view expressed in the paradox itself, referred to it disparagingly as 'this eristic and lazy argument'.[1] Taylor liked neither the argument nor Meno's reasons for bringing it up: 'Meno', he wrote, 'again tries to run off on an irrelevant issue. He brings up the sophistic puzzle . . .'.[2] Klein thought of the negative influence of the paradox on all desire to learn anything new and wrote that Meno himself 'was conspicuously reluctant to make the effort Socrates requested of him. It seems that his behaviour throughout the conversation was in agreement with the consequence that flows from the argument he has just presented.'[3] Bernard Phillips, who with many other writers takes the argument itself quite seriously, nevertheless insists that for Meno personally 'it is merely a dodge'.[4] Even Bluck, who is slightly more sympathetic to Meno than other writers are, cannot approve of him in this instance: 'So far as Meno is concerned, this question may be regarded as a convenient dodge, an eristic trick; but for Plato, it had important philosophical implications.'[5]

Plato himself certainly took Meno's paradox seriously, as we can see from the care with which he develops his own controversial and complicated solution to the problem (*Meno* 81a5–86c2) and from the intimate connection of that solution, the theory of recollection, to the Theory of Forms when the latter eventually appears, as it does not in the *Meno*, in Plato's texts.[6] But does Plato take only the argument, and not Meno himself, seriously? Is Meno merely dodging the issue and trying to win a debating point from

Socrates? Is his paradox simply a pretext for Plato to present his own, recently acquired, epistemological ideas?

This view is invested with considerable authority, but does not seem to me to be true. To see that it is not, we must first examine the general situation that prompts Meno to present his paradox as well as the precise wording of his statement. If we can show that Plato thinks that Meno himself has good reason to raise this difficulty then we shall be able to connect this passage with certain other issues, some of which were of considerable importance in Plato's philosophical thinking.

## I

The question whether *aretē* is teachable, inborn, or acquired in some other way, with which Meno so abruptly opens the dialogue (71a,1–4), was a commonplace of early Greek speculation. That it concerned not only Socrates but also, more generally, the sophistic movement is already indicated by the Gorgianic style of Meno's question.[7] More traditionally, the issue applied not only to *aretē* but also to *sophia* (wisdom); this may appear surprising in view of the fact that Socrates finds it uncontroversial to claim that if *aretē* is *epistēmē* (knowledge or understanding, often used interchangeably with *sophia*) then it is surely teachable (*Meno* 87c5–6).[8] Already by the end of the fifth century, the author of *Dissoi Logoi* (403–395 BC) can refer to the 'neither true nor new argument that *sophiē* and *aretā* can neither be taught nor learned' (6.1).[9] In a famous passage of *Olympian* II. 86–8, Pindar had already claimed that the wise (which in this case refers to the poet) is so by nature, the rest being to him like cacophonous crows in comparison.[10] Isocrates was to argue that *aretē* and *dikaiosunē* (justice) are not purely teachable, without, that is, the proper nature (*Contra Sophistas* 14–18, 21)[11] – a position with some affinities to Plato's view in the *Republic*. Finally, a similar position in regard to *andreia* (courage) is attributed to Socrates by Xenophon at *Memorabilia* III. 9.

But though this question was commonplace, there was little, if any agreement as to the nature of what it concerned, the nature of *aretē*. What concerns me is not the specific debate over the distinction between 'quiet' or 'co-operative' and competitive virtues. Mine is the much simpler point that *aretē* has an immensely broader range of application than its conventional English translation 'virtue', while the more recent 'excellence' strikes me as too weak and vague. *Aretē* not only applies to more human qualities than 'virtue' does, but it also covers features that are in no way specifically human. This is, of course, perfectly clear from *Republic* 352d–354a, where Plato discusses explicitly the *aretē* of instruments and, by implication, that of animals. But this usage is not found only in Plato. Already in Homer, horses are said to possess *aretē* (*Iliad* XXIII. 276, 374). Even inanimate objects can have their characteristic excellence: fertile soil (Thucydides I. 2, 4) and fine cotton (Herodotus III. 106, 2) are cases in point. If it were not for this, we might do well to construe *aretē* as 'success' or as the quality that constitutes or that accounts for it. If nothing else, this would show that the ancient debate is relevant to the many contemporary promises to ensure success, for an appropriate fee, in all sorts of fields and endeavours and which prompt Socratic and Platonic responses from all those who look down upon the notion of success implicit in these promises and upon the endeavours themselves. We may thus be able to answer Jowett, who, construing *aretē* as virtue, claimed that 'no one would either ask or answer such a question (as Meno's) in modern times'.[12]

In order to account for the application of *aretē* to animals as well as to inanimate objects, it might be better to construe it as that quality or set of qualities, whatever that may be, that makes something *outstanding* in its group. We might even consider it as what accounts for an object's *justified notability*. Both suggestions concern not only intrinsic features of such objects but also, in one way or another, their reputation. And this is as it should be. For from the earliest times on, the notion of *aretē* was intrinsically social, sometimes almost equivalent to fame (*kleos*). That this was so even in late periods is shown by Hypereides, who in his *Epitaph* wrote that those who die for their city 'leave *aretē* behind them' (41). Also, an epigraph commemorating the Athenians who fell at Potidaea states that 'having placed their lives onto the scale, they received *aretē* in return'.[13]

The question, therefore, whether *aretē* can be taught is the question whether one can be taught what it takes to have a justifiably high reputation among one's peers.[14] But this, of course, leaves the prior question unanswered; the term is not non-controversially connected with any particular set of human qualities. We still do not know the proper domain within which one is supposed to be outstanding or, even more importantly, in what being outstanding itself consists.

This last reasonable doubt, expressed in appropriate Socratic vocabulary, suggests that Socrates' own response to Meno's opening question makes rather good sense. In the persona of an imaginary Athenian, Socrates tells Meno not only that he does not know whether it can be taught but also that he doesn't know 'in any way at all (*to parapan*) what *aretē* itself is' (71a5–7).[15] Now as long as we think of *aretē* as virtue we have enough intuitions about what that is to think that Socrates' reply must be prompted by metaphysical or epistemological considerations. He, too, we suppose, has a pretty good idea of what virtue is, but insists that he does not in order to make a purely philosophical point about the priority of definition. Yet, though not without important metaphysical implications, Socrates' response to Meno's precipitate question is quite independently reasonable. Meno asks without preamble a commonplace question which none the less depends on many disputable presuppositions. Socrates' reaction is, simply, to try to slow Meno and the discussion down.[16]

In light of this, I follow Bluck (p. 209) in taking *to parapan* at 71a6 closely with *oude*. Socrates is disclaiming all knowledge of the nature of *aretē*, and he does exactly the same at 71b4: *ouk eidōs peri aretēs to parapan* ('not knowing about *aretē* at all'). I also take it that his very next point, that one cannot know whether Meno is beautiful, rich, or noble, if one does not in any way (*to parapan*) know who Meno is, is strictly parallel. Socrates is not appealing to a distinction between knowledge by acquaintance and knowledge by description as Bluck (pp. 32–3, 213–14) among others, has claimed, nor is he introducing, at least implicitly, a technical distinction between knowledge and belief and claiming that though one can have all sorts of beliefs about the object of one's inquiry, these beliefs cannot become knowledge unless they are supplemented by knowledge of the definition of the nature of the object in question.[17] His point is simple and intuitive: if he has *no* idea who Meno is, how can he answer any questions about him? That this is so is shown by the fact that Meno immediately accepts Socrates' general view, as he should not on either of the two interpretations above. What he cannot believe is that Socrates is quite as ignorant as he claims to be about the nature of *aretē*.

Nevertheless, and in characteristic fashion, Socrates insists on his ignorance and asks Meno, who claims to know, to tell him what *aretē* is. Meno makes three efforts (71e ff, 73c ff, 76b ff). But in each case he can only produce many *aretai* instead of the one that

Socrates wants in answer to his question. Meno is originally unwilling to agree that *aretē* is one (73a1–5). He then agrees to go along with Socrates without necessarily accepting his view (*eiper hen ge ti zēteis kata pantōn* – 'if what you're searching for is some one thing which covers them all', 73d1). He finally appears to accept Socrates' arguments to that effect (79a7–e4). Willing as he is to co-operate with Socrates, Meno is led from thinking that he knew what *aretē* is to being unable to say anything satisfactory about his topic, each time unexpectedly, and in a different way, being shown to make the very same error.

It is only after the failure of his third effort that Meno begins to lose his patience. Even so, he very politely concedes that Socrates seems correct in what he says (cf. 79d5, 79e4) and rather ingenuously confesses that he cannot answer the question. Through his famous comparison of Socrates to the torpedo fish, he claims that though he had earlier spoken at length and well about *aretē* his contact with Socrates seems to have robbed him of all ability to do so now (79c7–80b3).

It is very important to notice the exact expression Meno uses at this point: '*nūn de oud' hoti estin to parapan echō eipein*' ('but now I can't even say what [*aretē*] is at all') (80b4). He admits that he is unable to say even in the most general terms what *aretē* is, that he is totally lost and confused. And by the repetition of the crucial term *to parapan*, through which Socrates had earlier disavowed all ability to lead the discussion, Plato now places Meno, even if against his will, in the very same position which Socrates had eagerly taken up at the opening of the dialogue.

Socrates refuses to return Meno's compliment and offer a simile in his turn (80c3–6). If he has reduced Meno to perplexity, he says, it is only because he is himself perplexed.

καὶ νῦν περὶ ἀρετῆς ὃ ἔστιν ἐγὼ μὲν οὐκ οἶδα, σὺ μέντοι ἴσως πρότερον μὲν ᾔδησθα πρὶν ἐμοῦ ἅψασθαι, νῦν μέντοι ὅμοιος εἶ οὐκ εἰδότι.

('and with *aretē* now, I on my side *don't* know about it, while you on yours *did* know, perhaps, till you came into contact with me, while now you are similar to someone who *doesn't* know'.) (80d1–3)

This passage is important. We should notice, for one thing, the irony of the final phrase, in which Socrates, despite his earlier disclaimer, does after all offer a simile for Meno; though, of course, to say as he does that Meno is 'similar to someone who does not know' is literally true.[18] We should also notice that in saying that Meno may have known earlier what *aretē* is, Socrates suggests, equally ironically, that something that is known can actually be forgotten. In one sense this is quite true and it forms the central point of the theory of recollection. But once something comes to be known, once (in Plato's terms) it is recollected, then it becomes more difficult to forget it or to be persuaded to change one's mind about it. This, after all, is how Socrates distinguishes *doxa* from *epistēmē* at 97d6–98b5. True beliefs, he claims, like Daedalus' statues, are always escaping from the soul. But when they are bound down by an 'account of the explanation', which, 'as we earlier agreed, is recollection' (98a3–5), they are transformed into *epistēmē* and become permanent. There is a serious question here about the sorts of things that, once learned, become permanent. Does Plato believe, for example, that if you know the road to Larisa (97a9–11) you cannot ever forget it? Or would he more plausibly be willing to allow gradations of permanence which would prevent geometrical or ethical truths from being forgotten but which would allow lower-level truths to escape the soul either through forgetfulness or through contrary argument? We shall return to this question toward the end of this essay.

Our present passage, 80d1–3, is finally important because it completes the stage-setting for the raising of Meno's paradox. Since Meno has now admitted that he is totally lost with respect to *aretē* and since Socrates has repeated his earlier complete inability to say anything about it, neither of them can even know where to begin the investigation. It is only at this point and faced with yet a further exhortation by Socrates to say what *aretē* is (80d3–4) that the much-maligned Meno raises the not unreasonable question how, if this is indeed their situation, they can possibly go on with the inquiry. In stating the paradox Meno once again repeats Socrates' word *to parapan*: 'In what way', he asks, 'can you search for something when you are altogether ignorant of what it is?' (80d5–6). Plato has gone to great lengths in order to emphasize Socrates' ignorance and to strip Meno of all claims to knowledge. Given this situation, and far from being a contentious move, Meno's raising of the paradox of inquiry is natural and well motivated.

## II

Plato takes Meno's paradox, that you can't look for what you don't know and don't need to look for what you know, very seriously in its own right.[19] In addition, he provides Meno with good reason to raise it. He uses the paradox not only in order to discuss serious epistemological issues, but also to resolve a number of dialectical difficulties to which Socrates' practice had given rise.

Of course, Meno's paradox could easily be put to contentious use, as it was, in two related versions, in the *Euthydemus*. At 275d3–4, Euthydemus asks Cleinias whether those who learn are the wise or the ignorant; at 276d7–8, he asks him whether one learns things one already knows or things one does not. In each case Cleinias is made to contradict himself. Having claimed that it is the wise who learn, he is forced to admit that it has to be the ignorant instead (276b4–5) and immediately following, he is made to concede that in fact those who learn are, after all, the wise (276c6–7). Having claimed that one learns what one does not know, he is forced to agree that what one learns one actually knows (277a8–277b4) and, at that point, Dionysiodorus enters the argument and argues that one learns only what one does not know (277c6–7).

Socrates replies on Cleinias' behalf that such paradoxes depend merely on verbal trickery. They equivocate between two senses of *manthanein* (to learn), one involving the acquisition at some time of knowledge that was not at all possessed previously and the other involving the exercising of knowledge that has already been acquired in the past (277e3–278b2). In this he is followed to the letter by Aristotle, who, in *Sophistici Elenchi* 4 (165b30–4), classifies this as a paradox due to verbal homonymy.

When such paradoxes, therefore, are offered contentiously, Plato is perfectly capable of giving them a short and easy reply. His reply in the *Euthydemus* depends crucially and unselfconsciously on the notion of the absolute acquisition of knowledge. But, in the *Meno*, Plato finds this reply deeply problematic. At the very least, he does not think that the paradox to which he can also supply a merely verbal solution has merely verbal force. What, then, accounts for this difference in attitude?

We have already said that Meno uses the term *to parapan* in stating his paradox. Some commentators have taken it that Meno simply overstates his case, and that Plato solves the problem by pointing this out. Their case depends primarily on the fact that Socrates omits this qualification in his restatement of Meno's problem (80e1–5). Thomas, for example, writes:

> This immediately destroys the thrust of the original puzzle for, lacking '*parapan*', the crucial premise reads 'if a man does not have some knowledge' rather than 'if a man has no knowledge whatsoever'. The reformulated dilemma is consistent with the possession of some knowledge. . . . Plato is not making much of an effort to meet the eristics in their . . . own terms. How could he, since to do so would be to concede them victory? Why should he, when the dilemma proscribes the possible? One is not obliged to take seriously intellectual chicanery that prohibits us from doing what we already do.[20]

But to assume that this is chicanery and that we can perfectly well do what the paradox denies, being a begging of the question, is itself a prime case of chicanery. Despite the similar views of Moravcsik[21] and Scolnicov,[22] it does not seem to me that Socrates refutes Meno by changing the terms of the argument. He may try to show that we do all possess some knowledge already but he cannot begin from that fact. In this respect, at least, White is correct in writing that there is no substantive difference between Meno's and Socrates' statement of the paradox: 'What Socrates does is simply to make clear that Meno's puzzle can be cast in the form of a dilemma' (p. 290 [168 here], n. 4). The function of *to parapan* is important and ineliminable.

Discussions of this passage often claim that Plato is only concerned with one among the many species of learning. Gregory Vlastos, for example, writes that:

> *Manthanein* . . . is being used in this context in the restricted sense of *learning to have propositional knowledge*. The acquisition of inarticulate skills, though well within the scope of the word in ordinary usage, is tacitly excluded.[23]

Moravcsik also believes that the paradox concerns only 'learning taking the form of inquiry' (pp. 53–4 [112–13 here]). Plato, he continues, is not concerned with the learning of non-intellectual skills, with learning by being told, or with learning by imitation (p. 54 [112–13 here]).

This is in a way correct, since the *Meno* does discuss only learning by inquiry.[24] But we must avoid the implication, which perhaps these writers themselves do not want, that Plato acknowledges many ways of learning but discusses only one in this context. Instead, Plato seems to hold the view that any learning and *epistēmē* worth the name must be achieved through inquiry and that therefore all learning, not just one particular form of it, must, in Moravcsik's words, 'be given direction by the learner himself' (p. 54 [p. 113 here]). Plato is not simply excluding the learning of inarticulate skills from his discussion. Rather, he seems at least implicitly to be denying that inarticulate skills are acquired through learning and that they are therefore, strictly speaking, objects of *epistēmē*. Similarly, he appears to deny that being told or imitation can, in themselves, constitute learning and produce understanding.

But if learning can proceed only through inquiry and if neither Socrates nor Meno know how to go on, then their impasse is very serious indeed. Where can the elenchus even begin? In addition, Gorgias, who had been earlier mentioned as a possible teacher of *aretē* and who might have helped the discussion, has already been disqualified. Since Meno accepts his views, it was agreed that to include him in the discussion would have been superfluous (71c5–d5). And in any case, his account of what *aretē* is (71e1–72a5; cf. Aristotle, *Politics* I. 13, 1260a20–8) did not survive Socrates' arguments.

## III

It would seem, then, that for the discussion to proceed, Socrates and Meno are in need of another teacher who might guide them out of their impasse. Such teachers are mentioned later on in the *Meno*. Why does Plato not bring them into the discussion now? Is it simply because he is not interested in the case of learning by being told by another or is the matter, as I shall now try to suggest, considerably more complicated?

Three classes of possible teachers of *aretē* are brought up in the *Meno*: Sophists, notably successful citizens, and, in a rather cursory way, poets (89e–96b). The Sophists are disqualified because they cannot agree among themselves whether *aretē* can or cannot be taught (95b–c); also because, unlike the case of any other subject, those who claim to teach what *aretē* is are not acknowledged as proper teachers of their subject by others and are even claimed to lack that which they profess to teach (96a6–b1; cf. 91c1–92c5). Good and noble citizens, men like Pericles,

Themistocles, Aristides, and Thucydides, are disqualified because not one of them has been capable of teaching his own sons what *aretē* is (93b–94e); also because they, no less than the Sophists, cannot agree on whether this is a teachable topic (95a–b, 96b1–3).[25] Finally, the poets, through a quick examination of Theognis, are summarily dismissed because they cannot even produce internally coherent views on the subject (95c–96a).

These arguments against particular sorts of teachers of *aretē* are common, indeed, commonplace.[26] In addition to them, however, Plato offers a more subtle and much more far-ranging argument against any self-professed teachers of success. The argument is implicit in a not very widely discussed passage of the *Protagoras* (313a1–314c2). In this passage, Socrates is warning Hippocrates against going to the Sophist for instruction without first thinking the matter through very carefully. In addition, however, his warning involves an important paradox with some serious implications for our own discussion.

Socrates, we said, warns Hippocrates not to rush into Protagoras' company. He describes the Sophist as 'a merchant or pedlar of the goods by which the soul is nourished' (313c4–5). The soul, he continues, is nourished by what it learns (*mathēmata*, 313c7). He then offers an analogy between Sophists, so construed, and those who sell any sort of food for the body (*ponēron ē chrēston*) but praise everything they sell indiscriminately (313d1–3). The buyers of such food also lack the necessary knowledge, unless they happen to be experts on such issues, gymnasts or physicians (313d3–5). The same is at least possible in the case of the pedlars of mental nourishment: some of them, too, may well be 'ignorant of whether what they sell is harmful or beneficial to the soul' (*chrēston ē ponēron pros tēn psuchēn*, 313d8–e1). And the analogy holds further true of their clients, unless one among them happens to be 'a physician with regard to the soul' (*peri tēn psuchēn iatrikos*, 313e1–2). Now if, Socrates continues, 'you happen to be an expert regarding which of those things are beneficial or harmful, then it is safe for you to buy learning from Protagoras or from anyone else' (313e2–5). But if not, the danger is great, much greater indeed in this case than in the case of physical nourishment. Physical food can be taken away from the pedlars in a separate vessel and examined by an expert (*epaiōn*) before it is consumed (314a3–b1). But this is not possible with food for thought:

You cannot carry learning away in a jar. Once you have paid for it you must receive it directly into the soul and having learned it you must leave already harmed or benefited. (314b1–4)

The discussion is at least cautionary, but it makes an additional point. Buying, or more generally receiving, learning presents some special difficulties of its own. When buying food one can always ask a third party, an acknowledged expert, for advice before the fact and act accordingly. But when buying learning the expert cannot be consulted, so to speak, after the initial transaction. One must determine in advance of all contact whether listening to the Sophist or to any other professor of *aretē* is likely to help or harm one's soul. But at least part of the additional problem in regard to learning is that in this case there are no acknowledged experts. And therefore the same difficulty that applied to the Sophists will also apply to such putative experts: how is one to tell whether their advice is itself harmful or beneficial?

The predicament gets worse. The dangers involved in approaching the Sophist, concerning as they do, what is most dear and precious to us, the soul, are immense. The implication, though it is not explicitly drawn in the text, is that one should not approach such a professor unless one is certain that one knows that what is offered will be beneficial. Now to benefit or harm the soul, is, obviously, to make it better or worse (cf. 318a6–9, d7–e5). And a discussion in the *Laches* adds a special urgency to this connection.

In the *Laches*, Lysimachus and Milesias ask Socrates, Laches, and Nicias whether they should train their sons in armed combat. The two generals having disagreed on this issue, Socrates questions whether any one of them there is an expert (*technikos*, 185a1) on the issue at hand. In typical fashion, he immediately generalizes that issue to apply not only to fighting but to the large question whether the boys will or will not become good (*agathoi*, 185a6). This in turn he construes as the problem of how to make the boys' souls as good as possible (186a5–6). But to know how to accomplish this, he continues, they must know what it is that makes the soul better when it is present in it. And to know this, of course, is to know what *aretē* is (189d–190a).

In order to know whether a course of learning, therefore, will harm or benefit the soul, the expert (*iatrikos, epaiōn*) of the

*Protagoras* must, like the expert (*technikos*) of the *Laches*, know what *aretē* is. But if the expert knows this, why bother to go to the Sophist at all, why not learn instead from one who has already been determined to know? But the point is that there are no such acknowledged experts. Therefore, learners can only be certain that their soul will not be harmed by the Sophist (or by the expert) if they themselves can tell whether such advice or instruction will be beneficial or harmful. But to know this, we have just shown, is to know oneself what *aretē* is. Therefore, unless one already knows what *aretē* is, and thus precisely what Sophists claim to teach, one should never approach any professors of *aretē*. The Sophists, and all who claim to teach what *aretē* is, are quite useless!

## IV

None of the problems discussed here, of course, could ever be problems for Socrates, since he never claimed to teach what *aretē* is. It is true that in *Alcibiades* I Socrates makes some startlingly extravagant claims about his importance to Alcibiades and his political ambitions (105d ff). But his point there, I should think, is to satirize the wooing practices of Athenian men.[27] In general, Socrates steadfastly refuses the teacher's role or function in Plato's early dialogues.[28]

These problems, therefore, could not have seriously disturbed Socrates. But they did become very serious indeed for Plato, who gradually, in the very process of portraying him as refusing that role, came to see Socrates not only as 'the best, the wisest, and the most just' man of his generation (*Phaedo* 118a16–17) but also as the ablest, thus far, teacher of *aretē*. For Socrates' sons, like the sons of Pericles, Aristides, and Themistocles, did little to distinguish themselves in their city. His friends and companions, like the friends and companions of Protagoras and Gorgias, remained mediocre, like Crito, or became vicious, like Charmides, Critias, or especially Alcibiades. Though perhaps ironically motivated, his views on whether *aretē* can be taught did not remain stable. And he certainly was not universally acknowledged as an expert on *aretē*. On the contrary, his life no less than his reputation suffered worse in the hands of the Athenians than the lives and reputations of many who, in Plato's eyes, had no claim to *aretē* whatsoever compared to him.

How, we should finally ask, could Socrates be exempt from the paradox that the teacher of *aretē* is useless? How could Plato, the disciple who may have thought he learned something from him, believe that Socrates could be approached even if one did not already know what was good and what was bad?

The answer to this question goes to the heart of Socrates' personality as well as of his method. It is that Socrates, unlike all other teachers of *aretē*, does not constitute a danger to his students precisely because he refuses to tell anyone what *aretē* is, especially since he denies having that knowledge in the first place. Whatever claim Socrates has to the teaching of *aretē* lies exactly in his disclaiming any such ability. The contrast around which the *Protagoras* and many other early Platonic dialogues revolve is a contrast between a method that depends on telling one's students what *aretē* is, on transmitting information to them, and one that does not.

But if Socrates' refusal or inability to offer positive views makes it safe to approach him, it generates another problem: how does the elenctic method result in any learning? How do two people who are ignorant of the answer to a given question discover that answer and how do they realize that they have discovered it? If the elenchus presents a serious methodological question, this is it. And this is the very question that Meno raises in the paradox with which we have been concerned.

Plato tries to answer this question in the *Meno* through the examination of the slave and the theory of recollection, though his views on these issues never remain unchanged. In claiming that Meno's paradox is well motivated and that it goes to the heart of Socratic dialectic, I find myself in agreement with Irwin, who writes that 'the examination of the slave is a scale-model of a Socratic elenchos, with a commentary to explain and justify the procedure' (p. 139). However, I cannot agree with Irwin on the question of the resolution of the paradox. He thinks that the paradox depends on the view that if I know nothing about an object, I cannot identify it as the subject of my inquiry and I cannot therefore inquire into it at all (pp. 138–9).[29] According to Irwin, Socrates rejects this view and claims that

> though the slave does not know, he has true beliefs about the questions discussed. . . . To inquire into x we need only enough true beliefs about x to fix the reference of the term 'x'

so that when the inquiry is over, we can still see we refer to the same thing (p. 139).

To support his view, Irwin relies crucially on 85c6–7, where Socrates asks whether one who does not know does not still possess true beliefs about the things he does not know (p. 316, n. 14). But, for one thing, the position of the passage announces it more as an intermediate step of the argument rather than as a conclusion to it.[30] More importantly, the question of identification does not seem to me so crucial to Plato's resolution of the paradox. It is quite true that Plato writes that before the inquiry begins the slave has true beliefs concerning the geometrical problem discussed. But these beliefs were in no way available to him as such at the time. They were mixed together with all sorts of false beliefs, some of which were both elicited and eliminated by Socrates during his questioning. These true beliefs are recovered by the slave at the end of his examination by Socrates; they could not therefore play the identificatory role Irwin asks of them, and which requires them to be there consciously at its very beginning. Further, the knowledge that the slave is said to be eventually able to recover is also said to be in him, just as those true beliefs are (85d3–7). But if this is so, it is not clear that true beliefs are possessed in a particular manner, different from that in which knowledge is possessed and which therefore would enable them to have the different function Irwin's account assigns to them.

For true belief to secure the stable identification of the object of inquiry, it is necessary for it and for knowledge to be independent of each other. But this does not seem to be the case. Plato writes that the slave who now has only belief will acquire knowledge through repeated questioning (85c9–d1). This statement is not by itself very explicit, but it becomes a bit more clear when we connect it to the later discussion of 'the reasoning out of the explanation' at 97e–98a. Once this is achieved, Plato writes, true beliefs 'become *epistēmai*' ('items of knowledge'). That is, these beliefs do not simply fix the object of which knowledge is to be acquired or, in Plato's terms, recovered; rather once acquired (recovered) themselves they become that knowledge when they have been properly organized and systematized.[31]

But before we offer some tentative remarks about Plato's resolution of the paradox we must raise one further, rather complicated problem. What exactly does recollection cover for Plato? Does it apply to the whole process of learning or only to part of it? Or, not to beg any questions about learning, which part of the slave's examination actually involves him in recollection?

The manner in which Socrates introduces the theory of recollection and his rather general statements at 81d2–3, 81d4–5, and 82a1–2, suggest that recollection applies to all the different stages that may be, however loosely, associated with the process of learning. Accordingly, we expect that everything that takes place during the slave's examination constitutes an instance of recollection. Socrates strengthens this expectation when he prefaces his examination by urging Meno to see whether the slave will be recollecting or learning from him (82b6–7), and by saying at the end of its first stage that he is only asking questions of the slave and not telling him anything (82e4–6).

But doesn't Socrates teach or tell the slave all sorts of things during their discussion? How else can we construe the questions of 82c7–8 and 82d1–2 or the leading (that is, misleading) question of 82d8–e2 that prompts the slave to offer one of his many wrong solutions to the geometrical problem? In addition, we must not forget the passages 83c8–d1 and 83d4–5, where Socrates does not even bother to ask a question but himself draws the inference, marked in each case by *ara*, for the slave.

Bluck, who was exercised by this problem, answered that Socrates does not teach the slave 'in the sophistic way, by merely presenting him with propositions that he must accept'. He gradually 'leads' the slave to the correct solution and at that point the slave is 'able to "see" that what was said was true. The argument is simply that such "seeing" or comprehension would not be possible if the slave had not had previous acquaintance with the truth . . .'(p. 12).

But is it so clear that there was such a thing as 'the' sophistic way of teaching? And if there were, is Bluck's description of it accurate? Some Sophists, Hippias and sometimes Protagoras (*Protagoras* 320c2–4), may have taught in this manner. But Euthydemus and Dionysiodorus used a questioning method which, at least superficially, did not differ so drastically from the elenchus.[32] Bluck's appeal to 'seeing', in addition, seems to me rather empty. The point is not simply that, especially in the *Meno*, the text gives little warrant to the identification of the slave's understanding with 'his feeling of inner conviction' (p. 12). More importantly, it is not clear that, even if such a feeling exists, the slave has it only when he 'sees' the right answer and not also when he gives the wrong one. On the contrary, Socrates' comment at 82e5–6 to the effect that the slave now thinks he knows the solution suggests that subjectively there is no difference between merely thinking one has knowledge and actually having it. If there were, and assuming that everyone knows at least one thing, learning should proceed on its own until this feeling of inner conviction is acquired.

In the course of questioning the slave, Socrates produces in him, or elicits from him, a number of false geometric beliefs. In the present case, he continues to clear them out and to replace them by true ones instead. But what if he had not? What if, in particular, their conversation concerned *aretē*, of which Socrates is himself ignorant, and thus the very soul of the slave? Would Socrates not be capable of causing at least as much harm to the slave as the Sophists have earlier been said to cause their students unless these already know the answers to their questions?

It is at this point that we should take Socrates very seriously, if rather liberally, when he insists that he does not teach anyone anything. He does not mean that he will ask no obvious or leading questions, or that he will not make statements or even sometimes long speeches.[33] He does mean that he requires his interlocutor to assent only to what he thinks is true, nothing more and nothing less. This is what Vlastos has recently called the 'say what you believe' requirement of the elenchus.[34] Socrates' practice is in stark contrast with the method of Euthydemus, despite their apparent similarity. For Euthydemus insists that Socrates answer his questions in ways with which he is deeply dissatisfied, dropping a number of essential qualifications, in order to prove to him that (again in a way superficially and perhaps deliberately reminiscent of the *Meno*) he has always known everything, even before he or the whole universe came into being, provided Euthydemus 'wants it that way' (*Eud.* 295e–296d).

If knowledge consisted in a feeling of inner conviction, Socrates would have been quite dangerous to his interlocutors. For since knowledge and belief, true or false, do not differ subjectively, there might in fact be no way of telling, from the inside, whether a particular answer reached to a problem is true or false. But, of course, Socrates never ends his questioning when he has simply elicited a statement. The major burden of the elenchus is to *test* such statements and Socrates assumes that no false statement can survive these tests. Whether he is engaged in the more negative elenchus of the earlier dialogues or in the more positive investigation of the *Gorgias*,[35] Socrates consistently makes his interlocutors answer for their beliefs. What determines whether a belief is true or false has nothing to do with how the respondent feels and everything to do with that belief's dialectical impregnability.

The elenchus, therefore, depends solely on a dialectical test for truth: a belief is true if it cannot be overthrown by sound, noncontentious argument. To which, of course, one might be tempted to reply: but how can we know that a belief will not be overthrown? Socrates, I think, had no clear answer to this question. Plato may have tried to devise one: we can know this to be the case when we master the whole interconnected set of truths to which our particular belief refers. We have *epistēmē* when we have learned the axiomatic structure of the system in question and can prove any one of its elements.[36]

But even though Socrates' leading questions may be harmless to the slave, his claim that the whole examination involves recollection is misleading for the readers of the *Meno*. The slave only produces a false belief in the first stretch of the argument (82b9–83e3). Are we to infer that coming to have (or recovering) false beliefs is a case of recollection?[37]

By opening the second stretch of the examination by asking Meno to watch how the slave will now properly engage in orderly recollection (82e11–12), Socrates again suggests that the slave will be actually recollecting in what follows. What occurs here, of course, is that the slave is made to realize that he does not know the answer to Socrates' question (82e14–84a2). Are we to infer that recollection applies to the realization that one's beliefs about a topic are false?

Part of the answer to this question depends on the interpretation of Socrates' next question, which occurs in his summary of this second stretch of argument:

Ἐννοεῖς αὖ, ὦ Μένων, οὗ ἐστιν ἤδη βαδίζων ὅδε τοῦ ἀναμιμνήσκεσθαι. (84a3–4)

Thompson construes this as asking 'what point on the track of reminiscence he has now reached', and believes that recollection has already begun.[38] On the other hand, we could take the question to concern 'what point on the track *to* reminiscence he has now reached', in which case Socrates would be saying that the path to recollection is now open, not that recollection has already begun. In that case, we may take his earlier remarks about the slave's recollecting to apply not specifically to the first part of the discussion but, more generally and programmatically, to the whole examination. Recollection may be more restricted than is sometimes supposed.

This impression is reinforced by Socrates' summary of the last section of his questioning. He and Meno agree that the slave has only replied with beliefs that were his own (85b8–9) and that he has true beliefs about what he does not yet know (85c2–7). Socrates now claims that if 'someone asks him the same question many times and in many ways' he will finally have as much knowledge about these topics as anyone else (85c9–d1).[39] From this it is clear that the slave still does not have *epistēmē* of the subject and Socrates drives the point home by locating the slave's knowledge in the future in his very next question (*epistēsetai*, 85d3–4). He then goes on to say that it is just this recovery of knowledge which is still all in the *future* for the slave, that is recollection (85d6–7). Recollection thus seems limited to a very small part of the process of learning.

Despite the tension it creates with the general statement at 81d4–5, such a restricted interpretation of recollection fits well with Socrates' later distinction between *doxa* and *epistēmē*: the former, he says, 'is worth little until it is tied down by reasoning about the explanation' (98a3–4). And it is *this* (*touto*, 98a4), he continues, that, 'as we agreed earlier, is recollection' (98a4–5). But the *aitiās logismos* (this 'reasoning out the explanation'), as far as I can see, corresponds to nothing in the first stages of the slave's interrogation. The only process to which it can be connected is the repeated questioning that will eventually lead to the recovery of *epistēmē* (85c–d) and which we were just now, on independent grounds, considering as a candidate for recollection.

Suppose now that we restrict recollection in this way. Since we are explicitly told that the slave does not yet have any *epistēmē* does it not follow that he has not engaged in recollection in the dialogue? And if this is so, what is the point of his long examination? What has Plato succeeded in demonstrating by its means?

It is quite possible that recollection, strictly speaking, is not shown to occur anywhere in the *Meno*. Nevertheless, I think that the last stage of the slave's questioning, in which Socrates elicits the correct solution to the problem from him, is deeply representative of the process. It represents it, that is, because it is a part of it. The slave, Socrates says, will come to have knowledge 'if one asks him the very same questions [or: questions about the very same things] many times and in many ways' (85c10–11). What brings about the *aitiās logismos* and transforms *doxa*, into *epistēmē* is not a new operation, additional to the eliciting of true *doxa*, but rather the eliciting of enough true *doxai* about the subject to make having them *constitute* the *aitiās logismos*. The very same true beliefs the slave now has, Socrates claims at 86a7–8, 'having been aroused by questioning, become knowledge' (*epistēmai*).

Plato does not explain how this transformation is to occur, and it is very difficult to know what is involved in the transition. Certainly, simply having many *doxai* about geometry cannot be itself sufficient for *epistēmē*. One must also acquire the ability to organize them systematically, to become able to move from one of them to another properly and on one's own, to know how they are supported by one another. This is one of the reasons Plato emphasizes the role of questioning in the recovery of knowledge. Having the answers to as many questions as one pleases does not constitute *epistēmē* unless one is also capable of answering ever new questions as well as of formulating questions of one's own. The *aitiās logismos* and recollection, strictly speaking, consist in this ability, which transcends merely having answers to different questions but which is acquired (or revealed) only in the course of learning them.[40]

Implicitly, true beliefs are in one in just the way that knowledge is supposed to be; explicitly, they enter the process of learning and recollection midway. It is therefore unlikely that Meno's paradox is resolved by appealing to them in order to secure, from the very beginning of the inquiry, reference to the object which the inquiry concerns. Plato seems to deny the claim, on which the paradox depends, that 'one cannot search for what one does not know for one does not even know what to search for' (80e5), on slightly different grounds. One does know what one does not know because questioning and the inability to answer continued questions determine that knowledge is lacking. Conversely, the continued ability to answer such questions suggests that knowledge has been reached and that 'you have happened upon' what you did not know (80d8). On the other hand, he also denies the claim that 'one cannot search for what one knows – for one knows, and one who knows does not need to search' (80e3–5). For one need not know what one knows since knowledge may be, and usually is, forgotten and is brought out only by questioning. Knowledge is reached when what one knew that one does not know is matched with what one did not know that one knows. The role of questioning in bringing this matching about is crucial: Plato's resolution of Meno's paradox is dialectical rather than logical.

## V

The dialectical resolution of Meno's paradox, even when supported by the non-dialectical explanation offered through the theory of recollection,[41] does not by itself account for Socrates' continued insistence that he is not, in this or in any other case, engaged in teaching. We have seen that part of this account is that had Socrates been willing to offer positive views on the nature of *aretē*, he should not have been approached any more than the Sophists should. But in the *Meno* the question does not concern *aretē* and Socrates is quite aware of the correct answer. Why does Plato insist that the slave must come to it on his own? Why is he so eager to point out that even when Socrates is transmitting information to the slave (which he has him do on a number of occasions) the slave is still only recovering knowledge from within himself?

Plato appears to believe that even in matters that do not concern the soul's welfare as directly as *aretē* does, *epistēmē* cannot and must not be reached through the transmission of information. But knowledge depends essentially on the transmission of information and is itself transmissible. What is crucial to knowledge is that the information in which it consists has been acquired in the proper way, no less and no more. As Bernard Williams has written, in regard to knowledge in general

> not only is it not necessary that the knower be able to support or ground his belief by reference to other propositions, but it is not necessary that he be in any special state in regard to this belief at all, at least at the level of what he can consciously rehearse. What is necessary . . . is that one or more of a class of conditions should obtain . . . conditions which can best be summarized by the formula that, given the truth of *p*, it is no accident that *A* believes that *p* rather than not *p*.[42]

Though this formulation, as Williams himself admits, needs much further refinement, it seems to me quite true. However, Williams's conditions are remarkably weaker than Plato's and even explicitly exclude what Plato considers most crucial to *epistēmē*: the ability to 'support or ground (a) belief', to give an account, a *logos* of the object of *epistēmē*.[43]

We might want to say that Plato insists upon an unduly restrictive notion of knowledge; but we would do better, I think, to say that when he is discussing *epistēmē* he is not producing unreasonable conditions on knowledge, but rather, quite reasonable conditions on what it is to understand something. For unlike knowledge, understanding involves, in rough and ready terms, the ability to *explain* what one understands. By contrast, many items of knowledge, for example, particular facts, are not even the sorts of things to which explanation is applicable in this context.[44]

In the case of mathematical knowledge, at least so far as non-elementary propositions are concerned, Williams accepts 'the Platonic view' that such knowledge involves *aitiās logismos* which he glosses as 'a chain of proof'. But he goes on to claim that whether or not having such proof makes true beliefs more permanent, as Plato believes, is irelevant to the main point

> that the access to mathematical truth must necessarily be through proof, and that therefore the notion of non-accidental true belief in mathematics essentially involves the notion of mathematical proof (the points which the Platonic model of *recollection* precisely serves to obscure). (p. 9)

But Plato's emphasis on the permanence of *epistēmē* is anything but irrelevant. For one thing, the permanence of one's understanding of a topic is in itself a measure of the degree to which one understands it. At some earlier time, I was capable of dealing with quadratic equations; my present total inability to do so strongly argues that I never understood that subject very well. For understanding the nature of quadratic equations is not an isolated act concerning an isolated object; it involves, at least in principle, the understanding of a vast number of mathematical propositions and operations, perhaps of all of algebra. And the more of a field one understands, the more systematically one's abilities with respect to it are organized, the less likely it is that the relevant beliefs will be forgotten: the more likely it is that they will be, in Plato's word, permanent (*monimoi*, 96a6). It is very easy, it is in fact inevitable, to forget whether it rained here three years ago today or to be persuaded that my recollection is wrong. It is also easy to forget how to get from one part of one's country to another. It is easy to forget how to determine the circumference of the circle, if you were only taught it once at school. But it seems more difficult to say that one has forgotten geometry, and almost totally absurd to claim to have forgotten what *aretē* is.[45] The broader and more encompassing the field to which a proposition belongs, the more permanent beliefs concerning that field, once mastered, are likely to be. The more worthy, therefore, that field is, in Plato's eyes, as an object of *epistēmē*.

Plato's model of recollection, though it may obscure Williams's points about knowledge, is crucial in emphasizing the necessity of working out a proof or of reaching any sort of understanding through and for oneself. Knowledge of fact, we have said, is transmissible and the

> mechanism by which knowledge is transmitted is *belief*. More precisely . . . it is sufficient and necessary for the transmission of your knowledge that *p* to me that I *believe you* when, speaking (or writing) from knowledge, you tell me that *p*.[46]

But, as Augustine also saw and argued in the *De Magistro* (40), understanding cannot be handed down in this manner. In an important discussion of this dialogue that connects it to Plato's concerns, Burnyeat describes its main thesis, 'that no man can teach another knowledge (*scientia*)', as

> the claim that no man can teach another to understand something. The argument will not be that information cannot be transmitted from one person to another, but that the appreciation or understanding of any such information is something that each person must work out for himself . . . The conveying of information is not enough for teaching in the sense of bringing the learner to know something.[47]

Burnyeat wants to connect Augustine's view that learning comes about through 'first-hand learning, by the intellect or by my own sense-perception' with a number of cases discussed by Plato. He mentions in particular Plato's insistence that the slave in the *Meno* can learn mathematics only through reasoning and his claim that only someone who has actually gone on the road to Larisa knows the way there (97a–b). He also brings in the view of the *Theaetetus* (201b–c) that only an eyewitness to a crime can have knowledge about it (p. 16). My own view is that Plato considers the examples of the traveller and of the eyewitness not as instances of *epistēmē* but as indispensable analogies by which to explain his view of it. Their function is to highlight the crucial condition that *epistēmē* must be acquired first hand; and in so far as they satisfy this condition, they may be, catachrestically, considered as cases of *epistēmē*. But in a stricter sense,[48] *epistēmē* applies only to cases which in addition to first-hand acquisition also involve systematization, proof, explanation, or account: this is the *aitiās logismos* of the *Meno* and the *logos* of the *Theaetetus* (202d5). Neither the case of the traveller nor that of the eyewitness seems to me capable of satisfying this additional constraint.

What, then, is the difference between *epistēmē* and *orthē doxa*? According to Burnyeat, the case of the eyewitness shows that if he tells me I may come to know much of what he knows himself (though not, of course, on his grounds); still, there will 'typically' be other things I will not know because eyewitnesses 'nearly always' know more than they tell. What marks the difference between us is the eyewitness' synoptic grasp of something of which I at best know some isolated elements. And Burnyeat concludes that

> the important difference between knowledge and understanding is this, that knowledge can be piecemeal, can grasp related truths one by one, but understanding always involves seeing the connections and relations between the items known.
> (p. 17)

The conclusion itself is quite correct, but I doubt that the case of the eyewitness testifies in its favour. First, I am not sure that it would be correct to say that the eyewitness does have understanding of what occurs. More importantly, the manner in which Burnyeat constructs his case (through the qualifications 'typically' and 'nearly always') suggests that he may think that eyewitnesses can on occasion tell all they see. But the difference between the eyewitness and me (if we attribute understanding to the eyewitness) cannot be, as this construal implies, merely one of degree. For if it depends simply on the amount of the information transmitted, then teaching may be after all, at least in principle, a matter of degree: what we would need would simply be a *very good* eyewitness. I think that the problem is caused by taking this case to constitute for Plato an actual instance of *epistēmē*. If, as I suggest, we take it only as a partial illustration of what *epistēmē* involves, then we will not feel it necessary to locate the difference between *epistēmē* and *orthē doxa* through it.

Instead, we can turn to the case of the slave and of mathematical knowledge. For here, the difference between belief (or even knowledge) and understanding is more clearly qualitative. Here, the connections and relations between the objects of knowledge, which were not easy to discern in the previous case, are much more central. For it is these relations and connections that produce understanding, and this limits understanding to fields which, unlike empirical low-level matters, involve them crucially. And it is precisely the mastering of these connections and relations that cannot be transmitted (cf. Plato, *Rep.* 518b6–7) because these connections are methods and rules for proceeding in a properly justified manner, from one item of knowledge to another. And even if such rules and methods can be formulated, and in that sense, transmitted, what cannot be transmitted in the same manner is the ability to follow the methods and to apply the rules.[49] And if we can formulate methods and rules for following the previous set, we will again face the question how these new rules and methods are to be correctly applied. The notion of recollection provides Plato both with an account of the inward, first-hand nature of all *epistēmē* and with a way of ending this regress: its power lies in its double contribution to Plato's philosophical purposes.[50]

In relation to *aretē* the connections we have been discussing are what allows one to do the right thing on all occasions and not only sometimes or capriciously. Unless it is in order to fool someone, the geometrician will not consciously produce a fallacious proof of a theorem. And unless it is in order to harm someone, the *agathos* will not willingly do the wrong thing. But part of being *agathos* of course, is never to want to harm anyone, as Socrates consistently argued in Plato's dialogues. The *agathos*, therefore, will never do the wrong thing.

Socrates, in Plato's eyes, never did the wrong thing and thus seemed to him to be the best man of his generation. But Socrates steadfastly refused the role of teacher: he claimed not to know how to make people good, and not even to understand at all what *aretē* itself consisted in. For practical and ethical reasons, Socrates had never wanted to tell his students (for students he certainly wanted, and had no less than any of the distinguished Sophists) anything about the subject which they wanted to learn from him. For epistemological reasons, Plato came not to want Socrates to have believed that he was capable of doing so. Meno's paradox brought together Socrates' immediate concern with not harming his friends (a rather old-fashioned conception of *aretē* in its own right) with Plato's theoretical interest in the nature of understanding. The theory of recollection, whatever its ultimate shortcomings, succeeded in accounting systematically for both, even if in the process some of the mystery of Socrates gave way to the mysticism of Plato.[51]

## NOTES

1 Paul Shorey, *What Plato Said* (Chicago, 1983), p. 157.
2 A. E. Taylor, *Plato: The Man and His Work*, 4th edn (London, 1937), p. 137.
3 Jacob Klein, *A Commentary on Plato's Meno* (Chapel Hill, 1965), p. 92.
4 Bernard Phillips, 'The significance of Meno's paradox', in *Plato's Meno: Text and Criticism*, Alexander Sesonske and Noel Fleming (eds) (Belmont, 1965), p. 78.
5 R. S. Bluck, *Plato's Meno* (Cambridge, 1961), p. 8. Bluck's mixed view of Meno can be found on pp. 125–6.
6 The contrary views of Cherniss and Guthrie have been recently discussed by Michael Morgan, 'Belief, knowledge and learning in Plato's middle dialogues' (unpublished manuscript), pp. 8–9, with full references.
7 Cf. also G. B. Kerferd, *The Sophistic Movement* (Cambridge, 1981), pp. 131–8.
8 Cf. *Protagoras* 361a5–b3 and contrast *Euthydemus* 282c1–8.
9 On the date of the *Dissoi Logoi*, cf. T. M. Robinson, *Contrasting Arguments: An Edition of the Dissoi Logoi* (New York, 1979), pp. 34–41.
10 Cf. *Nemean* III. 41.
11 Cf. *Antidosis* 186–92, 274–5. For further references, cf. Klein, above n. 3, p. 39 n. 18.
12 B. Jowett, *The Dialogues of Plato*, 4th edn by D. J. Allan and H. E. Dale (Oxford, 1953), p. 252.
13 W. Peek, *Griechische Versinschriften*, vol. I (Berlin, 1955), 20. 11.
14 The question of the public aspects of *aretē*, though very complicated, has not been widely discussed. My suspicion, though highly speculative and in need of extensive support before it can be taken seriously, is that Plato was centrally concerned with it. Part of his purpose in the *Republic*, I would want (and have) to argue, is to ensure that *aretē* will always have a proper audience, and that those who possess it will necessarily be recognized as such by everyone in their social group.
15 There is considerable irony in putting this reply in the mouth of an imaginary Athenian, since Anytus is later shown not to have any doubts about the fact that any good Athenian citizen can make another better (92e ff).
16 The abrupt opening of the *Meno* concerns both Bluck (above n. 5, p. 199) and Klein (above n. 3, p. 38). The discussion above may offer an adequate dramatic justification for it.

17 This view has become popular recently. It is supported for example, by Terence Irwin, *Plato's Moral Theory* (Oxford, 1977), pp. 40–1, 63; by Gerasimos Xenophon Santas, *Socrates* (London, Boston, and Henley, 1979), pp. 118–22, 311 n. 26; and by Paul Woodruff, *Plato: Hippias Major* (Indianapolis, 1982), pp. 138, 141. The issue is much too complicated to be discussed here, and it will occupy me on a further occasion. A careful examination of the passages cited in this connection (*Laches* 190b8–c2; *Protag.* 361c3–6; *Charmides* 157e7–159a3; *Meno* 100b4–6; *Lysis* 223b4–8; *Hippias Major* 286c8–d2, 304d4–e3; *Republic* 345b3–c3) has convinced me that Socrates does not, and need not, appeal to the distinction between knowledge and belief in order to justify his views on the priority of definition. The present case is, I think, even more straightforward.

18 Cp. 80d3 with *homoiotatos . . . narkēi* (80a5–6) and cf. Bluck, above n. 5, p. 271.

19 Cf. Nicholas White, 'Inquiry', *Review of Metaphysics* XXVIII (1974) [reprinted in this volume, pp. 152–71. Ed.] p. 289 [152] with n. 1.

20 John E. Thomas, *Musings on the Meno* (The Hague, 1980), pp. 123, 128–9.

21 J. M. E. Moravcsik, 'Learning as recollection' in *Plato: Metaphysics and Epistemology*, Gregory Vlastos (ed.) (Garden City: New York, 1971) [reprinted in this volume, pp. 112–28. Ed.], p. 57 [115–16].

22 Samuel Scolnicov, 'Three aspects of Plato's philosophy of learning and instruction', *Paideia* V (1976), p. 52.

23 Gregory Vlastos, '*Anamnesis* in the *Meno*', *Dialogue* 4 (1965) [reprinted in this volume, pp. 88–111. Ed.], p. 143 [105] n. 1.

24 Cf. White, above n. 19, and Irwin, above n. 17, p. 315 n. 13.

25 Similar arguments can be found at *Protag.* 319e–320b, *Alcibiades* 118c–119a.

26 Cf. *Dissoi Logoi* 6. 3, 4.

27 On which see Kenneth Dover, *Greek Homosexuality* (Cambridge, Mass., 1978), pp. 81–100. In the course of the dialogue Socrates insists that he is not telling Alcibiades anything as their discussion proceeds (112d ff) and he readily admits that he, no less than Alcibiades, is in need of an education (124b1–c2). In a final ironic reversal, moreover, the dialogue ends with Alcibiades assuming the teacher's role and assigning to Socrates the student's position (135d–e).

28 Socrates often describes himself as a willing disciple of someone who claims to know something about *aretē*; cf., e.g., *Euthyphro* 5a3–b7.

29 White (above n. 13) offers a related account, more concerned with identifying the object inquired into throughout the inquiry, on pp. 294–7. [pp. 155–8 here]

30 Cf. Michael Morgan, 'An interpretation of *Meno* 85b8–86b4' (unpublished manuscript, 1982), p. 8.

31 I have discussed some of the issues involved in this transition in '*Epistēmē* and *Logos* in Plato's later thought', *Archiv für Geschichte der Philosophie* LXVI (1984), pp. 11–36.

32 For some material on sophistic teaching methods, cf. Kerferd, above n. 7, pp. 59–67.

33 For example, despite his insistence on short questions and answers at *Gorgias* 448e–449a, 449b4–c7, Socrates makes many longer speeches than Gorgias in the course of their conversation (451a3–c9, 452a1–4, 455a8–e 5, 457c3–458c8).

34 Gregory Vlastos, 'The Socratic elenchus', *Oxford Studies in Ancient Philosophy*, Vol. I (Oxford, 1983), pp. 27–58, with full references.

35 Vlastos' evidence, in 'The Socratic elenchus', for his construal of the elenchus as a method for reaching positive ethical conclusions mainly comes, as he himself admits, from the *Gorgias*.

36 This view is supported in '*Epistēmē* and *Logos* in Plato's later thought' (above n. 31).

37 Theodor Ebert, *Meinung und Wissen in der Philosophie Platons* (Berlin, 1974), pp. 83–104, and 'Plato's theory of recollection reconsidered: an interpretation of *Meno* 80a–86c', *Man and World* VI (1973), pp. 163–81, thinks that it is because he thinks that Plato believes that learning is only analogous to recollection, and not an instance of it. But, I think, Plato's view is much stronger than that, and it would be very strange of him to consider that both the recovery of knowledge and the recovery of false beliefs are equally cases of recollection.

38 E. S. Thompson, *Plato's Meno* (London, 1901), p. 137.

39 Plato radically qualifies this extremely optimistic view, of course, in the *Republic*. The myth of *Er* and the theory of recollection as presented in the *Phaedrus* provide a rationale for his more cautious claims about the ability of people to reach *epistēmē*.

40 Restricting recollection in this way may help account for Socrates' argument of 96d ff that though *aretē* is beneficial it may still not be *epistēmē* but *orthē doxa* instead and thus not teachable. For recollection provides Socrates' alternative account of teaching and learning. If it applied to the recovery of a single true belief (or to a small number of them), then this recovery would definitely be a matter of teaching, and Socrates would have no grounds for arguing that *aretē* cannot be taught. But if recollection only follows the recovery, or mere possession, of true belief, he may have just such a reason: teaching produces orderly recollection.

41 On the question whether the paradox is resolved primarily by the examination or by the theory of recollection, I agree with Irwin (above n. 17, p. 139 and n. 13; contra White, above n. 19, p. 289 [152 here], and *Plato on Knowledge and Reality* (Indianapolis, 1976), pp. 40–1): the paradox is disarmed in the examination, and recollection explains how that is possible.

42 Bernard Williams, 'Knowledge and Reasons' in *Problems in the Theory of Knowledge*, G. H. von Wright (ed.) (The Hague, 1972), p. 5.

43 I have presented a full case for that claim in '*Epistēmē* and *Logos* in Plato's later thought' (above n. 31); cf. also Jon Moline, *Plato's Theory of Understanding* (Madison 1981), pp. 32–51.

44 This is not to say that the fact, which I know, that it is raining cannot be explained. It is only to say that my knowledge of that (meteorological) explanation has no bearing on whether I know the fact in question. Most people know the latter, when it is the case, and ignore the former.

45 Cf. Hesiod, *Works and Days* pp. 293–4: 'He is the very best who understands everything having considered it himself and knows what is good later and to the end' (quoted by Moline, above n. 43, p. 19; the translation is different).

46 Michael Welbourne, 'The Transmission of Knowledge', *Philosophical Quarterly* XXIX (1979), p. 3.

47 M. F. Burnyeat, 'Augustine *De Magistro*' (unpublished manuscript, 1982), pp. 9, 11. [Cf. now Burnyeat, 'Wittgenstein and Augustine *De Magistro*' in *Proceedings of the Aristotelian Society*, Supplementary Volume 61 (1987), pp. 1–24. Ed.].

48 This stricter sense, as I proceed to suggest, can be found in the *Meno* and in the *Theaetetus*, contrary to Burnyeat's suggestion, above n. 47, p. 16.

49 The problem is discussed, but not resolved, by Gilbert Ryle, 'Teaching and Training' in *Plato's Meno*, Malcolm Brown (ed.) (Indianapolis, 1971), pp. 243–6.

50 Recollection does not perpetuate the regress, for the requisite abilities have, according to Plato (85e–86b), always been in the soul.

51 For comments on an earlier version of this essay, I am grateful to M. F. Burnyeat, Rosemary Desjardins, Steven Strange, and Gregory Vlastos. I must also thank Paul Kalligas, who discussed these issues exhaustively with me and who gave me extensive and helpful comments. The generous support of the Guggenheim Foundation is gratefully acknowledged.

# NOTES ON CONTRIBUTORS

**I. M. Crombie** was, until his retirement in 1983, Fellow and Tutor in Philosophy at Wadham College, Oxford.

**I. G. Kidd** was Professor in the Department of Greek at the University of St Andrews until his retirement in 1987.

**Julius Moravcsik** is Professor of Philosophy at Stanford University.

**George Nakhnikian** retired in 1990 from his position as Professor of Philosophy at Indiana University.

**Alexander Nehamas** was Professor of Philosophy at Pittsburgh University when he wrote the article in this volume. He is now at the University of Pennsylvania.

**Gregory Vlastos** was Professor of Philosophy at Princeton University when he wrote the article in this volume. Upon his retirement in 1976 he moved to Berkeley, California, as a Visiting Professor. He died in 1991.

**Nicholas P. White** is Professor of Philosophy at the University of Michigan.

**Kathleen V. Wilkes** is Fellow and Tutor in Philosophy at St Hilda's College, Oxford.

# GLOSSARY

Each entry below includes (1) the Greek term transliterated, (2) the term in Greek script, and (3) a translation or range of translations covering the meanings of the term most relevant to the *Meno*. The main renderings in my translation in this volume are asterisked, except that the words *einai* and *logos* are treated differently (qqv). Where not otherwise stated, nouns are listed in the nominative singular, adjectives in the nominative masculine singular, and verbs in the present infinitive.

*agathos* (ἀγαθός)   good★
*aitia* (αἰτία)   reason, cause, explanation★
  *aitias logismos* (αἰτίας λογισμός)   reasoning out the explanation★
*alēthēs* (ἀληθής)   true★
  *alētheia* (ἀλήθεια)   truth★
*anamnēsis* (ἀνάμνησις)   recollection★
*andreia* (ἀνδρεία)   courage★
*aporia* (ἀπορία)   (1) impassability, difficulty, bafflement, perplex-
    ity★ (80a–d,84c); (2) lack of resource, non-achievement★ (78e)
  *aporein* (ἀπορεῖν)   be at a loss, baffled, perplexed★
*aretē* (ἀρετή)   goodness, excellence, virtue★
*boulesthai* (βούλεσθαι)   wish★, wish for★, would like★, want★
*didaskein* (διδάσκειν)   teach★
  *didakton* (διδακτόν)   (neuter form of the verbal adjective *didaktos*
    from the above) – something taught, teachable, that comes
    from teaching★
*dikaiosunē* (δικαιοσύνη)   justice★
  *dikaios* (δίκαιος)   just★
*doxa* (δόξα)   opinion★, belief
*eidos* (εἶδος)   form★, shape, character

250

*einai* (εἶναι) be – in many of the same senses as the English word and some others besides; e.g., 'exist', 'be the case', 'consist of', 'belong to', 'apply to', etc. I have often translated as 'be' or 'be so', but have not attempted consistency with this word

*epistēmē* (ἐπιστήμη) knowledge*, understanding

*epithūmein* (ἐπιθυμεῖν) desire* (verb)

*hosiotēs* (ὁσιότης) holiness*, piety

  *hosios* (ὅσιος) holy*, pious

*hupothesis* (ὑπόθεσις) hypothesis*

*kakia* (κακία) badness, vice*

  *kakos* (κακός) bad*, evil

*kalos* (καλός) beautiful*, fine*, noble

  *kaloi kāgathoi* (καλοὶ καγαθοί) fine and good* – a description for the elite within a Greek city

*logos* (λόγος) broadly, anything said, spoken, or expressing reasoning; also, reason itself. Consistency in translation is unattainable. I have mainly used 'account', 'argument', or 'discussion', but not always

  *logismos* (λογισμός) reckoning, reasoning*, reasoning out*

*manthanein* (μανθάνειν) learn*, apprehend, understand*

  *mathēsis* (μάθησις) learning*

*megaloprepeia* (μεγαλοπρέπεια) grandeur*, magnificence, munificence

*ōphelimos* (ὠφέλιμος) beneficial*, useful

*orthos* (ὀρθός) right*, correct

  *orthē doxa* (ὀρθὴ δόξα) right opinion*

*ousia* (οὐσία) being, nature*, essence

*phronēsis* (φρόνησις) wisdom*, prudence, sagacity

*poion ti esti* (ποῖόν τί ἐστι) what it is like*, its properties, what sort of thing it is

*sophia* (σοφία) wisdom*, expert skill

  *sophos* (σοφός) wise*, expert

*sophistēs* (σοφιστής) Sophist* (but at 85b4 expert*)

*sōphrosunē* (σωφροσύνη) temperance*, moderation, self-control

  *sōphrōn* (σώφρων) temperate*, moderate, self-controlled

*ti esti* (τί ἐστι) what it is*, its nature, essence

*xenos* (ξένος) stranger, visitor* from abroad; often, more specifically, one with whom one has links of hospitality, thus 'guest-friend*'

*zētein* (ζητεῖν) search for*, inquire

  *zētēsis* (ζήτησις) search*, inquiry

# BIBLIOGRAPHY

## 1 EDITIONS, TRANSLATIONS AND COMMENTARIES

### Collected works of Plato

Burnet, J. (ed.), *Platonis Opera*, vols I–V, Oxford Classical Texts series. The *Meno* is in vol. III (Oxford, 1903) (Greek text.)

Hamilton, E. and Cairns, H. (eds), *Plato, the Collected Dialogues including the Letters*, translated by various hands (New York, 1961).

Jowett, B., *The Dialogues of Plato*, translated into English with analyses and introductions, 4th edn revised by D. J. Allan and H. E. Dale (Oxford, 1953).

### The *Meno*

Bluck, R. S., *Plato's Meno*. Greek text, introduction and commentary (Cambridge, 1961).

Canto Sperber, M., *Platon, Ménon*. French translation with introduction, notes, and classified bibliography (Flammarian: Paris, 1991).

Grube, G. M. A., *Plato's Meno*. Translation with short introduction (Indianapolis, 1976).

Guthrie, W. K. C., *Plato, Protagoras and Meno*. Translation with introduction (Penguin: London, 1956).

Klein, J., *A Commentary on Plato's Meno* (Chapel Hill, 1965).

Reich, K., *Platon, Menon*. Greek text, with O. Apelt's German translation revised in collaboration with E. Zekl, introduction, notes, and substantial bibliography (Hamburg, 1982).

Sharples, R. W., *Plato: Meno*. Greek text, translation, introduction, notes, and select bibliography (Aris and Phillips: Warminster, 1985).

Thompson, E. Seymour, *The Meno of Plato*. Greek text and commentary, (London, 1901).

## 2 OTHER BOOKS, INCLUDING COLLECTIONS OF ARTICLES

Adkins, A. W. H., *Merit and Responsibility* (Oxford, 1960).

# BIBLIOGRAPHY

Allen, R. E., *Plato's Euthyphro and the Earlier Theory of Forms* (London, 1970).

Allen, R. E. (ed.), *Studies in Plato's Metaphysics* (London, 1965).

Ast, D. F., *Lexicon Platonicum* (Lipsiae 1835–8).

Brown, M. (ed.), *Plato's Meno*. Guthrie's translation with essays by various authors (Indianapolis and New York, 1971).

Canto Sperber, M. (ed.), *Les Paradoxes de la Connaissance. Essais sur le Ménon de Platon*, (Odile Jacob: Paris, 1991)

Cornford, F. M., *Principium Sapientiae* (Cambridge, 1952).

Crombie, I. M., *An Examination of Plato's Doctrines*, 2 vols (London, 1962 and 1963).

Dodds, E. R., *Plato, Gorgias*. Greek text with introduction and commentary (Oxford, 1959).

Field, G. C., *Plato and his Contemporaries* (London, 1930).

Gould, J., *The Development of Plato's Ethics* (Cambridge, 1955).

Grimm, L., *Definition in Plato's Meno* (Oslo, 1962).

Gulley, N., *Plato's Theory of Knowledge* (New York, 1962).

Guthrie, W. K. C., *A History of Greek Philosophy* (Cambridge, six volumes: (I) 1962, (II) 1965, (III) 1969, (IV) 1975, (V) 1978, (VI) 1981)

Hare, R. M., *Plato*. Past Masters Series (Oxford, 1982).

Irwin, T., *Plato's Moral Theory: The Early and Middle Dialogues* (Oxford, 1977).

Kerford, G. B., *The Sophistic Movement* (Cambridge, 1981).

Melling, D. J., *Understanding Plato* (Opus: Oxford, 1987).

Robinson, R., *Plato's Earlier Dialectic*, 2nd edn (Oxford, 1953).

Robinson, T. M., *Contrasting Arguments – An Edition of the Dissoi Logoi* (New York, 1979).

Santas, G., *Socrates* (Boston, London and Henley, 1979).

Taylor, A. E., *Plato: The Man and his Work*, 4th edn (London, 1937); reprinted in paperback 1960.

Vlastos, G., *Platonic Studies*, 2nd edn (Princeton, 1981).

Vlastos, G., *Socrates* (Cambridge, 1991).

Vlastos, G. (ed.), *Plato: A Collection of Critical Essays*, 2 vols (New York and London, 1971); reprinted Notre Dame, 1978.

Vlastos, G. (ed.), *The Philosophy of Socrates: A Collection of Critical Essays* (New York and London, 1971; reprinted Notre Dame, 1980).

White, N., *Plato on Knowledge and Reality* (Indianapolis, 1976).

## 3 ARTICLES

Allen, R. E., 'Anamnesis in Plato's *Meno* and *Phaedo'*, *Review of Metaphysics* 13 (1959–60), pp. 165–74.

Anscombe, G. E. M., 'Understanding proofs: *Meno* 85d9–86c2', *Philosophy* 54 (1979), pp. 149–58.

Bedu-Addo, J. T., 'Recollection and the argument "from a hypothesis" in Plato's *Meno'*, *Journal of Hellenic Studies* 104 (1984), pp. 1–14.

Bedu-Addo, J. T., 'Sense-experience and recollection in Plato's *Meno'*, *American Journal of Philology* 104 (1983), pp. 228–48.

Benson, H. H., 'Meno, the slave-boy and the elenchus', *Phronesis* 35 (1990), pp. 128–58.

Bluck, R. S., 'Plato's *Meno*' (reply to Hoerber, q.v. below), *Phronesis* 6 (1961), pp. 94–101.

Boter, G. J., '*Meno* 82c2–3', *Phronesis* 33 (1988), pp. 208–15.

Brickhouse, T. C. and Smith, N. D., 'Socrates on goods, virtue and happiness', *Oxford Studies in Ancient Philosophy* 5 (1987), pp. 1–27.

Brickhouse, T. C. and Smith, N. D., 'Vlastos on the elenchus' (reply to Vlastos 1983, q.v. below), *Oxford Studies in Ancient Philosophy* 2 (1984), pp. 85–95.

Brown, M., 'Plato disapproves of the slaveboy's answer', *Review of Metaphysics* 20 (1967), pp. 57–93: reprinted in Brown (ed.) q.v. in section 2 above, pp. 198–242.

Brown, T. S., 'Meno of Thessaly', *Historia* 35 (1986), pp. 387–404.

Burnyeat, M. F., 'Examples in epistemology: Socrates, Theaetetus and G. E. Moore', *Philosophy* 52 (1977), pp. 381–98.

Burnyeat, M. F., 'Wittgenstein and Augustine *De Magistro*', *Proceedings of the Aristotelian Society, Supplementary Volume* 61 (1987), pp. 1–24.

Burnyeat, M. F. and Barnes, J., 'Socrates and the jury: paradoxes in Plato's distinction between knowledge and true belief' (a symposium), *Proceedings of the Aristotelian Society*, Supplementary Volume 54 (1980), pp. 173–206.

Cahn, S. M., 'A puzzle concerning the *Meno* and the *Protagoras*', *Journal of the History of Philosophy* 11 (1973), pp. 535–37.

Cherniss, H., 'The philosophical economy of the theory of Ideas', *American Journal of Philology* 57 (1936), pp. 445–56; reprinted in Allen (ed.), 1965, q.v. in section 2 above, pp. 1–12.

Devereux, D. T., 'Nature and teaching in Plato's *Meno*', *Phronesis* 23 (1978), pp. 118–26.

Ebert, T., 'Plato's theory of recollection reconsidered: *Meno* 80a–86a', *Man and the World* 6 (1973), pp. 163–81.

Davidson, D., 'Plato's philosopher', *London Review of Books*, 1 August 1985, pp. 15–16.

Fowler, D. H., 'Yet more on *Meno* 82a–85b', *Phronesis* 35 (1990), pp. 175–81.

Gaiser, K., 'Platons *Menon* und die Akademie', *Archiv für Geschichte der Philosophie* 46 (1964), 241–92; reprinted in Wippern, J. (ed.), *Das Probleme der Ungeschriebenen Lehre Platons* (Darmstadt, 1972) pp. 329–93.

Hare, R. M., 'Philosophical discoveries', *Mind* new series 69 (1960), pp. 145–62; reprinted in Hare's *Essays on Philosophical Method* (London, 1971), pp. 19–37.

Hare, R. M., 'Platonism in moral education: two varieties', *Monist* 58 (1974), pp. 568–80.

Hoerber, R. G., 'Plato's *Meno*', *Phronesis* 5 (1960), pp. 78–102.

Lloyd, G. E. R., 'The *Meno* and the mysteries of mathematics', *Phronesis* 37 (1992), pp. 166–83.

Moline, J., 'Meno's paradox', *Phronesis* 14 (1969), pp. 153–61.

Morrison, J. S., 'Meno of Pharsalus, Polycrates and Ismenias', *Classical Quarterly* 36 (1942), pp. 57–68.

Narcy, M., 'Enseignement et dialectique dans le "Menon" ', *Revue Internationale de Philosophie* 23 (1969), pp. 474–94.

Nehamas, A., '*Episteme* and *Logos* in Plato's later thought', *Archiv für Geschichte der Philosophie* 66 (1984), pp. 11–36.

Penner, T., 'Socrates on virtue and motivation', *Phronesis, Supplementary Volume* 1 (1973), pp. 133–51.

Penner, T., 'The unity of virtue', *Philosophical Review* 82 (1973), pp. 35–68.

Powers, L. H., 'Knowledge by deduction', *Philosophical Review* 87 (1978), pp. 337–71.

Robinson, R., 'Plato's consciousness of fallacy', *Mind* new series 51 (1942), 97–114; reprinted in Robinson's *Essays in Greek Philosophy* (Oxford 1969), pp. 16–38.

Rose, G., 'Plato's *Meno* 86–89', *Journal of the History of Philosophy* 8 (1970), pp. 1–8.

Ryle, G., 'Many things are odd about our *Meno*', *Paideia* 5 (1976), pp. 1–9.

Ryle, G., 'Plato', in Edwards, P. (ed.), *The Encyclopedia of Philosophy* (New York, 1967) vol. 6, pp. 314–33.

Ryle, G., 'Teaching and training', in Peters, R. S. (ed.), *The Concept of Education* (London 1957), pp. 105–19; reprinted in Brown (ed.), q.v. in section 2 above, pp. 243–61.

Santas, G., 'The Socratic fallacy', *Journal of the History of Philosophy* 10 (1972), pp. 127–41.

Scolnikov, S., 'Three aspects of Plato's philosophy of learning and instruction', *Paideia* 5 (1976), pp. 50–62.

Scott, D., 'Platonic Anamnesis revisited', *Classical Quarterly* 37 (1987), pp. 346–66.

Sharon, B., '*Meno* – a cognitive-psychological view', *British Journal for the Philosophy of Science* 35 (1984), pp. 129–47.

Sharples, R. W., 'More on Plato, *Meno* 82c3', *Phronesis* 34 (1989), pp. 220–6.

Stahl, H. P., 'Ansätze zur Satzlogic bei Platon', *Hermes* 88 (1960), pp. 409–51. A translation, by G. Weiler, is in Brown (ed.), q.v. in section 2 above, pp. 180–97.

Sternfield, R. and Zyskind, H., 'Plato's *Meno* 86e–87a: the geometrical illustration of the argument by hypothesis', *Phronesis* 22 (1977), 206–11.

Stokes, M. C., Review of Bluck, *Plato's Meno*, *Archiv für Geschichte der Philosophie* 45 (1963), 292–9.

Tigner, S. S., 'On the kinship of all nature in Plato's *Meno*', *Phronesis* 15 (1970), pp. 1–4.

Verdenius, W. J., 'Notes on Plato's *Meno*', *Mnemosune* 4th series 10 (1957), pp. 289–99, and 'Further notes on Plato's *Meno*', ibid. 17 (1964), pp. 261–80.

Vlastos, G., 'Socrates on the parts of virtue', in Vlastos 1973, q.v. in section 2 above, pp. 417–23.

Vlastos, G., 'The Socratic elenchus' and 'Afterthoughts on the Socratic elenchus', *Oxford Studies in Ancient Philosophy* 1 (1983), pp. 27–58 and 71–4.

Vlastos, G., 'What did Socrates understand by his "What is *F*?" question?' in Vlastos 1973, q.v. in section 2 above, pp. 410–17.

Woodruff, P., 'Socrates on the parts of virtue', *Canadian Journal of Philosophy*, Supplementary Volume 2 (1976), pp. 101–16.

Zyskind, H. and Sternfield, R., 'Plato's *Meno* 89c: "Virtue is knowledge": a hypothesis?', *Phronesis* 21 (1976), pp. 130–4.

# INDEX